Workshop on Linking Natural Language Processing and Biology: Towards Deeper Biological Literature Analysis 2006

(BioNLP 06)

Held at HLT/NAACL 2006

New York, New York, USA
8 June 2006

ISBN: 978-1-61738-492-9

Printed from e-media with permission by:

Curran Associates, Inc.
57 Morehouse Lane
Red Hook, NY 12571
www.proceedings.com

Some format issues inherent in the e-media version may also appear in this print version.

Printed by Curran Associates, Inc. (2010)

Association for Computational Linguistics
209 N. Eighth Street
Stroudsburg, Pennsylvania 18360

Phone: 1-570-476-8006
Fax: 1-570-476-0860

acl@aclweb.org

Introduction to BioNLP'06

Welcome to the HLT-NAACL'06 BioNLP Workshop, Linking Natural Language Processing and Biology: Towards Deeper Biological Literature Analysis.

The late 1990s saw the beginning of a trend towards significant growth in the area of biomedical language processing, and in particular in the use of natural language processing techniques in the molecular biology and related computational bioscience domains. The figure below gives an indication of the amount of recent activity in this area: it shows the cumulative number of documents returned by searching PubMed, the premiere repository of biomedical scientific literature, with the query `((natural language processing) OR (text mining)) AND (gene OR protein)`, limiting the search by year for every year from 1999 through 2005: the three papers in 1999 had grown to 227 by the end of 2005.

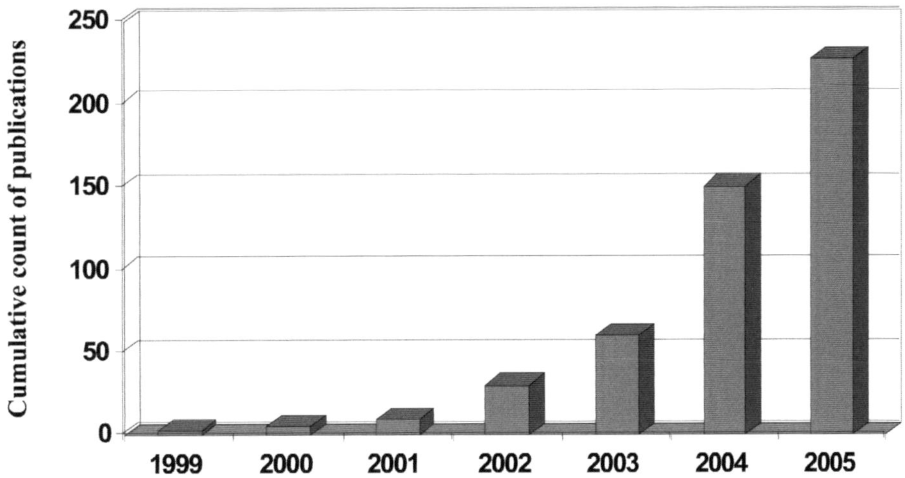

Figure 1: Cumulative hits returned by searching PubMed with the terms `((natural language processing) OR (text mining)) AND (gene OR protein)` for the years 1999-2005.

Significant challenges to biological literature exploitation remain, in particular for such biological problem areas as automated function prediction and pathway reconstruction and for linguistic applications such as relation extraction and abstractive summarization. In light of the nature of these remaining challenges, the focus of this workshop was intended to be applications that move towards deeper semantic analysis. We particularly solicited work that addresses relatively under-explored areas such as summarization and question-answering from biological information.

Papers describing applications of semantic processing technologies to the biology domain were especially invited. That is, the primary topics of interest were applications which require deeper linguistic analysis of the biological literature. We also solicited papers exploring issues in porting NLP systems originally constructed for other domains to the biology domain. What makes the biology domain special? What hurdles must be overcome in performing linguistic analysis of biological text? Are any special linguistic or knowledge resources required, beyond a domain-specific lexicon? What relations in biological text are most interesting to biologists, and hence should be the focus of our future efforts?

The workshop received 31 submissions: 29 full-paper submissions, and two poster submissions. A strong program committee, representing BioNLP researchers in North America, Europe, and Asia, provided thorough reviews, resulting in the acceptance of eleven full papers and nineteen posters, for an acceptance rate for full papers of 38% (11/29), which we believe made this one of the most competitive BioNLP workshop or conference sessions to date.

A notable trend in the accepted papers is that only one of them was on the topic of entity identification. The subject areas of the papers presented at BioNLP'06 included an exceptionally wide range of topics: question-answering, computational lexical semantics, information extraction, entity normalization, semantic role labelling, image classification, and syntactic aspects of the sublanguage of molecular biology.

The intent of this workshop was to bring researchers in text processing in the bioinformatics and biomedical domains together to discuss how techniques from natural language processing and information retrieval can be exploited to address biological information needs. Credit for its successes in reaching that goal is due entirely to the authors of the papers and posters presented in this volume and to the exceptional program committee.

Finally, Procter & Gamble generously donated money to sponsor the workshop. We were able to invite Andrey Rzhetsky from Columbia University to speak thanks to this donation. We thank P&G for their contribution, and Andrey for accepting the invitation to speak.

Karin Verspoor
K. Bretonnel Cohen
Ben Goertzel
Inderjeet Mani

Organizers:

Karin Verspoor, Los Alamos National Laboratory
Kevin Bretonnel Cohen, Center for Computational Pharmacology, U. Colorado
Ben Goertzel, Biomind LLC
Interjeet Mani, MITRE

Program Committee:

Aaron Cohen, Oregon Health & Science University
Alexander Morgan, MITRE
Alfonso Valencia, Centro Nacional de Biotecnologia, Universidad Autonoma, Madrid
Andrey Rzhetsky, Columbia University
Ben Wellner, MITRE
Bob Carpenter, Alias I, Inc.
Bonnie Webber, University of Edinburgh
Breck Baldwin, Alias I, Inc.
Carol Friedman, Columbia University
Christian Blaschke, Bioalma (Madrid)
Hagit Shatkay, Queen's University
Henk Harkema, Cognia Corporation
Hong Yu, Columbia University
Jeffrey Chang, Duke Institute for Genome Sciences and Policy
Jun-ichi Tsujii, National Center for Text Mining, UK and University of Tokyo
Lan Aronson, National Library of Medicine
Larry Hunter, University of Colorado Health Sciences Center
Lorraine Tanabe, National Library of Medicine
Luis Rocha, University of Indiana
Lynette Hirschman, MITRE
Marc Light, University of Iowa
Mark Mandel, University of Pennsylvania
Marti Hearst, UC Berkeley
Olivier Bodenreider, National Library of Medicine
Patrick Ruch, University Hospital of Geneva and Swiss Federal Institute of Technology
Robert Futrelle, Northeastern University
Sophia Ananiadou, National Center for Text Mining, UK and University of Manchester
Thomas Rindflesch, National Library of Medicine
Vasileios Hatzivassiloglou, University of Texas at Dallas
W. John Wilbur, National Library of Medicine

Additional Reviewers:

Helen L. Johnson, U. Colorado
Martin Krallinger, Centro Nacional de Biotecnologia, Universidad Autonoma, Madrid
Zhiyong Lu, U. Colorado

Invited Speaker:

Andrey Rzhetsky, Columbia University

Table of Contents

Poster Papers

Conference Program

Thursday, June 8, 2006

9:00–9:10 Welcome and Opening Remarks

Session 1: Linking NLP and Biology

9:10–9:30 *The Semantics of a Definiendum Constrains both the Lexical Semantics and the Lexicosyntactic Patterns in the Definiens*
Hong Yu and Ying Wei

9:30–9:50 *Ontology-Based Natural Language Query Processing for the Biological Domain*
Jisheng Liang, Thien Nguyen, Krzysztof Koperski and Giovanni Marchisio

9:50–10:10 *Term Generalization and Synonym Resolution for Biological Abstracts: Using the Gene Ontology for Subcellular Localization Prediction*
Alona Fyshe and Duane Szafron

10:10–10:30 *Integrating Ontological Knowledge and Textual Evidence in Estimating Gene and Gene Product Similarity*
Antonio Sanfilippo Christian Posse, Banu Gopalan, Stephen Tratz and Michelle Gregory

10:30–11:00 Break

Session 2: Towards deeper biological literature analysis

11:00-11:20 *A Priority Model for Named Entities*
Lorraine Tanabe and W. John Wilbur

11:20–11:40 *Human Gene Name Normalization using Text Matching with Automatically Extracted Synonym Dictionaries*
Haw-ren Fang, Kevin Murphy, Yang Jin, Jessica Kim and Peter White

11:40–12:00 *Integrating Co-occurrence Statistics with Information Extraction for Robust Retrieval of Protein Interactions from Medline*
Razvan Bunescu, Raymond Mooney, Arun Ramani and Edward Marcotte

12:00–12:20 *BIOSMILE: Adapting Semantic Role Labeling for Biomedical Verbs*
Richard Tzong-Han Tsai, Wen-Chi Chou, Yu-Chun Lin, Cheng-Lung Sung, Wei Ku, Ying-Shan Su, Ting-Yi Sung and Wen-Lian Hsu

12:30-14:00 Lunch

Thursday, June 8, 2006 (continued)

Session 3: Exploring Document Properties

The Procter & Gamble Keynote Speech

15:30-16:00 Break

Session 4: Insights from Corpus Analysis

Wrapup and Poster Session

16:20-16:30 Wrapup and Discussion

16:30-18:00 Poster Session

Sponsorship by

P&G

The Semantics of a Definiendum Constrains both the Lexical Semantics and the Lexicosyntactic Patterns in the Definiens

Hong Yu
Department of Health Sciences
University of Wisconsin-Milwaukee
Milwaukee, WI 53201
Hong.Yu@uwm.edu

Ying Wei
Department of Biostatistics
Columbia University
New York, NY 10032
Ying.Wei@columbia.com

Abstract

Most current definitional question answering systems apply one-size-fits-all lexicosyntactic patterns to identify definitions. By analyzing a large set of online definitions, this study shows that the semantic types of definienda constrain both lexical semantics and lexicosyntactic patterns of the definientia. For example, "heart" has the semantic type *[Body Part, Organ, or Organ Component]* and its definition (e.g., "heart locates between the lungs") incorporates semantic-type-dependent lexicosyntactic patterns (e.g., "*TERM locates …*") and terms (e.g., "lung" has the same semantic type *[Body Part, Organ, or Organ Component]*). In contrast, "AIDS" has a different semantic type *[Disease or Syndrome]*; its definition (e.g., "An infectious disease caused by human immunodeficiency virus") consists of different lexicosyntactic patterns (e.g., "*…causes by…*") and terms (e.g., "infectious disease" has the semantic type *[Disease or Syndrome]*). The semantic types are defined in the widely used biomedical knowledge resource, the Unified Medical Language System (UMLS).

1 Introduction

Definitional questions (e.g., "What is X?") constitute an important question type and have been a part of the evaluation at the Text Retrieval Conference (TREC) Question Answering Track since 2003. Most systems apply one-size-fits-all lexicosyntactic patterns to identify definitions (Liang et al. 2001; Blair-Goldensohn et al. 2004; Hildebrandt et al. 2004; Cui et al. 2005). For example, the pattern "*NP, (such as|like|including) query term*" can be used to identify the definition "*New research in mice suggests that drugs such as Ritalin quiet hyperactivity*" (Liang et al. 2001).

Few existing systems, however, have explored the relations between the semantic type (denoted as S_{DT}) of a definiendum (i.e., a defined term (DT)) and the semantic types (denoted as S_{Def}) of terms in its definiens (i.e., definition). Additionally, few existing systems have examined whether the lexicosyntactic patterns of definitions correlate with the semantic types of the defined terms.

By analyzing a large set of online definitions, this study shows that 1) S_{Def} correlates with S_{DT}, and 2) S_{DT} constrains the lexicosyntactic patterns of the corresponding definitions. In the following, we will illustrate our findings with the following four definitions:

a. ***Heart***[Body Part, Organ, or Organ Component]: The hollow[Spatial Concept] muscular[Spatial Concept] organ[Body Part, Organ, or Organ Component,Tissue] located[Spatial Concept] behind[Spatial Concept] the sternum[Body Part, Organ, or Organ Component] and between the lungs[Body Part, Organ, or Organ Component].

b. ***Kidney***[Body Part, Organ, or Organ Component]: The kidneys are a pair of glandular organs[Body Part, Organ, or Organ Component] located[Spatial Concept] in the abdominal_cavities[Body Part, Organ, or Organ Component] of mammals[Mammal] and reptiles[Reptile].

c. ***Heart attack***[Disease or Syndrome]: also called myocardial_infarction[Disease or Syndrome]; damage[Functional Concept] to the heart_muscle[Tissue] due to insufficient

Proceedings of the BioNLP Workshop on Linking Natural Language Processing and Biology at HLT-NAACL 06, pages 1–8,
New York City, June 2006. ©2006 Association for Computational Linguistics

blood supply[Organ or Tissue Function] for an extended[Spatial Concept] time_period[Temporal Concept].

d. ***AIDS***[Disease or Syndrome]: An infectious_disease[Disease or Syndrome] caused[Functional Concept] by human_immunodeficiency_virus[Virus].

In the above four definitions, the superscripts in [brackets] are the semantic types (e.g., [Body Part, Organ, or Organ Component] and [Disease or Syndrome]) of the preceding terms. A multiword term links words with the underscore "_". For example, "heart" IS-A [Body Part, Organ, or Organ Component] and "heart_muscle" IS-A [Tissue]. The semantic types are defined in the *Semantic Network (SN)* of the Unified Medical Language System (UMLS), the largest biomedical knowledge resource. Details of the UMLS and SN will be described in Section 2. We applied MMTx (Aronson et al. 2004) to automatically map a string to the UMLS semantic types. MMTx will also be described in Section 2.

Simple analysis of the above four definitions shows that given a defined term (DT) with a semantic type S_{DT} (e.g., [Body Part, Organ, or Organ Component]), terms that appear in the definition tend to have the same or related semantic types (e.g., [Body Part, Organ, or Organ Component] and [Spatial Concept]). Such observations were first reported as "Aristotelian definitions" (Bodenreider and Burgun 2002) in the limited domain of anatomy. (Rindflesch and Fiszman 2003) reported that the hyponym related to the definiendum must be in an IS-A relation with the hypernym that is related to the definiens. However, neither work demonstrated statistical patterns on a large corpus as we report in this study. Additionally, none of the work explicitly suggested the use of patterns to support question answering.

In addition to statistical correlations among semantic types, the lexicosyntactic patterns of the definitions correlate with S_{DT}. For example, as shown by sentences a~d, when S_{DT} is [Body Part, Organ, or Organ Component], its lexicosyntactic patterns include "*…located…*". In contrast, when S_{DT} is [Disease or Syndrome], the patterns include "*…due to…*" and "*… caused by…*".

In this study, we empirically studied statistical correlations between S_{DT} and S_{Def} and between S_{DT} and the lexicosyntactic patterns in the definitions. Our study is a result of detailed statistical analysis of 36,535 defined terms and their 226,089 online definitions. We built our semantic constraint model based on the widely used biomedical knowledge resource, the UMLS. We also adapted a robust information extraction system to generate automatically a large number of lexicosyntactic patterns from definitions. In the following, we will first describe the UMLS and its semantic types. We will then describe our data collection and our methods for pattern generation.

2 Unified Medical Language System

The Unified Medical Language System (UMLS) is the largest biomedical knowledge source maintained by the National Library of Medicine. It provides standardized biomedical concept relations and synonyms (Humphreys et al. 1998). The UMLS has been widely used in many natural language processing tasks, including information retrieval (Eichmann et al. 1998), extraction (Rindflesch et al. 2000), and text summarization (Elhadad et al. 2004; Fiszman et al. 2004).

The UMLS includes the Metathesaurus (MT), which contains over one million biomedical concepts and the Semantic Network (SN), which represents a high-level abstraction from the UMLS Metathesaurus. The SN consists of 134 semantic types with 54 types of semantic relations (e.g., *is-a* or *part-of*) that relate the semantic types to each other. The UMLS Semantic Network provides broad and general world knowledge that is related to human health. Each UMLS concept is assigned one or more semantic types.

The National Library of Medicine also makes available MMTx, a programming implementation of MetaMap (Aronson 2001), which maps free text to the UMLS concepts and associated semantic types. MMTx first parses text into sentences, then chunks the sentences into noun phrases. Each noun phrase is then mapped to a set of possible UMLS concepts, taking into account spelling and morphological variations; each concept is weighted, with the highest weight representing the most likely mapped concept. One recent study has evaluated MMTx to have 79% (Yu and Sable 2005) accuracy for mapping a term to the semantic type(s) in a small set of medical questions. Another study (Lacson and Barzilay 2005) measured MMTx to have a recall of 74.3% for capturing the semantic types in another set of medical texts.

In this study, we applied MMTx to identify the semantic types of terms that appear in their definitions. For each candidate term, MMTx ranks a list of UMLS concepts with confidence. In this study, we selected the UMLS concept that was assigned with the highest confidence by MMTx. The UMLS concepts were then used to obtain the corresponding semantic types.

3 Data Collection

We collected a large number of online definitions for the purpose of our study. Specifically, we applied more than 1 million of the UMLS concepts as candidate definitional terms, and searched for the definitions from the World Wide Web using the *Google:Definition* service; this resulted in the downloads of a total of 226,089 definitions that corresponded to a total of 36,535 UMLS concepts (or 3.7% of the total of 1 million UMLS concepts). We removed from definitions the defined terms; this step is necessary for our statistical studies, which we will explain later in the following sections. We applied MMTx to obtain the corresponding semantic types.

4 Statistically Correlated Semantic Types

We then identified statistically correlated semantic types between S_{DT} and S_{Def} based on bivariate tabular chi-square (Fleiss 1981).

	Number of definitions that have STY_i	Number of definitions that don't have STY_i	Total
S_{Def}	$O(Def_i)$	$O(\underline{Def_i})$	N_{Def}
S_{All}	$O(All_i)$	$O(\underline{All_i})$	N_{All}
Total	N_i	$\underline{N_i}$	N

Specifically, given a semantic type $STY_{i,\ i=1,2,3,\dots,134}$ of any defined term, the observed numbers of definitions that were and were not assigned the STY_i are O(Def_i) and O($\underline{Def_i}$). *All* indicates the total 226,089 definitions. The observed numbers of definitions in which the semantic type STY_i did and did not appear were O(All_i) and O($\underline{All_i}$). 134 represents the total number of the UMLS semantic types. We applied formulas (1) and (2) to calculate expected frequencies and then the chi-square value (the degree of freedom is one). A high chi-square value indicates the importance of the semantic type that appears in the definition. We removed the defined terms from their definitions prior to the semantic-type statistical analysis in order to remove the bias introduced by the defined terms (i.e., defined terms frequently appear in the definitions).

$$E(Def_i) = \frac{N_{Def} * N_i}{N}, \quad E(\underline{Def_i}) = \frac{N_{Def} * \underline{N_i}}{N},$$

$$E(All_i) = \frac{N_{All} * N_i}{N}, \quad E(\underline{All_i}) = \frac{N_{All} * \underline{N_i}}{N} \qquad (1)$$

$$\chi^2 = \sum \frac{(E-O)^2}{E} \qquad (2)$$

To determine whether the chi-square value is large enough for statistical significance, we calculated its p-value. Typically, 0.05 is the cutoff of significance, i.e. significance is accepted if the corresponding p-value is less than 0.05. This criterion ensures the chance of false significance (incorrectly detected due to chance) is 0.05 for a single S_{DT}-S_{Def} pair. However, since there are 134*134 possible S_{DT}-S_{Def} pairs, the chance for obtaining at least one false significance could be very high. To have a more conservative inference, we employed a Bonferroni-type correction procedure (Hochberg 1988).

Specifically, let $p_{(1)} \le p_{(2)} \le \cdots \le p_{(m)}$ be the ordered raw p-values, where m is the total number of S_{DT}-S_{Def} pairs. A S_{Def} is significantly associated with a S_{DT} if S_{Def}'s corresponding p-value $\le p_{(i)} \le \alpha/(m-i+1)$ for some i. This correction procedure allows the probability of at-least-one-false-significance out of the total m pairs is less than alpha (=0.05).

The number of definitions for each S_{DT} ranges from 4 ([Entity]), 10 ([Event]), 17 ([Vertebrate]) to 8,380 ([Amino Acid, Peptide, or Protein]) and 18,461 ([Organic Chemical]) in our data collection. As the power of a statistical test relies on the sample size, some correlated semantic types might be undetected when the number of available definitions is small. It is therefore worthwhile to know what the necessary sample size is in order to have a decent chance of detecting difference statistically.

For this task, we assume P_0 and P_1 are true probabilities that a STY will appear in N_{Def} and N_{All}. Based upon that, we calculated the minimal required number of sentences n such that the probability of statistical significance will be larger than or equal to 0.8. This sample size is determined based on the following two assumptions: 1) the observed frequencies are approximately normally distributed, and 2) we use chi-square significance to test the hypothesis $P_0 = P_1$ at significance level 0.05 ($\bar{P} = \frac{P_0 + P_1}{2}$).

$$n > \frac{(z_{0.025}\sqrt{2\bar{P}(1-\bar{P})} + z_{0.2}\sqrt{P_1(1-P_1)+P_0(1-P_0)})^2}{(P_0 - P_1)^2} \quad (3)$$

5 Semantic Type Distribution

Our null hypothesis is that given any pair of $\{S_{DT}(X), S_{DT}(Y)\}$, $X \neq Y$, where X and Y represent two different semantic types of the total 134 semantic types, there are no statistical differences in the distributions of the semantic types of the terms that appear in the definitions.

We applied the bivariate tabular chi-square test to measure the semantic type distribution. Following similar notations to Section 4, we use $\underline{O}_{Xi}$ and $\underline{O}_{Yi}$ for the corresponding frequencies of not being observed in $S_{Def}(X)$ and $S_{Def}(Y)$.

For each semantic type STY, we calculate the expected frequencies of being observed and not being observed in $S_{Def}(X)$ and $S_{Def}(Y)$, respectively, and their corresponding chi-square value according to formulas (3) and (4):

$$E_{X_i} = \frac{N_{X_i} * (O_{X_i} + O_{Y_i})}{N_{X_i} + N_{Y_i}}, \quad \underline{E}_{X_i} = \frac{N_{X_i} * (\underline{O}_{X_i} + \underline{O}_{Y_i})}{N_{X_i} + N_{Y_i}},$$

$$E_{Y_i} = \frac{N_{Y_i} * (O_{X_i} + O_{Y_i})}{N_{X_i} + N_{Y_i}}, \quad \underline{E}_{Y_i} = \frac{N_{Y_i} * (\underline{O}_{X_i} + \underline{O}_{Y_i})}{N_{X_i} + N_{Y_i}} \quad (4)$$

$$\chi^2_{X,Y,i} = \sum \frac{(E_{X_i} - O_{X_i})^2}{E_{X_i}} + \sum \frac{(E_{Y_i} - O_{Y_i})^2}{E_{Y_i}} \quad (5)$$

where N_X and N_Y are the numbers of sentences in $S_{Def}(X)$ and $S_{Def}(Y)$, respectively, and in both (4) and (5), $i = 1,2,\ldots,134$, and $(X, Y) = 1,2,\ldots,134$ and $X \neq Y$. The degree of freedom is *1*. The chi-square value measures whether the occurrences of STY_i, are equivalent between $S_{Def}(X)$ and $S_{Def}(Y)$. The same multiple testing correction procedure will be used to determine the significance of the chi-square value. Note that if at least one STY_i has been detected to be statistically significant after multiple-testing correction, the distributions of the semantic types are different between $S_{Def}(X)$ and $S_{Def}(Y)$.

6 Automatically Identifying Semantic-Type-Dependent Lexicosyntactic Patterns

Most current definitional question answering systems generate lexicosyntactic patterns either manually or semi-automatically. In this study, we automatically generated large sets of lexicosyntactic patterns from our collection of online definitions. We applied the information extraction system Autoslog-TS (Riloff and Philips 2004) to automatically generate lexicosyntactic patterns in definitions. We then identified the statistical correlation between the semantic types of defined terms and their lexicosyntactic patterns in definitions.

AutoSlog-TS is an information extraction system that is built upon AutoSlog (Riloff 1996). AutoSlog-TS automatically identifies extraction patterns for noun phrases by learning from two sets of un-annotated texts *relevant* and *non-relevant*. AutoSlog-TS first generates every possible lexicosyntactic pattern to extract every noun phrase in both collections of text and then computes statistics based on how often each pattern appears in the relevant text versus the background and outputs a ranked list of extraction patterns coupled with statistics indicating how strongly each pattern is associated with *relevant* and *non-relevant* texts.

We grouped definitions based on the semantic types of the defined terms. For each semantic type, the *relevant* text incorporated the definitions, and the *non-relevant* text incorporated an equal number of sentences that were randomly selected from the MEDLINE collection. For each semantic type, we applied AutoSlog-TS to its associated *relevant* and *non-relevant* sentence collections to generate lexicosyntactic patterns; this resulted in a total of 134 sets of lexicosyntactic patterns that corresponded to different semantic types of defined terms. Additionally, we identified the common lexicosyntactic patterns across the semantic types and ranked the lexicosyntactic patterns based on their frequencies across semantic types.

We also identified statistical correlations between S_{DT} and the lexicosyntactic patterns in definitions based on chi-square statistics that we have described in the previous two sections. For formula 1~4, we replaced each STY with a lexicosyntactic pattern. Our null hypothesis is that given any S_{DT}, there are no statistical differences in the distributions of the lexicosyntactic patterns that appear in the definitions.

[Body Part, Organ, or Organ Component]:
[Body Part, Organ, or Organ Component]
[Spatial Concept]
[Tissue]
[Body Location or Region]
[Medical Device]

[Disease or Syndrome]:
[Disease or Syndrome]
[Pathologic Function]
[Body Part, Organ, or Organ Component]
[Sign or Symptom]
[Finding]

[Organization]:
[Organization]
[Regulation or Law]
[Governmental or Regulatory Activity]
[Social Behavior]
[Occupational Activity]

Figure 1: A list of semantic types of defined terms with the top five statistically correlated semantic types (P<<0.0001) that appear in their definitions.

7 Results

Our chi-square statistics show that for any pair of semantic types $\{S_{DT}(X), S_{DT}(Y)\}$, $X \neq Y$, the distributions of S_{Def} are statistically different at alpha=0.05; the results show that the semantic types of the defined terms correlate to the semantic types in the definitions. Our results also show that the syntactic patterns are distributed differently among different semantic types of the defined terms (alpha=0.05).

Our results show that many semantic types that appear in definitions are statistically correlated with the semantic types of the defined terms. The average number and standard deviation of statistically correlated semantic types is 80.6±35.4 at P<<0.0001.
Figure 1 shows three S_{DT} ([Body Part, Organ, or Organ Component], [Disease or Syndrome], and [Organization]) with the corresponding top five statistically correlated semantic types that appear in their definitions. Our results show that in a total of 112 (or 83.6%) cases, S_{DT} appears as one of the top five statistically correlated semantic types in S_{Def}, and that in a total of 94 (or 70.1%) cases, S_{DT} appears at the top in S_{Def}. Our results indicate that if a definitional term has a semantic type S_{DT}, then the terms in its definition tend to have the same or related semantic types.

We examined the cases in which the semantic types of definitional terms do not appear in the top five semantic types in the definitions. We found that in all of those cases, the total numbers of definitions that were used for statistical analysis were too small to obtain statistical significance. For example, when S_{DT} is "Entity", the minimum size for a S_{Def} was 4.75, which is larger than the total number of the definitions (i.e., 4). As a result, some actually correlated semantic types might be undetected due to insufficient sample size.

Our results also show that the lexicosyntactic patterns of definitional sentences are S_{DT}-dependent. Our results show that many lexicosyntactic patterns that appear in definitions are statistically correlated with the semantic types of defined terms. The average number and standard deviation of statistically correlated lexico-syntactic patterns is 1656.7±1818.9 at P<<0.0001. We found that the more definitions an S_{DT} has, the more lexicosyntactic patterns.

Figure 2 shows the top 10 lexicosyntactic patterns (based on chi-square statistics) that were captured by Autoslog-TS with three different S_{DT}; namely, *[Disease or Syndrome], [Body Part, Organ, or Organ Component],* and *[Organization].* Figure 3 shows the top 10 lexicosyntactic patterns ranked by AutoSlog-TS which incorporated the frequencies of the patterns (Riloff and Philips 2004).

Figure 4 lists the top 30 common patterns across all different semantic types S_{DT}. We found that many common lexicosyntactic patterns (e.g., "…known as…", "…called", "…include…") have been identified by other research groups through either manual or semi-automatic pattern discovery (Blair-Goldensohn et al. 2004).

[Disease or Syndrome]	[Body Part, Organ, or Organ Component]	[Organization]
Np_Prep_<NP>__INFLAMMATION_OF	Np_Prep_<NP>__PART_OF	Np_Prep_<NP>__UNION_IN
ActVp_Prep_<NP>__CHARACTERIZED_BY	<subj>_ActVp__LOCATED	<subj>_AuxVp_Dobj__BE_COURT
<subj>_ActVp__CHARACTERIZED	ActVp_<dobj>__CALLED	Np_Prep_<NP>__ORGANIZATION_TO
ActVp_<dobj>__CALLED	Np_Prep_<NP>__PORTION_OF	Np_Prep_<NP>__GOVERNMENT_WITH
<subj>_ActVp__OCCURS	<subj>_ActVp__CALLED	Subj_AuxVp_<dobj>__BE_ARMY
Np_Prep_<NP>__LOSS_OF	Np_Prep_<NP>__SIDE_OF	Np_Prep_<NP>__WORSHIP_FOR
<subj>_ActVp__CAUSES	ActVp_<dobj>__CONTAINS	ActVp_Prep_<NP>__FORMED_FOR
<subj>_ActVp__INCLUDE	Np_Prep_<NP>__BASE_OF	<subj>_ActVp_Dobj__OWN_PROPERTY
ActVp_<dobj>__CAUSES	Np_Prep_<NP>__ORGAN_IN	Subj_AuxVp_<dobj>__HAVE_CORPORATION
Np_Prep_<NP>__FORM_OF	Np_Prep_<NP>__LAYER_OF	Subj_AuxVp_<dobj>__BE_ORGANIZATIONS

Figure 2: The top 10 lexicosyntactic patterns that appear in definitions based on chi-square statistics. The defined terms have one of the three semantic types *[Disease_or_Syndrome], [Body Part, Organ, or Organ Component],* and *[Organization].*

[Disease or Syndrome]	[Body Part, Organ, or Organ Component]	[Organization]
Np_Prep_<NP>__INFLAMMATION_OF	Np_Prep_<NP>__PART_OF	Np_Prep_<NP>__GROUP_OF
<subj>_ActVp__DISEASE	<subj>_ActVp__LOCATED	Np_Prep_<NP>__HOUSE_OF
ActVp_Prep_<NP>__CHARACTERIZED_BY	ActVp_<dobj>__CALLED	Np_Prep_<NP>__PLACE_OF
<subj>_ActVp__CHARACTERIZED	Np_Prep_<NP>__PORTION_OF	ActVp_<dobj>__INCLUDING
ActVp_<dobj>__CALLED	<subj>_ActVp__CALLED	<subj>_ActVp__ESTABLISHED
ActVp_Prep_<NP>__CAUSED_BY	Np_Prep_<NP>__SIDE_OF	<subj>_ActVp__FORMED
<subj>_ActVp__OCCURS	ActVp_<dobj>__CONTAINS	Np_Prep_<NP>__COURT_OF
Np_Prep_<NP>__LOSS_OF	Np_Prep_<NP>__BASE_OF	<subj>_ActVp__INCLUDE
<subj>_ActVp__CAUSED	Np_Prep_<NP>__ORGAN_IN	ActVp_<dobj>__SEE
<subj>_ActVp__CAUSES	Np_Prep_<NP>__LAYER_OF	ActVp_Prep_<NP>__REFERS_TO

Figure 3: The top 10 lexicosyntactic patterns ranked by Autoslog-TS. The defined terms have one of the three semantic types *[Disease_or_Syndrome], [Body Part, Organ, or Organ Component],* and *[Organization].*

1. ActVp_<dobj>__SEE	11. <subj>_PassVp__USED	21. <subj>_ActVp__INCLUDES
2. <subj>_ActVp__USED	12. ActVp_Prep_<NP>__KNOWN_AS	22. <subj>_ActVp__INCLUDING
3. ActVp_<dobj>__CALLED	13. ActVp_<dobj>__INCLUDES	23. <subj>_ActVp__LIKE
4. Subj_AuxVp_<dobj>__BE_IT	14. Np_Prep_<NP>__TYPE_OF	24. <subj>_ActVp__DISEASE
5. <subj>_ActVp__CALLED	15. ActVp_Prep_<NP>__USED_IN	25. <subj>_ActVp__REFERS
6. Np_Prep_<NP>__PART_OF	16. ActVp_<dobj>__LIKE	26. Np_Prep_<NP>__NUMBER_OF
7. ActVp_<dobj>__INCLUDING	17. Np_Prep_<NP>__ONE_OF	27. ActVp_Prep_<NP>__FOUND_IN
8. <subj>_ActVp__INCLUDE	18. Np_Prep_<NP>__FORM_OF	28. <subj>_ActVp__KNOWN
9. ActVp_<dobj>__INCLUDE	19. Np_Prep_<NP>__GROUP_OF	29. Np_Prep_<NP>__PROCESS_OF
10. ActVp_Prep_<NP>__REFERS_TO	20. <subj>_PassVp__CALLED	30. <subj>_ActVp__OCCURS

Figure 4: The top 30 common lexicosyntactic patterns generated across patterns with different S_{DT}.

8 Discussion

The statistical correlations between S_{DT} and S_{Def} may be useful to enhance the performance of a definition-question-answering system by at least two means. First, the semantic types may be useful for word sense disambiguation. A simple application is to rank definitional sentences based on the distributions of the semantic types of terms in the definitions to capture the definition of a specific sense. For example, a biomedical definitional question answering system may exclude the definition of other senses (e.g., "feeling" as shown in the sentence "The locus of feelings and intuitions; 'in your heart you know it is true'; 'her story would melt your heart.'") if the semantic types that define "heart" do not include [Body Part, Organ, or Organ Component] of terms other than "heart".

Secondly, the semantic-type correlations may be used as features to exclude non-definitional sentences. For example, a biomedical definitional question answering system may exclude the following non-definitional sentence "Heart rate was unaffected by the drug" because the semantic types in the sentence do not include [Body Part, Organ, or Organ Component] of terms other than "heart".

S_{DT}-dependent lexicosyntactic patterns may enhance both the recall and precision of a definitional question answering system. First, the large sets of lexicosyntactic patterns we generated automatically may expand the smaller sets of lexicosyntactic patterns that have been reported by the existing question answering systems. Secondly, S_{DT}-dependent lexicosyntactic patterns may be used to capture definitions.

The common lexicosyntactic patterns we identified (in Figure 4) may be useful for a generic definitional question answering system. For example, a definitional question answering system may implement the most common patterns to detect any generic definitions; specific patterns may be implemented to detect definitions with specific S_{DT}.

One limitation of our work is that the lexicosyntactic patterns generated by Autoslog-TS are within clauses. This is a disadvantage because 1) lexicosyntactic patterns can extend beyond clauses (Cui et al. 2005) and 2) frequently a definition has multiple lexicosyntactic patterns. Many of the patterns might not be generalizible. For example, as shown in Figure 2, some of the top ranked patterns (e.g., "Subj_AuxVp_<dobj>_BE_ARMY>") identified by AutoSlog-TS may be too specific to the text collection. The pattern-ranking method introduced by AutoSlog-TS takes into consideration the frequency of a pattern and therefore is a better ranking method than the chi-square ranking (shown in Figure 3).

9 Related Work

Systems have used named entities (e.g., "PEOPLE" and "LOCATION") to assist in information extraction (Agichtein and Gravano 2000) and question answering (Moldovan et al. 2002; Filatova and Prager 2005). Semantic constraints were first explored by (Bodenreider and Burgun 2002; Rindflesch and Fiszman 2003) who observed that the principle nouns in definientia are frequently semantically related (e.g., hyponyms, hypernyms, siblings, and synonyms) to definiena. Semantic constraints have been introduced to definitional question answering (Prager et al. 2000; Liang et al. 2001). For example, an artist's work must be completed between his birth and death (Prager et al. 2000); and the hyponyms of defined terms might be incorporated in the definitions (Liang et al. 2001). Semantic correlations have been explored in other areas of NLP. For example, researchers (Turney 2002; Yu and Hatzivassiloglou 2003) have identified semantic correlation between words and views: positive words tend to appear more frequently in positive movie and product reviews and newswire article sentences that have a positive semantic orientation and vice versa for negative reviews or sentences with a negative semantic orientation.

10 Conclusions and Future Work

This is the first study in definitional question answering that concludes that the semantics of a definiendum constrain both the lexical semantics and the lexicosyntactic patterns in the definition. Our discoveries may be useful for the building of a biomedical definitional question answering system.

Although our discoveries (i.e., that the semantic types of the definitional terms determine both the lexicosyntactic patterns and the semantic types in the definitions) were evaluated with the knowledge framework from the biomedical, domain-specific knowledge resource the UMLS, the principles may be generalizable to any type of semantic classification of definitions. The semantic constraints may enhance both recall and precision of one-size-fits-all question answering systems, which may be evaluated in future work.

As stated in the Discussion session, one disadvantage of this study is that the lexicosyntactic patterns generated by Autoslog-TS are within clauses. Future work needs to develop pattern-recognition systems that are capable of detecting patterns across clauses.

In addition, future work needs to move beyond lexicosyntactic patterns to extract semantic-lexicosyntactic patterns and to evaluate how the semantic-lexicosyntactic patterns can enhance definitional question answering.

Acknowledgement: The author thanks Sasha Blair-Goldensohn, Vijay Shanker, and especially the three anonymous reviewers who provide valuable critics and comments. The concepts "Definiendum" and "Definiens" come from one of the reviewers' recommendation.

References

Agichtein E, Gravano L (2000) Snowball: extracting relations from large plain-text collections. . Paper presented at Proceedings of the 5th ACM International Conference on Digital Libraries

Aronson A (2001) Effective Mapping of Biomedical Text to the UMLS Metathesaurus: The MetaMap Program. Paper presented at American Medical Information Association

Aronson A, Mork J, Gay G, Humphrey S, Rogers W (2004) The NLM Indexing Initiative's Medical Text Indexer. Paper presented at MedInfo 2004

Blair-Goldensohn S, McKeown K, Schlaikjer A (2004) Answering Definitional Questions: A Hybrid Approach. In: Maybury M (ed) New Directions In Question Answering. AAAI Press

Bodenreider O, Burgun A (2002) Characterizing the definitions of anatomical concepts in WordNet and specialized sources. Paper presented at The First Global WordNet Conference

Cui H, Kan M, Cua T (2005) Generic soft pattern models for definitional question answering. . Paper presented at The 28th Annual International ACM SIGIR Salvado, Brazil

Eichmann D, Ruiz M, Srinivasan P (1998) Cross-language information retrieval with the UMLS metathesaurus. Paper presented at SIGIR

Elhadad N, Kan M, Klavans J, McKeown K (2004) Customization in a unified framework for summarizing medical literature. Journal of Artificial Intelligence in Medicine

Filatova E, Prager J (2005) Tell me what you do and I'll tell you what you are: learning occupation-related activities for biographies. Paper presented at HLT/EMNLP 2005. Vancouver, Canada

Fiszman M, Rindflesch T, Kilicoglu H (2004) Abstraction Summarization for Managing the Biomedical Research Literature. Paper presented at HLT-NAACL 2004: Computational Lexical Semantic Workshop

Fleiss J (1981) Statistical methods for rates and proportions.

Hildebrandt W, Katz B, Lin J (2004) Answering definition questions with multiple knowledge sources. . Paper presented at HLT/NAACL

Hochberg Y (1988) A sharper Bonferroni procedure for multiple tests of significance. Biometrika 75:800-802

Humphreys BL, Lindberg DA, Schoolman HM, Barnett GO (1998) The Unified Medical Language System: an informatics research collaboration. J Am Med Inform Assoc 5:1-11.

Lacson R, Barzilay R (2005) Automatic processing of spoken dialogue in the hemodialysis domain. Paper presented at Proc AMIA Symp

Liang L, Liu C, Xu Y-Q, Guo B, Shum H-Y (2001) Real-time texture synthesis by patch-based sampling. ACM Trans Graph 20:127--150

Moldovan D, Harabagiu S, Girju R, Morarescu P, Lacatusu F, Novischi A, Badulescu A, Bolohan O (2002) LCC tools for question answering. Paper presented at The Eleventh Text REtrieval Conference (TREC 2002)

Prager J, Brown E, Coden A, Radev D (2000) Quesiton-answering by predictive annotation. Paper presented at Proceeding 22nd Annual International ACM SIGIR Conference on Research and Development in Information Retrieval

Riloff E (1996) Automatically generating extraction patterns from untagged text. . Paper presented at AAAI-96

Riloff E, Philips W (2004) An introduction to the Sundance and AutoSlog Systems. Technical Report #UUCS-04-015. University of Utah School of Computing.

Rindflesch T, Tanabe L, Weinstein J, Hunter L (2000) EDGAR: extraction of drugs, genes and relations from the biomedical literature. Pac Symp Biocomput:517-528.

Rindflesch TC, Fiszman M (2003) The interaction of domain knowledge and linguistic structure in natural language processing: interpreting hypernymic propositions in biomedical text. J Biomed Inform 36:462-477

Turney P (2002) Thumbs up or thumbs down? Semantic orientation applied to unsupervised classification of reviews. Paper presented at ACL 2002

Yu H, Hatzivassiloglou V (2003) Towards answering opinion questions: Separating facts from opinions and identifying the polarity of opinion sentences. Paper presented at Proceedings of the 2003 Conference on Empirical Methods in Natural Language Processing (EMNLP 2003)

Yu H, Sable C (2005) Being Erlang Shen: Identifying answerable questions. Paper presented at Nineteenth International Joint Conference on Artificial Intelligence on Knowledge and Reasoning for Answering Questions

Ontology-Based Natural Language Query Processing for the Biological Domain

Jisheng Liang, Thien Nguyen, Krzysztof Koperski, Giovanni Marchisio

Insightful Corporation
1700 Westlake Ave N., Suite 500, Seattle, WA, USA
{jliang,thien,krisk,giovanni}@insightful.com

Abstract

This paper describes a natural language query engine that enables users to search for entities, relationships, and events that are extracted from biological literature. The query interpretation is guided by a domain ontology, which provides a mapping between linguistic structures and domain conceptual relations. We focus on the usability of the natural language interface to users who are used to keyword-based information retrieval. Preliminary evaluation of our approach using the GENIA corpus and ontology shows promising results.

1 Introduction

New scientific research methods have greatly increased the volume of data available in the biological domain. A growing challenge for researchers and health care professionals is how to access this ever-increasing quantity of information [Hersh 2003]. The general public has even more trouble following current and potential applications. Part of the difficulty lies in the high degree of specialization of most resources. There is thus an urgent need for better access to current data and the various domains of expertise. Key considerations for improving information access include: 1) accessibility to different types of users; 2) high precision; 3) ease of use; 4) transparent retrieval across heterogeneous data sources; and 5) accommodation of rapid language change in the domain.

Natural language searching refers to approaches that enable users to express queries in explicit phrases, sentences, or questions. Current information retrieval engines typically return too many documents that a user has to go through. Natural language query allows users to express their information need in a more precise way and retrieve specific results instead of ranked documents. It also benefits users who are not familiar with domain terminology.

With the increasing availability of textual information related to biology, including MEDLINE abstracts and full-text journal articles, the field of biomedical text mining is rapidly growing. The application of Natural Language Processing (NLP) techniques in the biological domain has been focused on tagging entities, such as genes and proteins, and on detecting relations among those entities. The main goal of applying these techniques is database curation. There has been a lack of effort or success on improving search engine performance using NLP and text mining results. In this effort, we explore the feasibility of bridging the gap between text mining and search by

- Indexing entities and relationships extracted from text,
- Developing search operators on entities and relationships, and
- Transforming natural language queries to the entity-relationship search operators.

The first two steps are performed using our existing text analysis and search platform, called InFact [Liang 2005; Marchisio 2006]. This paper concerns mainly the step of NL query interpretation and translation. The processes described above are all guided by a domain ontology, which provides a conceptual mapping between linguistic structures and domain concepts/relations. A major drawback to existing NL query interfaces is that their linguistic and conceptual coverage is not clear to the user

Proceedings of the BioNLP Workshop on Linking Natural Language Processing and Biology at HLT-NAACL 06, pages 9–16,
New York City, June 2006.

[Androutsopoulos 1995]. Our approach addresses this problem by pointing out which concepts or syntactic relations are not mapped when we fail to find a consistent interpretation.

There has been skepticism about the usefulness of natural language queries for searching on the web or in the enterprise. Users usually prefer to enter the minimum number of words instead of lengthy grammatically-correct questions. We have developed a prototype system to deal with queries such as "With what genes does AP-1 interact?" The queries do not have to be standard grammatical questions, but rather have forms such as: "proteins regulated by IL-2" or "IL-2 inhibitors". We apply our system to a corpus of molecular biology literature, the GENIA corpus. Preliminary experimental results and evaluation are reported.

2 Overview of Our Approach

Molecular biology concerns interaction events between proteins, drugs, and other molecules. These events include transcription, translation, dissociation, etc. In addition to basic events which focus on interactions between molecules, users are also interested in relationships between basic events, e.g. the causality between two such events [Hirschman 2002]. In order to produce a useful NL query tool, we must be able to correctly interpret and answer typical queries in the domain, e.g.:

- What genes does transcription factor X regulate?
- With what genes does gene G physically interact?
- What proteins interact with drug D?
- What proteins affect the interaction of another protein with drug D?

Figure 1 shows the process diagram of our system. The query interpretation process consists of two major steps: 1) Syntactic analysis – parsing and decomposition of the input query; and 2) Semantic analysis – mapping of syntactic structures to an intermediate conceptual representation. The analysis uses an ontology to extract domain-specific entities/relations and to resolve linguistic ambiguity and variations. Then, the extracted semantic expression is transformed into an entity-relationship query language, which retrieves results from pre-indexed biological literature databases.

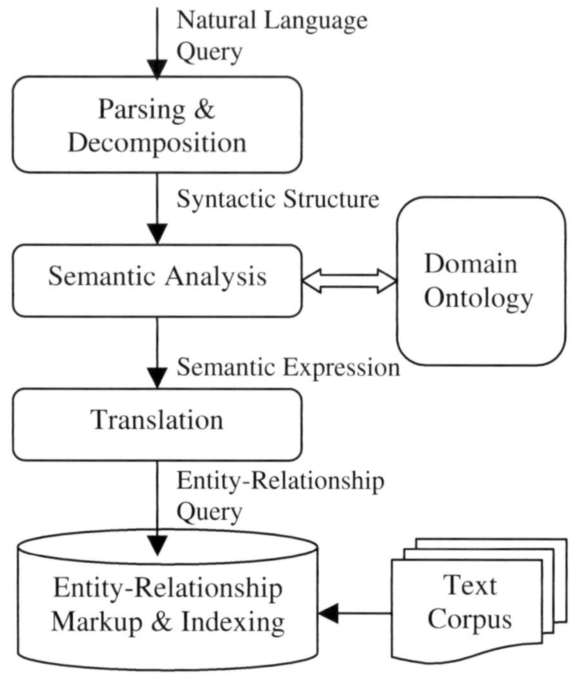

Figure 1 shows the query processing and retrieval process.

2.1 Incorporating Domain Ontology

Domain ontologies explicitly specify the meaning of and relation between the fundamental concepts in an application domain. A *concept* represents a set or class of entities within a domain. *Relations* describe the interactions between concepts or a concept's properties. Relations also fall into two broad categories: *taxonomies* that organize concepts into "is-a" and "is-a-member-of" hierarchy, and *associative* relationships [Stevens 2000]. The associative relationships represent, for example, the functions and processes a concept has or is involved in. A domain ontology also specifies how knowledge is related to linguistic structures such as grammars and lexicons. Therefore, it can be used by NLP to improve expressiveness and accuracy, and to resolve the ambiguity of NL queries.

There are two major steps for incorporating a domain ontology: 1) building/augmenting a lexicon for entity tagging, including lexical patterns that specify how to recognize the concept in text; and 2) specifying syntactic structure patterns for extracting semantic relationships among concepts. The existing ontologies (e.g. UMLS, Gene Ontology) are created mainly for the purpose of database annotation and consolidation. From those ontologies, we could extract concepts and taxonomic relations, e.g., is-a. However there is also a need for ontologies that specify relevant associative relations between concepts, e.g. "Protein acetylate Protein." In our experiment we investigate the problem of augmenting an existing ontology (i.e. GENIA) with associative relations and other linguistic information required to guide the query interpretation process.

2.2 Query Parsing and Normalization

Our NL parser performs the steps of tokenization, part-of-speech tagging, morphological processing, lexical analysis, and identification of phrase and grammatical relations such as subjects and objects. The lexical analysis is based on a customizable lexicon and set of lexical patterns, providing the abilities to add words or phrases as dictionary terms, to assign categories (e.g. entity types), and to associate synonyms and related terms with dictionary items. The output of our parser is a dependency tree, represented by a set of dependency relationships of the form (head, relation, modifier).

In the next step, we perform syntactic decomposition to collapse the dependency tree into subject-verb-object (SVO) expressions. The SVO triples can express most types of syntactic relations between various entities within a sentence. Another advantage of this triple expression is that it becomes easier to write explicit transformational rules that encode specific linguistic variations.

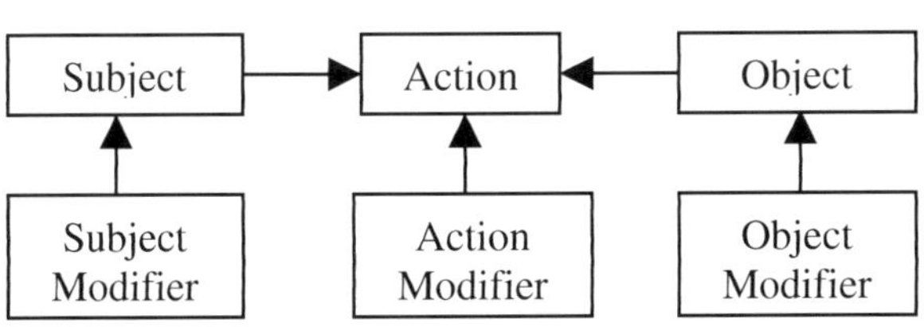

Figure 2 shows the subject-action-object triplet.

Verb modifiers in the syntactic structure may include prepositional attachment and adverbials. The modifiers add context to the event of the verb, including time, location, negation, etc. Subject/object modifiers include appositive, nominative, genitive, prepositional, descriptive (adjective-noun modification), etc. All these modifiers can be either considered as descriptors (attributes) or reformulated as triple expressions by assigning a type to the pair.

Linguistic normalization is a process by which linguistic variants that contain the same semantic content are mapped onto the same representational structure. It operates at the morphological, lexical and syntactic levels. Syntactic normalization involves transformational rules that recognize the equivalence of different structures, e.g.:

- Verb Phrase Normalization – elimination of tense, modality and voice.
- Verbalization of noun phrases – e.g. Inhibition of X by Y → Y inhibit X.

For example, queries such as:

Proteins activated by IL-2
What proteins are activated by IL-2?
What proteins does IL-2 activate?
Find proteins that are activated by IL-2

are all normalized into the relationship:

IL-2 > activate > Protein

As part of the syntactic analysis, we also need to catch certain question-specific patterns or phrases based on their part-of-speech tags and grammatical roles, e.g. determiners like "which" or "what", and verbs like "find" or "list".

2.3 Semantic Analysis

The semantic analysis typically involves two steps: 1) Identifying the semantic type of the entity sought by the question; and 2) Determining additional constraints by identifying relations that ought to hold between a candidate answer entity and other entities or events mentioned in the query [Hirschman 2001]. The semantic analysis attempts to map normalized syntactic structures to semantic entities/relations defined in the ontology. When the system is not able to understand the question, the cause of failure will be explained to the user, e.g. unknown word or syntax, no relevant concepts in the ontology, etc. The output of semantic analysis is a set of relationship triplets, which can be grouped into four categories:

Events, including interactions between entities and inter-event relations (nested events), e.g.
Inhibition("il-2", "erbb2")
Inhibition(protein, Activation(DEX, IkappaB))

Event Attributes, including attributes of an interaction event, e.g.

Location(Inhibition(il-2, erbb2), "blood cell")

Entity Attributes, including attributes of a given entity, e.g.
Has-Location("erbb2", "human")

Entity Types, including taxonomic paths of a given entity, e.g.
Is-A("erbb2", "Protein")

A natural language query will be decomposed into a list of inter-linked triplets. A user's specific information request is noted as "UNKNOWN."

Starting with an ontology, we determine the mapping from syntactic structures to semantic relations. Given our example "IL-2 > activate > Protein", we recognize "IL-2" as an entity, map the verb "activate" to a semantic relation "Activation," and detect the term "protein" as a designator of the semantic type "Protein." Therefore, we could easily transform the query to the following triplets:

- Activation(IL-2, UNKNOWN)
- Is-A(UNKNOWN, Protein)

Given a syntactic triplet of subject/verb/object or head/relation/modifier, the ontology-driven semantic analysis performs the following steps:

1. Assign possible semantic types to the pair of terms,
2. Determine all possible semantic links between each pair of assigned semantic types defined in the ontology,
3. Given the syntactic relation (i.e. verb or modifier-relation) between the two concepts, infer and validate plausible inter-concept semantic relationships from the set determined in Step 2,
4. Resolve linguistic ambiguity by rejecting inconsistent relations or semantic types.

It is simpler and more robust to identify the query pattern using the extracted syntactic structure, in which linguistic variations have been normalized into a canonical form, rather than the original question or its full parse tree.

2.4 Entity-Relationship Indexing and Search

In this section, we describe the annotation, indexing and search of text data. In the off-line indexing mode, we annotate the text with ontological concepts and relationships. We perform full linguistic analysis on each document, which involves splitting of text into sentences, sentence parsing, and the same syntactic and semantic analysis as described in previous sections on query processing. This step recognizes names of proteins, drugs, and other biological entities mentioned in the texts. Then we apply a document-level discourse analysis procedure to resolve entity-level coreference, such as acronyms/aliases and pronoun anaphora. Sentence-level syntactic structures (subject-verb-object triples) and semantic markups are stored in a database and indexed for efficient retrieval.

In the on-line search mode, we provide a set of entity-relationship (ER) search operators that allow users to search on the indexed annotations. Unlike keyword search engines, we employ a highly expressive query language that combines the power of grammatical roles with the flexibility of Boolean operators, and allows users to search for actions, entities, relationships, and events. We represent the basic relationship between two entities with an expression of the kind:

Subject Entity > Action > Object Entity

We can optionally constrain this expression by specifying modifiers or using Boolean logic. The arrows in the query refer to the directionality of the action. For example,

Entity 1 <> Action <> Entity 2

will retrieve all relationships involving *Entity 1* and *Entity 2*, regardless of their roles as subject or object of the action. An asterisk (*) can be used to denote unknown or unspecified sources or targets, e.g. "Il-2 > inhibit > *".

In the ER query language we can represent and organize entity types using taxonomy paths, e.g.:

[substance/compound/amino_acid/protein]
[source/natural/cell_type]

The taxonomic paths can encode the "is-a" relation (as in the above examples), or any other relations defined in a particular ontology (e.g. the "part-of" relation). When querying, we can use a taxonomy path to specify an entity type, e.g. *[Protein/Molecule]*, *[Source]*, and the entity type will automatically include all subpaths in the taxonomic hierarchy. The complete list of ER query features that we currently support is given in Table 1.

ER Query Features	Descriptions and Examples
Relationships between two entities or entity types	The query "*il-2 <> * <> Ap1*" will retrieve all relationships between the two entities.
Events involving one or more entities or types	The query "*il-2 > regulate > [Protein]*" will return all instances of il-2 regulating a protein.
Events restricted to a certain action type - categories of actions that can be used to filter or expand search	The query "*[Protein] > [Inhibition] > [Protein]*" will retrieve all events involving two proteins that are in the nature of inhibition.
Boolean Operators - AND, OR, NOT	Example: Il-2 OR "interleukin 2" > inhibit or suppress >* Phrases such as "interleukin 2" can be included in quotes.
Prepositional Constraints - Filter results by information found in a prepositional modifier.	Query *Il-2 > activate > [protein]^[cell_type]* will only return results mentioning a cell type location where the activation occurs.
Local context constraints - Certain keyword(s) must appear near the relationship (within one sentence).	Example: LPS > induce > NF-kappaB CONTEXT CONTAINS "human T cell"
Document keyword constraints - Documents must contain certain keyword(s)	Example: Alpha-lipoic acid > inhibit > activation DOC CONTAINS "AIDS" OR "HIV"
Document metadata constraints	Restrict results to documents that contain the specified metadata values.
Nested Search	Allow users to search the results of a given search.
Negation Filtering	Allow users to filter out negated results that are detected during indexing.

Table 1 lists various types of ER queries

2.5 Translation to ER Query

We extract answers through entity-relational matching between the NL query and syntactic/semantic annotations extracted from sentences. Given the query's semantic expression as described in Section 2.3, we translate it to one or more entity-relationship search operators. The different types of semantic triplets (i.e. Event, Attribute, and Type) are treated differently when being converted to ER queries.

- The Event relations can be converted directly to the subject-action-object queries.
- The inter-event relations are represented as local context constraints.
- The Event Attributes are translated to prepositional constraints.
- The Entity Attribute relations could be extracted either from same sentence or from somewhere else within document context, using the nested search feature.
- The Entity Type relations are specified in the ontology taxonomy.

For our example, "proteins activated by il-2", we translate it into an ER query: "il-2 > [activation] > [protein]". Figure 3 shows the list of retrieved subject-verb-object triples that match the query, where each triple is linked to a sentence in the corpus.

3 Experiment Results

We tested our approach on the GENIA corpus and ontology. The evaluation presented in this section focuses on the ability of the system to translate NL queries into their normalized representation, and the corresponding ER queries.

3.1 Test Data

The GENIA corpus contains 2000 annotated MEDLINE abstracts [Ohta 2002]. The main reason we chose this corpus is that we could extract the pre-annotated biological entities to populate a domain lexicon, which is used by the NL parser. Therefore, we were able to ensure that the system had complete terminology coverage of the corpus. During indexing, we used the raw text data as input by stripping out the annotation tags.

The GENIA ontology has a complete taxonomy of entities in molecular biology. It is divided into substance and source sub-hierarchies. The substances include sub-paths such as nucleic_acid/DNA and amino_acid/protein. Sources are biological locations where substances are found and their reactions take place. They are also hierarchically subclassified into organisms, body parts, tissues, cells

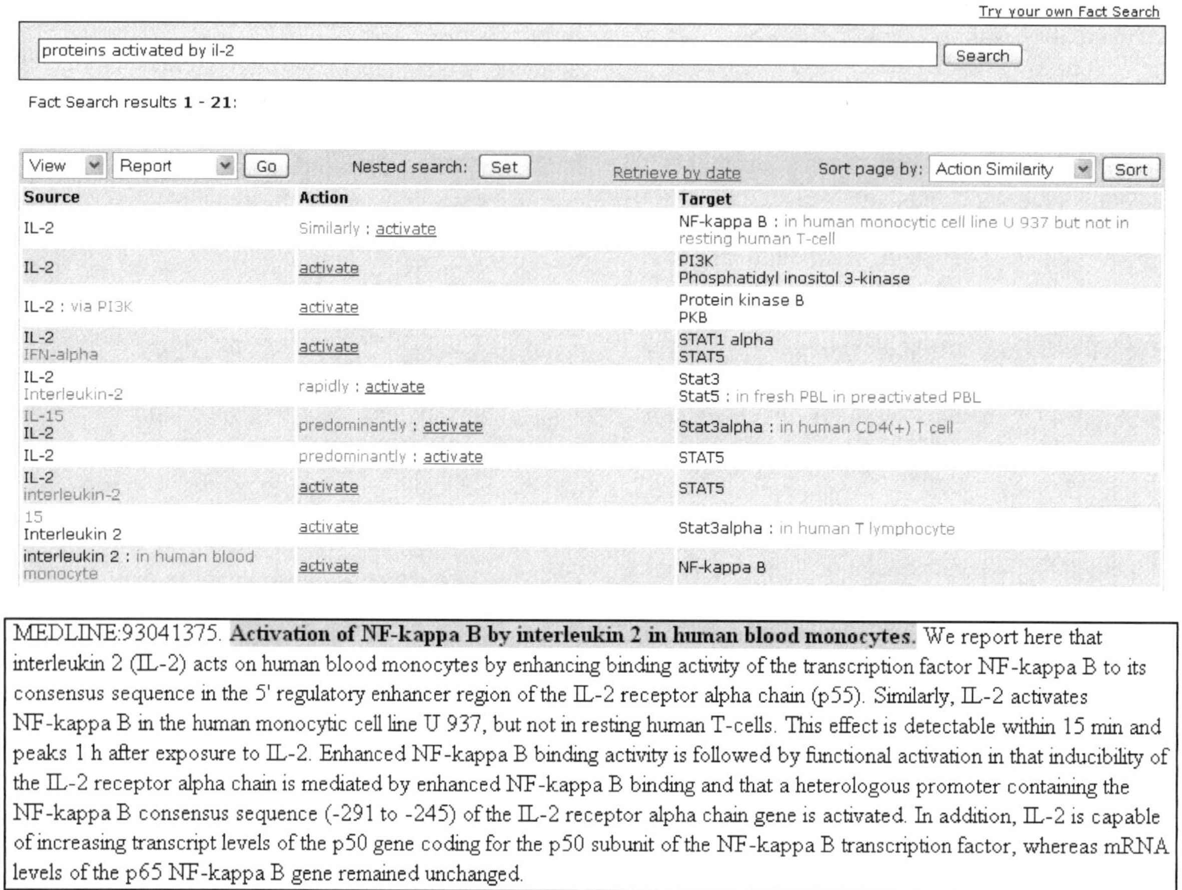
Try your own Fact Search

proteins activated by il-2 | Search

Fact Search results **1 - 21**:

View | Report | Go | Nested search: Set | Retrieve by date | Sort page by: Action Similarity | Sort

Source	Action	Target
IL-2	Similarly : activate	NF-kappa B : in human monocytic cell line U 937 but not in resting human T-cell
IL-2	activate	PI3K Phosphatidyl inositol 3-kinase
IL-2 : via PI3K	activate	Protein kinase B PKB
IL-2 IFN-alpha	activate	STAT1 alpha STAT5
IL-2 Interleukin-2	rapidly : activate	Stat3 Stat5 : in fresh PBL in preactivated PBL
IL-15 IL-2	predominantly : activate	Stat3alpha : in human CD4(+) T cell
IL-2	predominantly : activate	STAT5
IL-2 interleukin-2	activate	STAT5
15 Interleukin 2	activate	Stat3alpha : in human T lymphocyte
interleukin 2 : in human blood monocyte	activate	NF-kappa B

MEDLINE:93041375. **Activation of NF-kappa B by interleukin 2 in human blood monocytes.** We report here that interleukin 2 (IL-2) acts on human blood monocytes by enhancing binding activity of the transcription factor NF-kappa B to its consensus sequence in the 5' regulatory enhancer region of the IL-2 receptor alpha chain (p55). Similarly, IL-2 activates NF-kappa B in the human monocytic cell line U 937, but not in resting human T-cells. This effect is detectable within 15 min and peaks 1 h after exposure to IL-2. Enhanced NF-kappa B binding activity is followed by functional activation in that inducibility of the IL-2 receptor alpha chain is mediated by enhanced NF-kappa B binding and that a heterologous promoter containing the NF-kappa B consensus sequence (-291 to -245) of the IL-2 receptor alpha chain gene is activated. In addition, IL-2 is capable of increasing transcript levels of the p50 gene coding for the p50 subunit of the NF-kappa B transcription factor, whereas mRNA levels of the p65 NF-kappa B gene remained unchanged.

Figure 3 shows our natural language query interface. The retrieved subject-verb-object relationships are displayed in a tabular format. The lower screenshot shows the document display page when user clicks on the last result link <interleukin 2, activate, NF-kappa B>. The sentence that contains the result relationship is highlighted.

or cell types, etc. Our adoption of the GENIA ontology as a conceptual model for guiding query interpretation is described as follows.

Entities - For gene and protein names, we added synonyms and variations extracted from the Entrez Gene database (previously LocusLink).

Interactions – The GENIA ontology does not contain associative relations. By consulting a domain expert, we identified a set of relations that are of particular interest in this domain. Some examples of relevant relations are: activate, bind, interact, regulate. For each type of interaction, we created a list of corresponding action verbs.

Entity Attributes - We identified two types of entity attributes:

1. Location, e.g. body_part, cell_type, etc. identified by path [genia/source]
2. Subtype of proteins/genes, e.g. enzymes, transcription factors, etc., identified by types like protein_family_or_group, DNA_family_or_group

Event Attributes - Locations were the only event attribute we supported in this experiment.

Designators - We added a mapping between each semantic type and its natural language names. For example, when a term such as "gene" or "nucleic acid" appears in a query, we map it to the taxonomic path: [Substance/compound/nucleic_acid]

3.2 Evaluation

To demonstrate our ability to interpret and answer NL queries correctly, we selected a set of 50 natural language questions in the molecular biology domain. The queries were collected by consulting a domain expert, with restrictions such as:

1. Focusing on queries concerning entities and interaction events between entities.
2. Limiting to taxonomic paths defined within the GENIA ontology, which does not contain important entities such as drugs and diseases.

For each target question, we first manually created the ground-truth entity-relationship model. Then, we performed automatic question interpretation and answer retrieval using the developed software prototype. The extracted semantic expressions were verified and validated by comparison against the ground-truth. Our system was able to correctly interpret all the 50 queries and retrieve answers from the GENIA corpus. In the rest of this section, we describe a number of representative queries.

Query on events:
With what genes does ap-1 physically interact?
Relations:
Interaction("ap-1", UNKOWN)
IS-A(UNKNOWN, "Gene")
ER Query:
ap-1 <>[Interaction] <> [nucleic_acid]

Queries on association:
erbb2 and il-2
what is the relation between erbb2 and il-2?
Relations:
Association("erbb2", "il-2")
ER Query:
Erbb2 <>*<>il-2

Query of noun phrases:
Inhibitor of erbb2
Relation:
Inhibition(UNKNOWN, "erbb2")
ER Query:
[substance] > [Inhibition] > erbb2

Query on event location:
In what cell types is il-2 activated?
Relations:
Activation (*, "Il-2")
Location (Activation(), [cell_type])
ER Query:
* > [Activation] > il-2 ^ [cell_type]

Entity Attribute Constraints

An entity's properties are often mentioned in a separate place within the document. We translate these types of queries into DOC_LEVEL_AND of multiple ER queries. This AND operator is currently implemented using the feature of nested search. For example, given query**:**

What enzymes does HIV-1 Tat suppress?

we recognize the word "enzyme" is associated with the path: [protein/protein_family_or_group], and we consider it as an attribute constraint.

Relations:
Inhibition ("hiv-1 tat", UNKNOWN)
IS-A(UNKNOWN, "Protein")
HAS-ATTRIBUTE (UNKNOWN, "enzyme")
ER query:
(hiv-1 tat > [Inhibition]> [protein])
DOC_LEVEL_AND
([protein] > be > enzyme)

One of the answer sentences is displayed below:

"Thus, our experiments demonstrate that the C-terminal region of HIV-1 Tat is required to suppress Mn-SOD expression"

while Mn-SOD is indicated as an enzyme in a different sentence:

"… Mn-dependent superoxide dismutase (**Mn-SOD**), a mitochondrial **enzyme** … "

Inter-Event Relations

The inter-event relations or nested event queries (CLAUSE_LEVEL_AND) are currently implemented using the ER query's local context constraints, i.e. one event must appear within the local context of the other.

Query on inter-event relations:
What protein inhibits the induction of Ikappa-Balpha by DEX?
Relations:
Inhibition ([protein], Activation())
Activation ("DEX", "IkappaBalpha")
ER Query:
([protein] > [Inhibition] > *)
CLAUSE_LEVEL_AND
(DEX > [Activation] > IkappaBalpha)

One of the answer sentences is:

"In both cell types, the cytokine that inhibits the induction of IkappaBapha by DEX, also rescues these cells from DEX-induced apoptosis."

4 Discussions

We demonstrated the feasibility of our approach using the relatively small GENIA corpus and ontology. A key concern with knowledge or semantic based methods is the scalability of the methods to larger set of data and queries. As future work, we plan to systematically measure the effectiveness of the approach based on large-scale experiments in an information retrieval setting, as we increase the knowledge and linguistic coverage of our system.

We are able to address the large data size issue by using InFact as an ingestion and deployment platform. With a distributed architecture, InFact is capable of ingesting large data sets (i.e. millions of MEDLINE abstracts) and hosting web-based search services with a large number of users. We will investigate the scalability to larger knowledge coverage by adopting a more comprehensive ontology (i.e. UMLS [Bodenreider 2004]). In addition to genes and proteins, we will include other entity types such as drugs, chemical compounds, diseases and phenotypes, molecular functions, and biological processes, etc. A main challenge will be increasing the linguistic coverage of our system in an automatic or semi-automatic way.

Another challenge is to encourage keyword search users to use the new NL query format and the semi-structured ER query form. We are investigating a number of usability enhancements, where the majority of them have been implemented and are being tested.

For each entity detected within a query, we provide a hyperlink that takes the user to an ontology lookup page. For example, if the user enters "protein il-2", we let the user know that we recognize "protein" as a taxonomic path and "il-2" as an entity according to the ontology. If a relationship triplet has any unspecified component, we provide recommendations (or tips) that are hyperlinks to executable ER queries. This allows users who are not familiar with the underlying ontology to navigate through most plausible results. When the user enters a single entity of a particular type, we display a list of relations the entity type is likely to be involved in, and a list of other entity types that are usually associated to the given type. Similarly, we define a list of relations between each pair of entity types according to the ontology. The relations are ranked according to popularity. When the user enters a query that involves two entities, we present the list of relevant relations to the user.

Acknowledgements: This research was supported in part by grant number 1 R43 LM008464-01 from the NIH. The authors thank Dr. David Haynor for his advice on this work; the anonymous reviewers for their helpful comments; and Yvonne Lam for helping with the manuscript.

References

Androutsopoulos I, Ritchie GD and Thanisch P. "Natural Language Interfaces to Databases – An Introduction", *Journal of Natural Language Engineering,* Vol 1, pp. 29-81, 1995.

Bodenreider O. The Unified Medical Language System (UMLS): Integrating Biomedical Terminology. *Nucleic Acids Research,* 2004.

Hersh W and Bhupatiraju RT. "TREC Genomics Track Overview", In *Proc. TREC,* 2003, pp. 14-23.

Hirschman L and Gaizauskas R. Natural Language Question Answering: The View from Here. *Natural Language Engineering*, 2001.

Hirschman L, Park JC, Tsujii J, Wong L and Wu CH. Accomplishments and Challenges in Literature Data Mining for Biology. *Bioinformatics Review*, Vol. 18, No. 12, 2002, pp. 1553-1561.

Liang J, Koperski K, Nguyen T, and Marchisio G. Extracting Statistical Data Frames from Text. *ACM SIGKDD Explorations*, Volume 7, Issue 1, pp. 67 – 75, June 2005.

Marchisio G, Dhillon D, Liang J, Tusk C, Koperski K, Nguyen T, White D, and Pochman L. A Case Study in Natural Language Based Web Search. To appear in *Text Mining and Natural Language Processing*. A Kao and SR Poteet (Editors). Springer 2006.

Ohta T, Tateisi Y, Mima H, and Tsujii J. GENIA Corpus: an Annotated Research Abstract Corpus in Molecular Biology Domain. In *Proc. HLT* 2002.

Stevens R, Goble CA, and Bechhofer S. Ontology-based Knowledge Representation for Bioinformatics. *Briefings in Bioinformatics*, November 2000.

Term Generalization and Synonym Resolution for Biological Abstracts: Using the Gene Ontology for Subcellular Localization Prediction

Alona Fyshe
Department of Computing Science
University of Alberta
Edmonton, Alberta T6G 2E8
alona@cs.ualberta.ca

Duane Szafron
Department of Computing Science
University of Alberta
Edmonton, Alberta T6G 2E8
duane@cs.ualberta.ca

Abstract

The field of molecular biology is growing at an astounding rate and research findings are being deposited into public databases, such as Swiss-Prot. Many of the over 200,000 protein entries in Swiss-Prot 49.1 lack annotations such as subcellular localization or function, but the vast majority have references to journal abstracts describing related research. These abstracts represent a huge amount of information that could be used to generate annotations for proteins automatically. Training classifiers to perform text categorization on abstracts is one way to accomplish this task. We present a method for improving text classification for biological journal abstracts by generating additional text features using the knowledge represented in a biological concept hierarchy (the Gene Ontology). The structure of the ontology, as well as the synonyms recorded in it, are leveraged by our simple technique to significantly improve the F-measure of subcellular localization text classifiers by as much as 0.078 and we achieve F-measures as high as 0.935.

1 Introduction

Can computers extract the semantic content of academic journal abstracts? This paper explores the use of natural language techniques for processing biological abstracts to answer this question in a specific domain. Our prototype method predicts the subcellular localization of proteins (the part of the biological cell where a protein performs its function) by performing text classification on related journal abstracts.

In the last two decades, there has been explosive growth in molecular biology research. Molecular biologists organize their findings into a common set of databases. One such database is Swiss-Prot, in which each entry corresponds to a protein. As of version 49.1 (February 21, 2006) Swiss-Prot contains more than 200,000 proteins, 190,000 of which link to biological journal abstracts. Unfortunately, a much smaller percentage of protein entries are annotated with other types of information. For example, only about half the entries have subcellular localization annotations. This disparity is partially due to the fact that humans annotate these databases manually and cannot keep up with the influx of data. If a computer could be trained to produce annotations by processing journal abstracts, proteins in the Swiss-Prot database could be curated semi-automatically.

Document classification is the process of categorizing a set of text documents into one or more of a predefined set of classes. The classification of biological abstracts is an interesting specialization of general document classification, in that scientific language is often not understandable by, nor written for, the lay-person. It is full of specialized terms, acronyms and it often displays high levels of synonymy. For example, the "PAM complex", which exists in the mitochondrion of the biological cell is also referred to with the phrases "presequence translocase-associated import motor" and

Proceedings of the BioNLP Workshop on Linking Natural Language Processing and Biology at HLT-NAACL 06, pages 17–24,
New York City, June 2006.

“mitochondrial import motor”. This also illustrates the fact that biological terms often span word boundaries and so their collective meaning is lost when text is whitespace tokenized.

To overcome the challenges of scientific language, our technique employs the Gene Ontology (GO) (Ashburner et al, 2000) as a source of expert knowledge. The GO is a controlled vocabulary of biological terms developed and maintained by biologists. In this paper we use the knowledge represented by the GO to complement the information present in journal abstracts. Specifically we show that:

- the GO can be used as a thesaurus
- the hierarchical structure of the GO can be used to generalize specific terms into broad concepts
- simple techniques using the GO significantly improve text classification

Although biological abstracts are challenging documents to classify, solving this problem will yield important benefits. With sufficiently accurate text classifiers, the abstracts of Swiss-Prot entries could be used to automatically annotate corresponding proteins, meaning biologists could more efficiently identify proteins of interest. Less time spent sifting through unannotated proteins translates into more time spent on new science, performing important experiments and uncovering fresh knowledge.

2 Related Work

Several different learning algorithms have been explored for text classification (Dumais et al, 1998) and support vector machines (SVMs) (Vapnik, 1995) were found to be the most computationally efficient and to have the highest precision/recall break-even point (BEP, the point where precision equals recall). Joachims performed a very thorough evaluation of the suitability of SVMs for text classification (Joachims, 1998). Joachims states that SVMs are perfect for textual data as it produces sparse training instances in very high dimensional space.

Soon after Joachims' survey, researchers started using SVMs to classify biological journal abstracts. Stapley et al. (2002) used SVMs to predict the subcellular localization of yeast proteins. They created a data set by mining Medline for abstracts containing a yeast gene name, which achieved F-measures in the range [0.31,0.80]. F-measure is defined as

$$f = \frac{2rp}{r+p}$$

where p is precision and r is recall. They expanded their training data to include extra biological information about each protein, in the form of amino acid content, and raised their F-measure by as much as 0.05. These results are modest, but before Stapley et al. most localization classification systems were built using text rules or were sequence based. This was one of the first applications of SVMs to biological journal abstracts and it showed that text and amino acid composition together yield better results than either alone.

Properties of proteins themselves were again used to improve text categorization for animal, plant and fungi subcellular localization data sets (Höglund et al, 2006). The authors' text classifiers were based on the most distinguishing terms of documents, and they included the output of four protein sequence classifiers in their training data. They measure the performance of their classifier using what they call sensitivity and specificity, though the formulas cited are the standard definitions of recall and precision. Their text-only classifier for the animal MultiLoc data set had recall (sensitivity) in the range [0.51,0.93] and specificity (precision) [0.32,0.91]. The MultiLocText classifiers, which include sequence-based classifications, have recall [0.82,0.93] and precision [0.55,0.95]. Their overall and average accuracy increased by 16.2% and 9.0% to 86.4% and 94.5% respectively on the PLOC animal data set when text was augmented with additional sequence-based information.

Our method is motivated by the improvements that Stapley et al. and Höglund et al. saw when they included additional biological information. However, our technique uses knowledge of a textual nature to improve text classification; it uses no information from the amino acid sequence. Thus, our approach can be used in conjunction with techniques that use properties of the protein sequence.

In non-biological domains, external knowledge has already been used to improve text categorization (Gabrilovich and Markovitch, 2005). In their research, text categorization is applied to news documents, newsgroup archives and movie reviews. The authors use the Open Directory Project (ODP) as a source of world knowledge to help alleviate problems of polysemy and synonymy. The ODP is a hierarchy of concepts where each concept node has links to related web pages. The authors mined these web pages to collect characteristic words for each concept. Then a new document was mapped, based on document similarity, to the closest matching ODP concept and features were generated from that concept's meaningful words. The generated features, along with the original document, were fed into an SVM text classifier. This technique yielded BEP as high as 0.695 and improvements of up to 0.254.

We use Gabrilovich and Markovitch's (2005) idea to employ an external knowledge hierarchy, in our case the GO, as a source of information. It has been shown that GO molecular function annotations in Swiss-Prot are indicative of subcellular localization annotations (Lu and Hunter, 2005), and that GO node names made up about 6% of a sample Medline corpus (Verspoor et al, 2003). Some consider GO terms to be too rare to be of use (Rice et al, 2005), however we will show that although the presence of GO terms is slight, the terms are powerful enough to improve text classification. Our technique's success may be due to the fact that we include the synonyms of GO node names, which increases the number of GO terms found in the documents.

We use the GO hierarchy in a different way than Gabrilovich et al. use the ODP. Unlike their approach, we do not extract additional features from all articles associated with a node of the GO hierarchy. Instead we use synonyms of nodes and the names of ancestor nodes. This is a simpler approach, as it doesn't require retrieving all abstracts for all proteins of a GO node. Nonetheless, we will show that our approach is still effective.

3 Methods

The workflow used to perform our experiments is outlined in Figure 1.

3.1 The Data Set

The first step in evaluating the usefulness of GO as a knowledge source is to create a data set. This process begins with a set of proteins with known subcellular localization annotations (Figure 1). For this we use Proteome Analyst's (PA) data sets (Lu et al, 2004; Szafron et al, 2004). The PA group used these data sets to create very accurate subcellular classifiers based on the keyword fields of Swiss-Prot entries for homologous proteins. Here we use PA's current data set of proteins collected from Swiss-Prot (version 48.3) and impose one further criterion: the subcellular localization annotation may not be longer than four words. This constraint is introduced to avoid including proteins where the localization category was incorrectly extracted from a long sentence describing several aspects of localization. For example, consider the subcellular annotation "attached to the plasma membrane by a lipid anchor", which could mean the protein's functional components are either cytoplasmic or extracellular (depending on which side of the plasma membrane the protein is anchored). PA's simple parsing scheme could mistake this description as meaning that the protein performs its function in the plasma membrane. Our length constraint reduces the chances of including mislabeled training instances in our data.

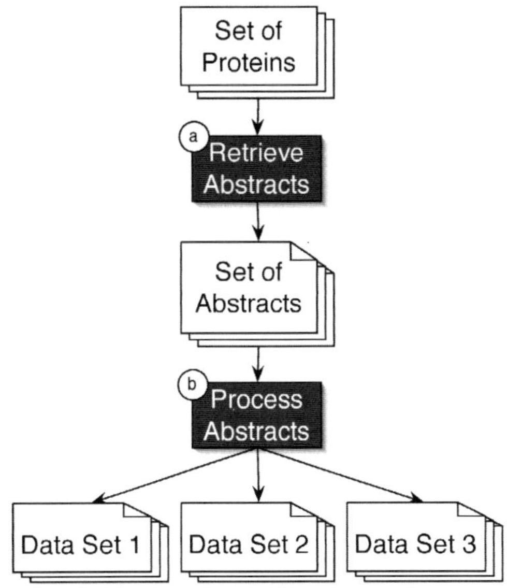

Figure 1: The workflow used to create data sets used in this paper. Abstracts are gathered for proteins with known localization (process *a*). Treatments are applied to abstracts to create three Data Sets (process *b*).

Class Name	Number of Proteins	Number of Abstracts
cytoplasm	1664	4078
endoplasmic reticulum	310	666
extracellular	2704	5655
golgi [a]	41	71
lysosome	129	599
mitochondrion	559	1228
nucleus	2445	5589
peroxisome	108	221
plasma membrane [a]	15	38
Total	**7652**	**17175**

[a]Classes with less than 100 abstracts were considered to have too little training data and are not included in our experiments.

Table 1: Summary of our Data Set. Totals are less than the sum of the rows because proteins may belong to more than one localization class.

PA has data sets for five organisms (animal, plant, fungi, gram negative bacteria and gram positive bacteria). The animal data set was chosen for our study because it is PA's largest and medical research has the most to gain from increased annotations for animal proteins. PA's data sets have binary labeling, and each class has its own training file. For example, in the nuclear data set a nuclear protein appears with the label "$+1$", and non-nuclear proteins appear with the label "-1". Our training data includes 317 proteins that localize to more than one location, so they will appear with a positive label in more than one data set. For example, a protein that is both cytoplasmic and peroxisomal will appear with the label "$+1$" in both the peroxisomal and cytoplasmic sets, and with the label "-1" in all other sets. Our data set has 7652 proteins across 9 classes (Table 1). To take advantage of the information in the abstracts of proteins with multiple localizations, we use a one-against-all classification model, rather than a "single most confident class" approach.

3.2 Retrieve Abstracts

Now that a set of proteins with known localizations has been created, we gather each protein's abstracts and abstract titles (Figure 1, process a). We do not include full text because it can be difficult to obtain automatically and because using full text does not improve F-measure (Sinclair and Webber, 2004). Abstracts for each protein are retrieved using the PubMed IDs recorded in the Swiss-Prot database. PubMed (`http://www.pubmed.gov`) is a database of life science articles. It should be noted that more than one protein in Swiss-Prot may point to the same abstract in PubMed. Because the performance of our classifiers is estimated using cross-validation (discussed in Section 3.4) it is important that the same abstract does not appear in both testing and training sets during any stage of cross-validation. To address this problem, all abstracts that appear more than once in the complete set of abstracts are removed. The distribution of the remaining abstracts among the 9 subcellular localization classes is shown in Table 1. For simplicity, the fact that an abstract may actually be discussing more than one protein is ignored. However, because we remove duplicate abstracts, many abstracts discussing more than one protein are eliminated.

In Table 1 there are more abstracts than proteins because each protein may have more than one associated abstract. Classes with less than 100 abstracts were deemed to have too little information for training. This constraint eliminated plasma membrane and golgi classes, although they remained as negative data for the other 7 training sets.

It is likely that not every abstract associated with a protein will discuss subcellular localization. However, because the Swiss-Prot entries for proteins in our data set have subcellular annotations, some research must have been performed to ascertain localization. Thus it should be reported in at least one abstract. If the topics of the other abstracts are truly unrelated to localization than their distribution of words may be the same for all localization classes. However, even if an abstract does not discuss localization directly, it may discuss some other property that is correlated with localization (e.g. function). In this case, terms that differentiate between localization classes will be found by the classifier.

3.3 Processing Abstracts

Three different data sets are made by processing our retrieved abstracts (Figure 1, process b). An ex-

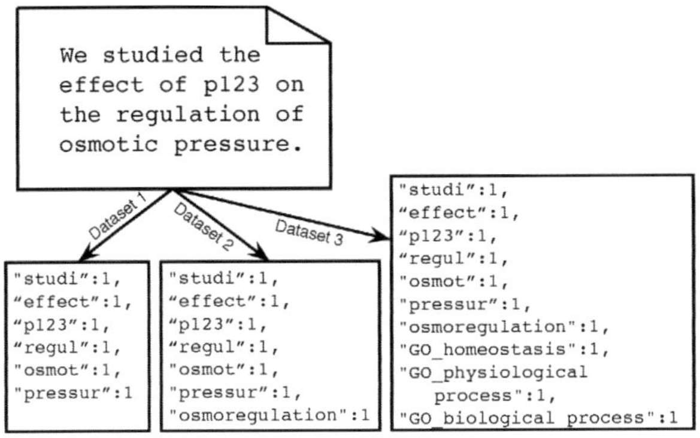

Figure 2: A sentence illustrating our three methods of abstract processing. Data Set 1 is our baseline, Data Set 2 incorporates synonym resolution and Data Set 3 incorporates synonym resolution and term generalization. Word counts are shown here for simplicity, though our experiments use TFIDF.

ample illustrating our three processing techniques is shown in Figure 2.

In Data Set 1, abstracts are tokenized and each word is stemmed using Porter's stemming algorithm (Porter, 1980). The words are then transformed into a vector of <word,TFIDF> pairs. TFIDF is defined as:

$$TFIDF(w_i) = f(w_i) * log(\frac{n}{D(w_i)})$$

where $f(w_i)$ is the number of times word w_i appears in documents associated with a protein, n is the total number of training documents and $D(w_i)$ is the number of documents in the whole training set that contain the word w_i. TFIDF was first proposed by Salton and Buckley (1998) and has been used extensively in various forms for text categorization (Joachims, 1998; Stapley et al, 2002). The words from all abstracts for a single protein are amalgamated into one "bag of words" that becomes the training instance which represents the protein.

3.3.1 Synonym Resolution

The GO hierarchy can act as a thesaurus for words with synonyms. For example the GO encodes the fact that "metabolic process" is a synonym for "metabolism"(see Figure 3). Data Set 2 uses GO's "exact_synonym" field for synonym resolution and adds extra features to the vector of words from Data Set 1. We search a stemmed version of the abstracts for matches to stemmed GO node names or synonyms. If a match is found, the GO node name (deemed the canonical representative for its set of synonyms) is associated with the abstract. In Figure 2 the phrase "regulation of osmotic pressure" appears in the text. A lookup in the GO synonym dictionary will indicate that this is an exact synonym of the GO node "osmoregulation". Therefore we associated the term "osmoregulation" with the training instance. This approach combines the weight of several synonyms into one representative, allowing the SVM to more accurately model the author's intent, and identifies multi-word phrases that are otherwise lost during tokenization. Table 2 shows the increase in average number of features per training instance as a result of our synonym resolution technique.

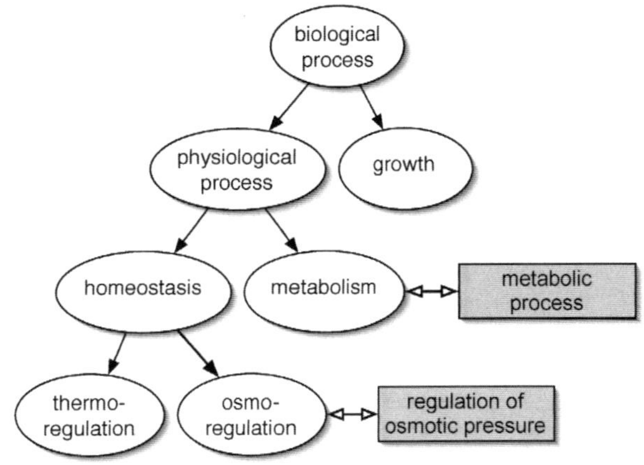

Figure 3: A subgraph of the GO biological process hierarchy. GO nodes are shown as ovals, synonyms appear as grey rectangles.

3.3.2 Term Generalization

In order to express the relationships between terms, the GO hierarchy is organized in a directed acyclic graph (DAG). For example, "thermoregulation" is a type of "homeostasis", which is a "physiological process". This "is a" relationship is expressed as a series of parent-child relationships (see Figure 3). In Data Set 3 we use the GO for synonym resolution (as in Data Set 2) and we also use its hierarchical structure to generalize specific terms into broader concepts. For Data Set 3, if a GO node name (or synonym) is found in an abstract, all names of ancestors to the match in the text are included in the

Class	Data Set 1	Data Set 2	Data Set 3
cytoplasm	166	177	203
endoplasmic reticulum	162	171	192
extracellular	148	155	171
lysosome	244	255	285
mitochondrion	155	163	186
nucleus	147	158	183
peroxisome	147	156	182
Overall Average	167	176	200

Table 2: Average number of features per training instance for 7 subcellular localization categories in animals. Data Set 1 is the baseline, Data Set 2 incorporates synonym resolution and Data Set 3 uses synonym resolution and term generalization.

training instance along with word vectors from Data Set 2 (see Figure 2). These additional node names are prepended with the string "GO_" which allows the SVM to differentiate between the case where a GO node name appears exactly in text and the case where a GO node name's child appeared in the text and the ancestor was added by generalization. Term generalization increases the average number of features per training instance (Table 2).

Term generalization gives the SVM algorithm the opportunity to learn correlations that exist between general terms and subcellular localization even if the general term never appears in an abstract and we encounter only its more specific children. Without term generalization the SVM has no concept of the relationship between child and parent terms, nor between sibling terms. For some localization categories more general terms may be the most informative and in other cases specific terms may be best. Because our technique adds features to training instances and never removes any, the SVM can assign lower weights to the generalized terms in cases where the localization category demands it.

3.4 Evaluation

Each of our classifiers was evaluated using 10 fold cross-validation. In 10 fold cross-validation each Data Set is split into 10 stratified partitions. For the first "fold", a classifier is trained on 9 of the 10 partitions and the tenth partition is used to test the classifier. This is repeated for nine more folds, holding out a different tenth each time. The results of all 10 folds are combined and composite precision, recall and F-measures are computed. Cross-validation accurately estimates prediction statistics of a classifier, since each instance is used as a test case at some point during validation.

The SVM implementation libSVM (Chang and Lin, 2001) was used to conduct our experiments. A linear kernel and default parameters were used in all cases; no parameter searching was done. Precision, recall and F-measure were calculated for each experiment.

4 Results and Discussion

Results of 10 fold cross-validation are reported in Table 3. Data Set 1 represents the baseline, while Data Sets 2 and 3 represent synonym resolution and combined synonym resolution/term generalization respectively. Paired t-tests ($p=0.05$) were done between the baseline, synonym resolution and term generalization Data Sets, where each sample is one fold of cross-validation. Those classifiers with significantly better performance over the baseline appear in bold in Table 3. For example, the lysosome classifiers trained on Data Set 2 and 3 are both significantly better than the baseline, and results for Data Set 3 are significantly better than results for Data Set 2, signified with an asterisk. In the case of the nucleus classifier no abstract processing technique was significantly better, so no column appears in bold.

In six of the seven classes, classifiers trained on Data Set 2 are significantly better than the baseline, and in no case are they worse. In Data Set 3, five of the seven classifiers are significantly better than the baseline, and in no case are they worse. For the lysosome and peroxisome classes our combined synonym resolution/term generalization technique produced results that are significantly better than synonym resolution alone. The average results of Data Set 2 are significantly better than Data Set 1 and the average results of Data Set 3 are significantly better than Data Set 2 and Data Set 1. On average, synonym resolution and term generalization combined give an improvement of 3%, and synonym

Class	Data Set 1 Baseline	Data Set 2 Synonym Resolution		Data Set 3 Term Generalization	
	F-measure	F-Measure	Δ	F-Measure	Δ
cytoplasm	0.740 (±0.049)	**0.758** (±0.042)	+0.017	**0.761** (±0.042)	+0.021
endoplasmic reticulum	0.760 (±0.055)	**0.779** (±0.068)	+0.019	**0.786** (±0.072)	+0.026
extracellular	0.931 (±0.009)	**0.935** (±0.009)	+0.004	**0.935** (±0.010)	+0.004
lysosome	0.746 (±0.107)	**0.787** (± 0.100)	+0.041	**0.820*** (±0.089)	+0.074
mitochondrion	0.840 (±0.041)	**0.848** (±0.038)	+0.008	0.852 (±0.039)	+0.012
nucleus	0.885 (±0.014)	0.885 (± 0.016)	+0.001	0.887 (±0.019)	+0.003
peroxisome	0.790 (±0.054)	**0.823** (±0.042)	+0.033	**0.868*** (±0.046)	+0.078
Average	0.815 (±0.016)	**0.832** (±0.012)	+0.017	**0.845*** (±0.009)	+0.030

Table 3: F-measures for stratified 10 fold cross-validation on our three Data Sets. Results deemed significantly improved over the baseline (p=0.05) appear in **bold**, and those with an asterisk (*) are significantly better than both other data sets. Change in F-measure compared to baseline is shown for Data Sets 2 and 3. Standard deviation is shown in parentheses.

resolution alone yields a 1.7% improvement. Because term generalization and synonym resolution never produce classifiers that are worse than synonym resolution alone, and in some cases the result is 7.8% better than the baseline, Data Set 3 can be confidently used for text categorization of all seven animal subcellular localization classes.

Our baseline SVM classifier performs quite well compared to the baselines reported in related work. At worst, our baseline classifier has F-measure 0.740. The text only classifier reported by Höglund et al. has F-measure in the range [0.449,0.851] (Höglund et al, 2006) and the text only classifiers presented by Stapley et al. begin with a baseline classifier with F-measure in the range [0.31,0.80] (Stapley et al, 2002). Although their approaches gave a greater increase in performance their low baselines left more room for improvement.

Though we use different data sets than Höglund et al. (2006), we compare our results to theirs on a class by class basis. For those 7 localization classes for which we both make predictions, the F-measure of our classifiers trained on Data Set 3 exceed the F-measures of the Höglund et al. text only classifiers in all cases, and our Data Set 3 classifier beats the F-measure of the MutliLocText classifier for 5 classes (see supplementary material `http://www.cs.ualberta.ca/~alona/bioNLP`). In addition, our technique does not preclude using techniques presented by Höglund et al. and Stapley et al., and it may be that using a combination of our approach and techniques involving protein sequence information may result in an even stronger subcellular localization predictor.

We do not assert that using abstract text alone is the best way to predict subcellular localization, only that if text is used, one must extract as much from it as possible. We are currently working on incorporating the classifications given by our text classifiers into Proteome Analyst's subcellular classifier to improve upon its already strong predictors (Lu et al, 2004), as they do not currently use any information present in the abstracts of homologous proteins.

5 Conclusion and Future work

Our study has shown that using an external information source is beneficial when processing abstracts from biological journals. The GO can be used as a reference for both synonym resolution and term generalization for document classification and doing so significantly increases the F-measure of most subcellular localization classifiers for animal proteins. On average, our improvements are modest, but they indicate that further exploration of this technique is warranted.

We are currently repeating our experiments for PA's other subcellular data sets and for function prediction. Though our previous work with PA is not text based, our experience training protein classifiers has led us to believe that a technique that works well for one protein property often succeeds for others as well. For example our general function classifier has F-measure within one percent of the F-measure of our Animal subcellular classifier. Although we test the technique presented here on subcellular localization only, we see no reason why it could not be used to predict any protein property (general function, tissue specificity, relation to disease, etc.). Finally, although our results apply to text classification for molecular biology, the principle of using an ontology that encodes synonyms and hierarchical relationships may be applicable to other applications with domain specific terminology.

The Data Sets used in these experiments are available at `http://www.cs.ualberta.ca/~alona/bioNLP/`.

6 Acknowledgments

We would like to thank Greg Kondrak, Colin Cherry, Shane Bergsma and the whole NLP group at the University of Alberta for their helpful feedback and guidance. We also wish to thank Paul Lu, Russell Greiner, Kurt McMillan and the rest of the Proteome Analyst team. This research was made possible by financial support from the Natural Sciences and Engineering Research Council of Canada (NSERC), the Informatics Circle of Research Excellence (iCORE) and the Alberta Ingenuity Centre for Machine Learning (AICML).

References

Michael Ashburner et al. 2000. Gene ontology: tool for the unification of biology the gene ontology consortium. *Nature Genetics*, 25(1):25–29.

Chih-Chung Chang and Chih-Jen Lin, 2001. *LIBSVM: a library for support vector machines*. Software available at `http://www.csie.ntu.edu.tw/~cjlin/libsvm`.

Susan T. Dumais et al. 1998. Inductive learning algorithms and representations for text categorization. In *Proc. 7th International Conference on Information and Knowledge Management CIKM*, pages 148–155.

Evgeniy Gabrilovich and Shaul Markovitch. 2005. Feature generation for text categorization using world knowledge. In *IJCAI-05, Proceedings of the Nineteenth International Joint Conference on Artificial Intelligence*, pages 1048–1053.

Annette Höglund et al. 2006. Significantly improved prediction of subcellular localization by integrating text and protein sequence data. In *Pacific Symposium on Biocomputing*, pages 16–27.

Thorsten Joachims. 1998. Text categorization with suport vector machines: Learning with many relevant features. In *ECML '98: Proceedings of the 10th European Conference on Machine Learning*, pages 137–142.

Zhiyong Lu and Lawrence Hunter. 2005. GO molecular function terms are predictive of subcellular localization. volume 10, pages 151–161.

Zhiyong Lu et al. 2004. Predicting subcellular localization of proteins using machine-learned classifiers. *Bioinformatics*, 20(4):547–556.

Martin F. Porter. 1980. An algorithm for suffix stripping. *Program*, 14(3):130–137.

Simon B Rice et al. 2005. Mining protein function from text using term-based support vector machines. *BMC Bioinformatics*, 6:S22.

Gail Sinclair and Bonnie Webber. 2004. Classification from full text: A comparison of canonical sections of scientific papers. In *COLING 2004 International Joint workshop on Natural Language Processing in Biomedicine and its Applications (NLPBA/BioNLP) 2004*, pages 69–72.

B. J. Stapley et al. 2002. Predicting the sub-cellular location of proteins from text using support vector machines. In *Pacific Symposium on Biocomputing*, pages 374–385.

Duane Szafron et al. 2004. Proteome analyst: Custom predictions with explanations in a web-based tool for high-throughput proteome annotations. *Nucleic Acids Research*, 32:W365–W371.

Vladimir N Vapnik. 1995. *The nature of statistical learning theory*. Springer-Verlag New York, Inc., New York, NY, USA.

Cornelia M. Verspoor et al. 2003. The gene ontology as a source of lexical semantic knowledge for a biological natural language processing application. *Proceedings of the SIGIR'03 Workshop on Text Analysis and Search for Bioinformatics*.

Integrating Ontological Knowledge and Textual Evidence in Estimating Gene and Gene Product Similarity

Antonio Sanfilippo, Christian Posse, Banu Gopalan, Stephen Tratz, Michelle Gregory

Pacific Northwest National Laboratory
Richland, WA 99352
{Antonio.Sanfilippo, Christian.Posse, Banu.Gopalan, Stephen.Tratz, Michelle.Gregory}@pnl.gov

Abstract

With the rising influence of the Gene Ontology, new approaches have emerged where the similarity between genes or gene products is obtained by comparing Gene Ontology code annotations associated with them. So far, these approaches have solely relied on the knowledge encoded in the Gene Ontology and the gene annotations associated with the Gene Ontology database. The goal of this paper is to demonstrate that improvements to these approaches can be obtained by integrating textual evidence extracted from relevant biomedical literature.

1 Introduction

The establishment of similarity between genes and gene products through homology searches has become an important discovery procedure that biologists use to infer structural and functional properties of genes and gene products–see Chang et al. (2001) and references therein. With the rising influence of the Gene Ontology[1] (GO), new approaches have emerged where the similarity between genes or gene products is obtained by comparing GO code annotations associated with them. The Gene Ontology provides three orthogonal networks of functional genomic concepts structured in terms of semantic relationships such as inheritance and meronymy, which encode biological process (BP), molecular function (MF) and cellular component (CC) properties of genes and gene products. GO code annotations explicitly relate genes and gene products in terms of participation in the same/similar biological processes, presence in the same/similar cellular components and expression of the same/similar molecular functions. Therefore, the use of GO code annotations in establishing gene and gene product similarity provides significant added functionality to methods such as BLAST (Altschul et al. 1997) and FASTA (Pearson and Lipman 1988) where gene and gene product similarity is calculated using string-based heuristics to select maximal segment pair alignments across gene and gene product sequences to approximate the Smith-Waterman algorithm (Smith and Waterman 1981).

Three main GO-based approaches have emerged so far to compute gene and gene product similarity. One approach assesses GO code similarity in terms of shared hierarchical relations within each gene ontology (BP, MF, or CC) (Lord et al. 2002, 2003; Couto et al. 2003; Azuaje et al. 2005). For example, the relative semantic closeness of two biological processes would be determined by the informational specificity of the most immediate parent that the two biological processes share in the BP ontology. The second approach establishes GO code similarity by leveraging associative relations across the three gene ontologies (Bodenreider et al. 2005). Such associative relations make predictions such as which cellular component is most likely to be the location of a given biological proc-

[1] http://www.geneontology.org.

Proceedings of the BioNLP Workshop on Linking Natural Language Processing and Biology at HLT-NAACL 06, pages 25–32,
New York City, June 2006.

ess and which molecular function is most likely to be involved in a given biological process. The third approach computes GO code similarity by combining hierarchical and associative relations (Posse et al. 2006).

Several studies within the last few years (Andrade et al. 1997, Andrade 1999, MacCallum et al. 2000, Chang at al. 2001) have shown that the inclusion of evidence from relevant scientific literature improves homology search. It is therefore highly plausible that literature evidence can also help improve GO-based approaches to gene and gene product similarity. Sanfilippo et al. (2004) propose a method for integrating literature evidence within an early version of the GO-based similarity algorithm presented in Posse et al. (2006). However, no effort has been made so far in evaluating the potential contribution of textual evidence extracted from relevant biomedical literature for GO-based approaches to the computation of gene and gene product similarity. The goal of this paper is to address this gap with specific reference to the assessment of protein similarity.

2 Background

GO-based similarity methods that focus on measuring intra-ontological relations have adopted the information theoretic treatment of semantic similarity developed in Natural Language Processing–see Budanitsky (1999) for an extensive survey. An example of such a treatment is given by Resnik (1995), who defines semantic similarity between two concept nodes *c1 c2* in a graph as the information content of the least common superordinate (*lcs*) of *c1* and *c2*, as shown in (1). The information content of a concept node *c*, *IC(c)*, is computed as *-log p(c)* where p*(c)* indicates the probability of encountering instances of *c* in a specific corpus.

(1) $$sim(c1,c2) = IC(lcs(c1,c2)) = -\log p(lcs(c1,c2))$$

Jiang and Conrath (1997) provide a refinement of Resnik's measure by factoring in the distance from each concept to the least common superordinate, as shown in (2).[2]

(2)
$$sim(c1,c2) = \frac{1}{IC(c1)+IC(c2)-2\times IC(lcs(c1,c2))}$$

Lin (1998) provides a slight variant of Jiang's and Conrath's measure, as indicated in (3).

(3) $$sim(c1,c2) = \frac{2\times IC(lcs(c1,c2))}{IC(c1)+IC(c2)}$$

The information theoretic approach is very well suited to assess GO code similarity since each gene subontology is formalized as a directed acyclic graph. In addition, the GO database[3] includes numerous curated GO annotations which can be used to calculate the information content of each GO code with high reliability. Evaluations of this methodology have yielded promising results. For example, Lord et al. (2002, 2003) demonstrate that there is strong correlation between GO-based similarity judgments for human proteins and similarity judgments obtained through BLAST searches for the same proteins. Azuaje et al. (2005) show that there is a strong connection between the degree of GO-based similarity and the expression correlation of gene products.

As Bodenreider et al. (2005) remark, the main problem with the information theoretic approach to GO code similarity is that it does not take into account associative relations across the gene ontologies. For example, the two GO codes 0050909 (*sensory perception of taste*) and 0008527 (*taste receptor activity*) belong to different gene ontologies (BP and MF), but they are undeniably very closely related. The information theoretic approach would simply miss associations of this kind as it is not designed to capture inter-ontological relations.

Bodenreider et al. (2005) propose to recover associative relations across the gene ontologies using a variety of statistical techniques which estimate the similarity of two GO codes inter-ontologically in terms of the distribution of the gene product annotations associated with the two GO codes in the GO database. One such technique is an adaptation of the vector space model frequently used in Information Retrieval (Salton et al. 1975), where

[2] Jiang and Conrath (1997) actually define the distance between two concepts nodes c1 c2, e.g.
$$dist(c1,c2) = IC(c1) + IC(c2) - 2\times IC(lcs(c1,c2))$$
For ease of exposition, we have converted Jiang's and Conrath's semantic distance measure to semantic similarity by taking its inverse, following Pedersen et al. (2005).

[3] http://www.godatabase.org/dev/database.

each GO code is represented as a vector of gene-based features weighted according to their distribution in the GO annotation database, and the similarity between two GO codes is computed as the cosine of the vectors for the two codes.

The ability to measure associative relations across the gene ontologies can significantly augment the functionality of the information theoretic approach so as to provide a more comprehensive assessment of gene and gene product similarity. However, in spite of their complementarities, the two GO code similarity measures are not easily integrated. This is because the two measures are obtained through different methods, express distinct senses of similarity (i.e. intra- and inter-ontological) and are thus incomparable.

Posse et al. (2006) develop a GO-based similarity algorithm–XOA, short for Cross-Ontological Analytics–capable of combining intra- and inter-ontological relations by "translating" each associative relation across the gene ontologies into a hierarchical relation within a single ontology. More precisely, let *c1* denote a GO code in the gene ontology *O1* and *c2* a GO code in the gene ontology *O2*. The XOA similarity between *c1* and *c2* is defined as shown in (4), where[4]

- *cos(ci,cj)* denotes the cosine associative measure proposed by Bodenreider et al. (2005)
- *sim(ci,cj)* denotes any of the three intra-ontological semantic similarities described above, see (1)-(3)
- $\max_{ci \text{ in } Oj} \{f(ci)\}$ denotes the maximum of the function f() over all GO codes *ci* in the gene ontology *Oj*.

The major innovation of the XOA approach is to allow the comparison of two nodes *c1*, *c2* across distinct ontologies *O1, O2* by mapping *c1* into its closest node *c4* in *O2* and *c2* into its closest node *c3* in *O1*. The inter-ontological semantic similarity between *c1* and *c2* can be then estimated from the intra-ontological semantic similarities between *c1-c3* and *c2-c4*, using multiplication with the associative relations between *c2-c3* and *c1-c4* as a score enrichment device.

$$(4)\quad \mathrm{XOA}(c1, c2) = \max \left\{ \begin{array}{l} \max\limits_{c3\ in\ O1} \left\{ \begin{array}{l} \mathrm{sim}(c1, c3) \times \\ \cos(c2, c3) \end{array} \right\}, \\ \\ \max\limits_{c4\ in\ O2} \left\{ \begin{array}{l} \mathrm{sim}(c2, c4) \times \\ \cos(c1, c4) \end{array} \right\} \end{array} \right\}$$

Posse et al. (2006) show that the XOA similarity measure provides substantial advantages. For example, a comparative evaluation of protein similarity, following the benchmark study of Lord et al. (2002, 2003), reveals that XOA provides the basis for a better correlation with protein sequence similarities as measured by BLAST bit score than any intra-ontological semantic similarity measure. The XOA similarity between genes/gene products derives from the XOA similarity between GO codes. Let *GP1* and *GP2* be two genes/gene products. Let *c11,c12,…, c1n* denote the set of GO codes associated with *GP1* and *c21, c22,…., c2m* the set of GO codes associated with *GP2*. The XOA similarity between *GP1* and *GP2* is defined as in (5), where *i=1,…,n* and *j=1,…,m*.

$$(5)\ \mathrm{XOA}(GP1,GP2) = \max \{\mathrm{XOA}(c1i, c2j)\}$$

The results of the study by Posse et al. (2006) are shown in Table 1. Note that the correlation between protein similarities based on intra-ontological similarity measures and BLAST bit scores in Table 1 is given for each choice of gene ontology (MF, BP, CC). This is because intra-ontological similarity methods only take into account GO codes that are in the same ontology and can therefore only assess protein similarity from a single ontology viewpoint. By contrast, the XOA-based protein similarity measure makes use of GO codes that can belong to any of the three gene ontologies and needs not be broken down by single ontologies, although the contribution of each gene ontology or even single GO codes can still be fleshed out, if so desired.

Is it possible to improve on these XOA results by factoring in textual evidence? We will address this question in the remaining part of the paper.

---

[4] If *c1* and *c2* are in the same ontology, i.e. *O1=O2*, then *xoa(c1,c2)* is still computed as in (4). In most cases, the maximum in (4) would be obtained with *c3 = c2* and *c4 = c1* so that XOA*(c1,c2)* would simply be computed as *sim(c1,c2)*. However, there are situations where there exists a GO code *c3* (*c4*) in the same ontology which

- is highly associated with *c1* (*c2*),
- is semantically close to *c2* (*c1*), and
- leads to a value for *sim(c1,c3)* x *cos(c2,c3)* ((*sim(c2,c4)* x *cos(c1,c4)*) that is higher than *sim(c1,c2)*.

Semantic Similarity Measures		Resnik	Lin	Jiang & Conrath
Intra-ontological				
	Molecular Function	0.307	0.301	0.296
	Biological Process	0.195	0.202	0.203
	Cellular Component	0.229	0.234	0.233
XOA		**0.405**	**0.393**	**0.368**

Table 1: Spearman rank order correlation coefficients between BLAST bit score and semantic similarities, calculated using a set of 255,502 protein pairs–adapted from Posse et al. (2006).

3 Textual Evidence Selection

Our first step in integrating textual evidence into the XOA algorithm is to select salient information from biomedical literature germane to the problem. Several approaches can be used to carry out this prerequisite. For example, one possibility is to collect documents relevant to the task at hand, e.g. through PubMed queries, and use feature weighting and selection techniques from the Information Retrieval literature–e.g. *tf*idf* (Buckley 1985) and Information Gain (e.g. Yang and Pedersen 1997)–to distill the most relevant information. Another possibility is to use Information Extraction algorithms tailored to the biomedical domain such as *Medstract* (http://www.medstract.org, Pustejovsky et al. 2002) to extract entity-relationship structures of relevance. Yet another possibility is to use specialized tools such as GoPubMed (Doms and Schroeder 2005) where traditional keyword-based capabilities are coupled with term extraction and ontological annotation techniques.

In our study, we opted for the latter solution, using generic Information Retrieval techniques to normalize and weigh the textual evidence extracted. The main advantage of this choice is that tools such as GoPubMed provide very high quality term extraction at no cost. Less appealing is the fact that the textual evidence provided is GO-based and therefore does not offer information which is orthogonal to the gene ontology. It is reasonable to expect better results than those reported in this paper if more GO-independent textual evidence were brought to bear. We are currently working on using *Medstract* as a source of additional textual evidence.

GoPubMed is a web server which allows users to explore PubMed search results using the Gene Ontology for categorization and navigation purposes (available at http://www.gopubmed.org). As shown in Figure 1 below, the system offers the following functionality:

- It provides an overview of PubMed search results by categorizing abstracts according to the Gene Ontology
- It verifies its classification by providing an accuracy percentage for each
- It shows definitions of Gene Ontology terms
- It allows users to navigate PubMed search results by GO categories
- It automatically shows GO terms related to the original query for each result
- It shows query terms (e.g. "Rab5" in the middle windowpane of Figure 1)
- It automatically extracts terms from search results which map to GO categories (e.g. highlighted terms other than "Rab5" in the middle windowpane of Figure 1).

In integrating textual evidence with the XOA algorithm, we utilized the last functionality (automatic extraction of terms) as an Information Extraction capability. Details about the term extraction algorithm used in GoPubMed are given in Delfs et al. (2004). In short, the GoPubMed term extraction algorithm uses word alignment strategies in combination with stemming to match word sequences from PubMed abstracts with GO terms. In doing so, partial and discontinuous matches are allowed. Partial and discontinuous matches are weighted according to closeness of fit. This is indicated by the accuracy percentages associated with GO in Figure 1 (right side). In this study we did not make use of these accuracy percentages, but plan to do so in the future.

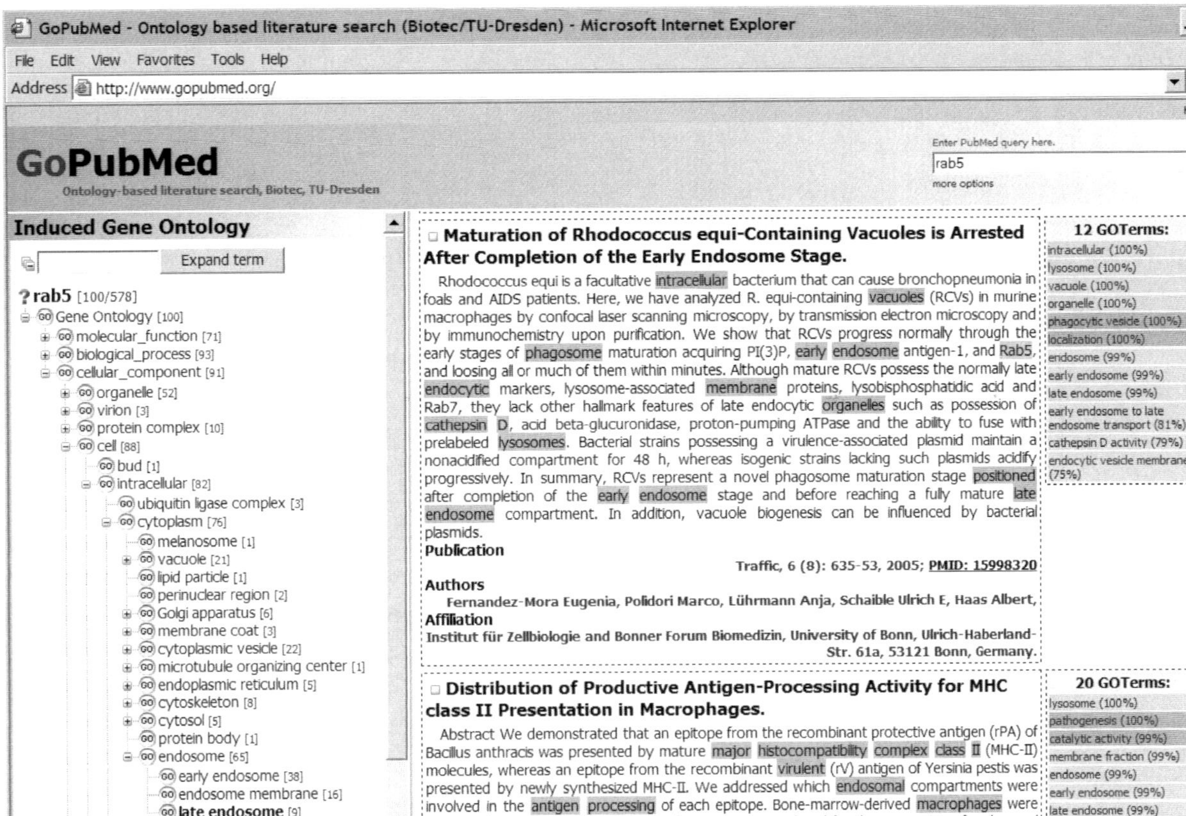

Figure 1: GoPubMed sample query for the "rab5" protein. The abstracts shown are automatically proposed by the system after the user issues the protein query and then selects the GO term "**late endosome**" (bottom left) as the discriminating parameter.

Our data set consists of 2360 human protein pairs containing 1783 distinct human proteins. This data set was obtained as a 1% random sample of the human proteins used in the benchmark study of Posse et al. (2006)–see Table 1.[5] For each of the 1783 human proteins, we made a GoPubMed query and retrieved up to 100 abstracts. We then collected all the terms extracted by GoPubMed for each protein across the abstracts retrieved. Table 2 provides an example of the output of this process.

nutrient, uptake, carbohydrate, metabolism, affecting, cathepsin, activity, protein, lipid, growth, rate, habitually, signal, transduction, fat, protein, cadherin, chromosomal, responses, exogenous, lactating, exchanges, affects, mammary, gland, ...

Table 2: Sample output of the GoPubMed term extraction process for the Cadherin-related tumor suppressor protein.

[5] We chose such a small sample to facilitate the collection of evidence from GoPubMed, which is not yet fully automated. Our XOA approach is very scalable, and we do not anticipate any problem running the full protein data set of 255,502 pairs, once we fully automate the GoPubMed extraction process.

4 Integrating Textual Evidence in XOA

Using the output of the GoPubMed term extraction process, we created vector-based signatures for each of the 1783 proteins, where

- features are obtained by stemming the terms provided by GoPubMed
- the value for each feature is derived as the *tf*idf* for the feature.

We then calculated the similarity between each of the 2360 protein pairs as the cosine value of the two vector-based signatures associated with the protein pair.

We tried two different strategies to augment the XOA score for protein similarity using the protein similarity values obtained as the cosine of the GoPubMed term-based signatures. The first strategy adopts a fusion approach in which the two similarity measures are first normalized to be commensurable and then combined to provide an interpretable integrated model. A simple normalization is obtained by observing that the Resnik's information content measure is commensurable to the log of the text based cosine (LC). This leads us to the fusion model shown in (5) for XOA, based on Resnik's semantic similarity measure (XOA_R).

(5) $Fusion(Resnik) = XOA_R + LC$

We then observe that the XOA measures based on Resnik, Lin (XOA_L) and Jiang & Conrath (XOA_{JC}) are highly correlated (correlations exceed 0.95 on the large benchmarking dataset discussed in section 2, see Table 1). This suggests the fusion model shown in (6), where the averages of the XOA scores are computed from the benchmarking data set.

(6) $Fusion(Lin) = XOA_L + LC*Ave(XOA_L)/Ave(XOA_R)$

$Fusion(Jiang\ \&\ Conrath) = XOA_{JC} + LC*Ave(XOA_{JC})/Ave(XOA_R)$

The second strategy consists in building a prediction model for BLAST bit score (BBS) using the XOA score and the log-cosine LC as predictors without the constraint of remaining interpretable. As in the previous strategy, a different model was sought for each of the three XOA variants. In each case, we restrict ourselves to cubic polynomial regression models as such models are quite efficient at capturing complex nonlinear relationships between target and predictors (e.g. Weisberg 2005). More precisely, for each of the semantic similarity measures, we fit the regression model to BBS shown in (7), where the subscript x denotes either R, L or JC, and the coefficients a to h are found by maximizing the Spearman rank order correlations between BBS and the regression model. This maximization is automatically carried out by using a random walk optimization approach (Romeijn 1992). The coefficients used in this study for each semantic similarity measure are shown in Table 3.

(7) $a*XOA_x + b*XOA_x^2 + c*XOA_x + d*LC + e*LC^2 + f*LC^3 + g*XOA_x*LC$

5 Evaluation

Table 4 summarizes the results for both strategies, comparing Spearman rank correlations between BBS and the models from the fusion and regression approaches with Spearman rank correlations between BBS and XOA alone. Note that the latter correlations are lower than the one reported in Table 2 due to the small size of our sample (1% of the original data set, as pointed out above). P-values associated with the changes in the correlation values are also reported, enclosed in parentheses.

	Resnik	Lin	Jiang & Conrath
a	-10684.43	2.83453e-05	0.2025174
b	1.786986	-31318.0	-1.93974
c	503.3746	45388.66	0.08461453
d	-3.952441	208.5917	4.939535e-06
e	0.0034074	1.55518e-04	0.0033902
f	1.4036e-05	9.972911e-05	-0.000838812
g	713.769	-1.10477e-06	2.461781

Table 3: Coefficients of the regression model maximizing Spearman rank correlation between BBS and the regression model for each of the three semantic similarity measures.

	XOA	Fusion	Regression
Resnik	0.295	0.325 (>0.20)	0.388 (0.0008)
Lin	0.274	0.301 (>0.20)	0.372 (0.0005)
Jiang & Conrath	0.273	0.285 (>0.20)	0.348 (0.008)

Table 4: Spearman rank order correlation coefficients between BLAST bit score BBS and XOA, BBS and the fusion model, and BBS and the regression model. P-values for the differences between the augmented models and XOA alone are given in parentheses.

An important finding from Table 4 is that integrating text-based evidence in the semantic similarity measures systematically improves the relationships between BLAST and XOA. Not surprisingly, the fusion models yield smaller improvements. However, these improvements in the order of 3% for the Resnik and Lin variants are very encouraging, even though they are not statistically significant. The regression models, on the other hand, provide larger and statistically significant improvements, reinforcing our hypothesis that textual evidence complements the GO-based similarity measures. We expect that a more sophisticated NLP treatment of textual evidence will yield significant improvements even for the more interpretable fusion models.

Conclusions and Further Work

Our early results show that literature evidence provides a significant contribution, even using very simple Information Extraction and integration methods such as those described in this paper. The employment of more sophisticated Information

Extraction tools and integration techniques is therefore likely to bring higher gains.

Further work using GoPubMed involves factoring in the accuracy percentage which related extracted terms to their induced GO categories and capturing complex phrases (e.g. *signal transduction*, *fat protein*). We also intend to compare the advantages provided by the GoPubMed term extraction process with Information Extraction tools created for the biomedical domain such as *Medstract* (Pustejovsky et al. 2002), and develop a methodology for integrating a variety of Information Extraction processes into XOA.

References

Altschul, S.F., T. L. Madden, A. A. Schaffer, J. Zhang, Z. Anang, W. Miller and D.J. Lipman (1997) Gapped BLAST and PSI-BLST: a new generation of protein database search programs. *Nucl. Acids Res.* 25:3389-3402.

Andrade, M.A. (1999) Position-specific annotation of protein function based on multiple homologs. *ISMB* 28-33.

Andrade, M.A. and A. Valencia (1997) Automatic annotation for biological sequences by extraction of keywords from MEDLINE abstracts. Development of a prototype system. *ISMB* 25-32.

Azuaje F., H. Wang and O. Bodenreider (2005) Ontology-driven similarity approaches to supporting gene functional assessment. In *Proceedings of the ISMB'2005 SIG meeting on Bio-ontologies* 2005, pages 9-10.

Bodenreider, O., M. Aubry and A. Burgun (2005) Non-lexical approaches to identifying associative relations in the Gene Ontology. In *Proceedings of Pacific Symposium on Biocomputing*, pages 104-115.

Buckley, C. (1985) Implementation of the SMART information retrieval system. *Technical Report 85-686*, Cornell University.

Budanitsky, A. (1999) Lexical semantic relatedness and its application in natural language processing. Technical report CSRG-390, Department of Computer Science, University of Toronto.

Chang, J.T., S. Raychaudhuri, and R.B. Altman (2001) Including biological literature improves homology search. In *Proc. Pacific Symposium on Biocomputing*, pages 374—383.

Couto, F. M., M. J. Silva and P. Coutinho (2003) Implementation of a functional semantic similarity measure between gene-products. *Technical Report*, Department of Informatics, University of Lisbon, http://www.di.fc.ul.pt/tech-reports/03-29.pdf.

Delfs, R., A. Doms, A. Kozlenkov, and M. Schroeder. (2004) GoPubMed: ontology based literature search applied to Gene Ontology and PubMed. In *Proc. of German Bioinformatics Conference*, Bielefeld, Germany. LNBI Springer.

Doms, A. and M. Schroeder (2005) GoPubMed: Exploring PubMed with the GeneOntology. *Nucleic Acids Research.* 33: W783-W786; doi:10.1093/nar/gki470.

Jiang J. and D. Conrath (1997) Semantic similarity based on corpus statistics and lexical taxonomy. In *Proceedings of International Conference on Research in Computational Linguistics*, Taiwan.

Romeijn, E.H. (1992) *Global Optimization by Random Walk Sampling Methods.* Tinbergen Institute Research Series, Volume 32. Thesis Publishers, Amsterdam.

Lin, D. (1998) An information-theoretic definition of similarity. In *Proceedings of the 15th International Conference on Machine Learning*, Madison, WI.

Lord P.W., R.D. Stevens, A. Brass, and C.A. Goble (2002) Investigating semantic similarity measures across the Gene Ontology: the relationship between sequence and annotation. *Bioinformatics* 19(10):1275-1283.

Lord P.W., R.D. Stevens, A. Brass, and C.A. Goble (2003) Semantic similarity measures as tools for exploring the Gene Ontology. In *Proceedings of Pacific Symposium on Biocomputing*, pages 601-612.

MacCallum, R. M., L. A. Kelley and Sternberg, M. J. (2000) SAWTED: structure assignment with text description--enhanced detection of remote homologues with automated SWISS-PROT annotation comparisons. *Bioinformatics* **16**, 125-9.

Pearson, W. R. and D. J. Lipman (1988) Improved tools for biological sequence analysis. In *Proceedings of the National Academy of Sciences* 85:2444-2448.

Pedersen, T., S. Banerjee and S. Patwardhan (2005) Maximizing Semantic Relatedness to Perform Word Sense Disambiguation. University of Minnesota Supercomputing Institute Research Report UMSI 2005/25, March. Available at http://www.msi.umn.edu/general/Reports/rptfiles/2005-25.pdf.

Posse, C., A. Sanfilippo, B. Gopalan, R. Riensche, N. Beagley, and B. Baddeley (2006) Cross-Ontological Analytics: Combining associative and hierarchical relations in the Gene Ontologies to assess gene product similarity. To appear in *Proceedings of International*

Workshop on Bioinformatics Research and Applications. Reading, U.K.

Pustejovsky, J., J. Castaño, R. Saurí, A. Rumshisky, J. Zhang, W. Luo (2002) Medstract: Creating large-scale information servers for biomedical libraries. *ACL 2002 Workshop on Natural Language Processing in the Biomedical Domain*. Philadelphia, PA.

Resnik, P. (1995) Using information content to evaluate semantic similarity. In *Proceedings of the 14th International Joint Conference on Artificial Intelligence*, pages 448–453, Montreal.

Sanfilippo A., C. Posse and B. Gopalan (2004) Aligning the Gene Ontologies. In *Proceedings of the Standards and Ontologies for Functional Genomics Conference 2*, Philadelphia, PA, http://www.sofg.org/meetings/sofg2004/Sanfilippo.ppt.

Salton, G., A. Wong and C. S. Yang (1975) A Vector space model for automatic indexing, *CACM* 18(11):613-620.

Smith, T. and M. S. Waterman (1981) Identification of common molecular subsequences. *J. Mol. Biol.* 147:195-197.

Weisberg, S. (2005) *Applied linear regression*. Wiley, New York.

Yang, Y. and J.O. Pedersen (1997) A comparative Study on feature selection in text categorization. In *Proceedings of the 14th International Conference on Machine Learning* (ICML), pages 412-420, Nashville.

A Priority Model for Named Entities

Lorraine Tanabe
National Center for Biotechnology Information
Bethesda, MD 20894
tanabe@ncbi.nlm.nih.gov

W. John Wilbur
National Center for Biotechnology Information
Bethesda, MD 20894
wilbur@ncbi.nlm.nih.gov

Abstract

We introduce a new approach to named entity classification which we term a Priority Model. We also describe the construction of a semantic database called SemCat consisting of a large number of semantically categorized names relevant to biomedicine. We used SemCat as training data to investigate name classification techniques. We generated a statistical language model and probabilistic context-free grammars for gene and protein name classification, and compared the results with the new model. For all three methods, we used a variable order Markov model to predict the nature of strings not represented in the training data. The Priority Model achieves an F-measure of 0.958-0.960, consistently higher than the statistical language model and probabilistic context-free grammar.

1 Introduction

Automatic recognition of gene and protein names is a challenging first step towards text mining the biomedical literature. Advances in the area of gene and protein named entity recognition (NER) have been accelerated by freely available tagged corpora (Kim et al., 2003, Cohen et al., 2005, Smith et al., 2005, Tanabe et al., 2005). Such corpora have made it possible for standardized evaluations such as Task 1A of the first BioCreative Workshop (Yeh et al., 2005).

Although state-of-the-art systems now perform at the level of 80-83% F-measure, this is still well below the range of 90-97% for non-biomedical NER. The main reasons for this performance disparity are 1) the complexity of the genetic nomenclature and 2) the confusion of gene and protein names with other biomedical entities, as well as with common English words. In an effort to alleviate the confusion with other biomedical entities we have assembled a database consisting of named entities appearing in the literature of biomedicine together with information on their ontological categories. We use this information in an effort to better understand how to classify names as representing genes/proteins or not.

2 Background

A successful gene and protein NER system must address the complexity and ambiguity inherent in this domain. Hand-crafted rules alone are unable to capture these phenomena in large biomedical text collections. Most biomedical NER systems use some form of language modeling, consisting of an observed sequence of words and a hidden sequence of tags. The goal is to find the tag sequence with maximal probability given the observed word sequence. McDonald and Pereira (2005) use conditional random fields (CRF) to identify the beginning, inside and outside of gene and protein names. GuoDong et al. (2005) use an ensemble of one support vector machine and two Hidden Markov Models (HMMs). Kinoshita et al. (2005) use a second-order Markov model. Dingare et al. (2005) use a maximum entropy Markov model (MEMM) with large feature sets.

Proceedings of the BioNLP Workshop on Linking Natural Language Processing and Biology at HLT-NAACL 06, pages 33–40,
New York City, June 2006.

NER is a difficult task because it requires both the identification of the boundaries of an entity in text, and the classification of that entity. In this paper, we focus on the classification step. Spasic et al. (2005) use the MaSTerClass case-based reasoning system for biomedical term classification. MaSTerClass uses term contexts from an annotated corpus of 2072 MEDLINE abstracts related to *nuclear receptors* as a basis for classifying new terms. Its set of classes is a subset of the UMLS Semantic Network (McCray, 1989), that does not include genes and proteins. Liu et al. (2002) classified terms that represent multiple UMLS concepts by examining the *conceptual relatives* of the concepts. Hatzivassiloglou et al. (2001) classified terms known to belong to the classes *Protein*, *Gene* and/or *RNA* using unsupervised learning, achieving accuracy rates up to 85%. The AZuRE system (Podowski et al., 2004) uses a separate modified Naive Bayes model for each of 20K genes. A term is disambiguated based on its contextual similarity to each model. Nenadic et al. (2003) recognized the importance of terminological knowledge for biomedical text mining. They used the C/NC-methods, calculating both the intrinsic characteristics of terms (such as their frequency of occurrence as substrings of other terms), and the context of terms as linear combinations. These biomedical classification systems all rely on the context surrounding named entities. While we recognize the importance of context, we believe one must strive for the appropriate blend of information coming from the context and information that is inherent in the name itself. This explains our focus on names without context in this work.

We believe one can improve gene and protein entity classification by using more training data and/or using a more appropriate model for names. Current sources of training data are deficient in important biomedical terminologies like cell line names. To address this deficiency, we constructed the SemCat database, based on a subset of the UMLS Semantic Network enriched with categories from the GENIA Ontology (Kim et al, 2003), and a few new semantic types. We have populated SemCat with over 5 million entities of interest from

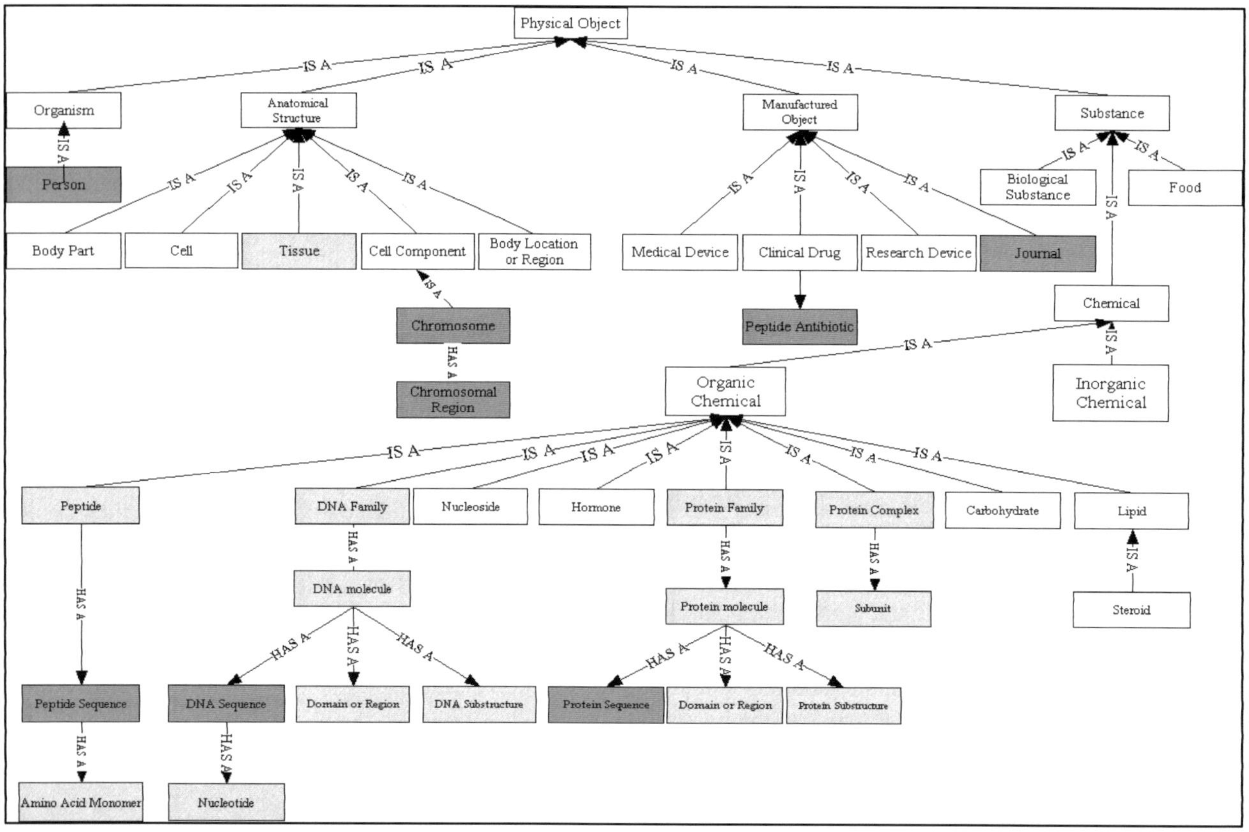

Figure 1. SemCat Physical Object Hierarchy. White = UMLS SN, Light Grey = GENIA semantic types, Dark Grey = New semantic types.

standard knowledge sources like the UMLS (Lindberg et al., 1993), the Gene Ontology (GO) (The Gene Ontology Consortium, 2000), Entrez Gene (Maglott et al., 2005), and GENIA, as well as from the World Wide Web. In this paper, we use SemCat data to compare three probabilistic frameworks for named entity classification.

3 Methods

We constructed the SemCat database of biomedical entities, and used these entities to train and test three probabilistic approaches to gene and protein name classification: 1) a statistical language model with Witten-Bell smoothing, 2) probabilistic context-free grammars (PCFGs) and 3) a new approach we call a Priority Model for named entities. As one component in all of our classification algorithms we use a variable order Markov Model for strings.

3.1 SemCat Database Construction

The UMLS Semantic Network (SN) is an ongoing project at the National Library of Medicine. Many users have modified the SN for their own research domains. For example, Yu et al. (1999) found that the SN was missing critical components in the genomics domain, and added six new semantic types including *Protein Structure* and *Chemical Complex*. We found that a subset of the SN would be sufficient for gene and protein name classification, and added some new semantic types for better coverage. We shifted some semantic types from suboptimal nodes to ones that made more sense from a genomics standpoint. For example, there were two problems with *Gene or Genome*. Firstly, genes and genomes are not synonymous, and secondly, placement under the semantic type *Fully Formed Anatomical Structure* is suboptimal from a genomics perspective. Since a gene in this context is better understood as an organic chemical, we deleted *Gene or Genome*, and added the GENIA semantic types for genomics entities under *Organic Chemical*. The SemCat Physical Object hierarchy is shown in Figure 1. Similar hierarchies exist for the SN Conceptual Entity and Event trees. A number of the categories have been supplemented with automatically extracted entities from MEDLINE, derived from regular expression pattern matching. Currently, SemCat has 77 semantic types, and 5.11M non-unique entries. Additional entities from MEDLINE are being manually classified via an annotation website. Unlike the Termino database (Harkema et al. (2004), which contains terminology annotated with morpho-syntactic and conceptual information, SemCat currently consists of gazetteer lists only.

For our experiments, we generated two sets of training data from SemCat, Gene-Protein (*GP*) and Not-Gene-Protein (*NGP*). *GP* consists of specific terms from the semantic types DNA MOLECULE, PROTEIN MOLECULE, DNA FAMILY, PROTEIN FAMILY, PROTEIN COMPLEX and PROTEIN SUBUNIT. *NGP* consists of entities from all other SemCat types, along with generic entities from the *GP* semantic types. Generic entities were automatically eliminated from *GP* using pattern matching to manually tagged generic phrases like *abnormal protein*, *acid domain*, and *RNA*.

Many SemCat entries contain commas and parentheses, for example, *"receptors, tgf beta."* A better form for natural language processing would be *"tgf beta receptors."* To address this problem, we automatically generated variants of phrases in *GP* with commas and parentheses, and found their counts in MEDLINE. We empirically determined the heuristic rule of replacing the phrase with its second most frequent variant, based on the observation that the most frequent variant is often too generic. For example, the following are the phrase variant counts for *"heat shock protein (dnaj)"*:

- heat shock protein (dnaj) 0
- dnaj heat shock protein 84
- heat shock protein 122954
- heat shock protein dnaj 41

Thus, the phrase kept for *GP* is *dnaj heat shock protein*.

After purifying the sets and removing ambiguous full phrases (ambiguous words were retained), *GP* contained 1,001,188 phrases, and *NGP* contained 2,964,271 phrases. From these, we randomly generated three train/test divisions of 90% train/10% test (*gp1*, *gp2*, *gp3*), for the evaluation.

3.2 Variable Order Markov Model for Strings

As one component in our classification algorithms we use a variable order Markov Model for strings. Suppose C represents a class and $x_1x_2x_3...x_n$ represents a string of characters. In order to estimate the probability that $x_1x_2x_3...x_n$ belongs to C we apply Bayes' Theorem to write

$$p(C \mid x_1x_2x_3...x_n) = \frac{p(x_1x_2x_3...x_n \mid C)\,p(C)}{p(x_1x_2x_3...x_n)} \quad (1)$$

Because $p(x_1x_2x_3...x_n)$ does not depend on the class and because we are generally comparing probability estimates between classes, we ignore this factor in our calculations and concentrate our efforts on evaluating $p(x_1x_2x_3...x_n \mid C)\,p(C)$. First we write

$$p(x_1x_2x_3...x_n \mid C) = \prod_{k=1}^{n} p(x_k \mid x_1x_2x_3...x_{k-1}, C) \quad (2)$$

which is an exact equality. The final step is to give our best approximation to each of the numbers $p(x_k \mid x_1x_2x_3...x_{k-1}, C)$. To make these approximations we assume that we are given a set of strings and associated probabilities $\{(s_i, p_i)\}_{i=1}^{M}$ where for each i, $p_i > 0$ and p_i is assumed to represent the probability that s_i belongs to the class C. Then for the given string $x_1x_2x_3...x_n$ and a given k we let $r \geq 1$ be the smallest integer for which $x_rx_{r+1}x_{r+2}...x_k$ is a contiguous substring in at least one of the strings s_i. Now let N' be the set of all i for which $x_rx_{r+1}x_{r+2}...x_k$ is a substring of s_i and let N be the set of all i for which $x_rx_{r+1}x_{r+2}...x_{k-1}$ is a substring of s_i. We set

$$p(x_k \mid x_1x_2x_3...x_{k-1}, C) = \frac{\sum_{i \in N'} p_i}{\sum_{i \in N} p_i}. \quad (3)$$

In some cases it is appropriate to assume that $p(C)$ is proportional to $\sum_{i=1}^{M} p_i$ or there may be other ways to make this estimate. This basic scheme works well, but we have found that we can obtain a modest improvement by adding a unique start character to the beginning of each string. This character is assumed to occur nowhere else but as the first character in all strings dealt with including any string whose probability we are estimating. This forces the estimates of probabilities near the beginnings of strings to come from estimates based on the beginnings of strings. We use this approach in all of our classification algorithms.

Table 1. Each fragment in the left column appears in the training data and the probability in the right column represents the probability of seeing the underlined portion of the string given the occurrence of the initial un-underlined portion of the string in a training string.

GP	
!apoe	9.55×10^{-7}
oe-e	2.09×10^{-3}
e-epsilon	4.00×10^{-2}
$p(apoe-epsilon \mid GP)$	7.98×10^{-11}
$p(GP \mid apoe-epsilon)$	0.98448
NGP	
!apoe	8.88×10^{-8}
poe-	1.21×10^{-2}
oe-e	6.10×10^{-2}
e-epsilon	6.49×10^{-3}
$p(apoe-epsilon \mid NGP)$	4.25×10^{-13}
$p(NGP \mid apoe-epsilon)$	0.01552

In Table 1, we give an illustrative example of the string apoe-epsilon which does not appear in the training data. A PubMed search for apoe-epsilon gene returns 269 hits showing the name is known. But it does not appear in this exact form in SemCat.

3.3 Language Model with Witten-Bell Smoothing

A statistical *n*-gram model is challenged when a bigram in the test set is absent from the training set, an unavoidable situation in natural language due to Zipf's law. Therefore, some method for assigning nonzero probability to novel *n*-grams is required. For our language model (LM), we used Witten-Bell smoothing, which reserves probability mass for out of vocabulary values (Witten and Bell, 1991, Chen and Goodman, 1998). The discounted probability is calculated as

$$\hat{P}(w_{i-n+1}...w_{i-1}) = \frac{\#(w_{i-n+1}...w_i)}{\#(w_{i-n+1}...w_{i-1}) + D(w_{i-n+1}...w_{i-1})} \quad (4)$$

where $D(w_{i-n+1}...w_{i-1})$ is the number of distinct words that can appear after $w_{i-n+1}...w_{i-1}$ in the training data. Actual values assigned to tokens outside the training data are not assigned uniformly but are filled in using a variable order Markov Model based on the strings seen in the training data.

3.4 Probabilistic Context-Free Grammar

The Probabilistic Context-Free Grammar (PCFG) or Stochastic Context-Free Grammar (SCFG) was originally formulated by Booth (1969). For technical details we refer the reader to Charniak (1993). For gene and protein name classification, we tried two different approaches. In the first PCFG method (PCFG-3), we used the following simple productions:

1) CATP → CATP CATP
2) CATP → CATP postCATP
3) CATP → preCATP CATP

CATP refers to the category of the phrase, *GP* or *NGP*. The prefixes *pre* and *post* refer to beginnings and endings of the respective strings. We trained two separate grammars, one for the positive examples, *GP*, and one for the negative examples, *NGP*. Test cases were tagged based on their score from each of the two grammars.

In the second PCFG method (PCFG-8), we combined the positive and negative training examples into one grammar. The minimum number of non-terminals necessary to cover the training sets *gp1-3* was six {CATP, preCATP, postCATP, NotCATP, preNotCATP, postNotCATP}. CATP represents a string from *GP*, and NotCATP represents a string from *NGP*. We used the following production rules:

1) CATP → CATP CATP
2) CATP → CATP postCATP
3) CATP → preCATP CATP
4) CATP → NotCATP CATP
5) NotCATP → NotCATP NotCATP
6) NotCATP → NotCATP postNotCATP
7) NotCATP→ preNotCATP NotCATP
8) NotCATP → CATP NotCATP

It can be seen that (4) is necessary for strings like "human p53," and (8) covers strings like "p53 pathway."

In order to deal with tokens that do not appear in the training data we use variable order Markov Models for strings. First the grammar is trained on the training set of names. Then any token appearing in the training data will have assigned to it the tags appearing on the right side of any rule of the grammar (essentially part-of-speech tags) with probabilities that are a product of the training. We then construct a variable order Markov Model for each tag type based on the tokens in the training data and the assigned probabilities for that tag type. These Models (three for PCFG-3 and six for PCFG-8) are then used to assign the basic tags of the grammar to any token not seen in training. In this way the grammars can be used to classify any name even if its tokens are not in the training data.

3.5 Priority Model

There are problems with the previous approaches when applied to names. For example, suppose one is dealing with the name "human liver alkaline phosphatase" and class C_1 represents protein names and class C_2 anatomical names. In that case a language model is no more likely to favor C_1 than C_2. We have experimented with PCFGs and have found the biggest challenge to be how to choose the grammar. After a number of attempts we have still found problems of the "human liver alkaline phosphatase" type to persist.

The difficulties we have experienced with language models and PCFGs have led us to try a different approach to model named entities. As a general rule in a phrase representing a named entity a word to the right is more likely to be the head word or the word determining the nature of the entity than a word to the left. We follow this rule and construct a model which we will call a Priority Model. Let T_1 be the set of training data (names) for class C_1 and likewise T_2 for C_2. Let $\{t_\alpha\}_{\alpha\in A}$ denote the set of all tokens used in names contained in $T_1 \cup T_2$. Then for each token t_α, $\alpha \in A$, we assume there are associated two probabilities p_α and q_α with the interpretation that p_α is the probability that the appearance of the token t_α in a name indicates that name belongs to class C_1 and q_α is the probability that t_α is a reliable indicator of the class of a name. Let $n = t_{\alpha(1)} t_{\alpha(2)} \cdots t_{\alpha(k)}$ be composed of the tokens on the right in the given order. Then we compute the probability

$$p(C_1 \mid n) = p_{\alpha(1)} \prod_{j=2}^{k} \left(1 - q_{\alpha(j)}\right) + \sum_{i=2}^{k} q_{\alpha(i)} p_{\alpha(i)} \prod_{j=i+1}^{k} \left(1 - q_{\alpha(j)}\right). \tag{5}$$

This formula comes from a straightforward interpretation of priority in which we start on the right side of a name and compute the probability the name belongs to class C_1 stepwise. If $t_{\alpha(k)}$ is the rightmost token we multiple the reliability $q_{\alpha(k)}$ times the significance $p_{\alpha(k)}$ to obtain $q_{\alpha(k)} p_{\alpha(k)}$, which represents the contribution of $t_{\alpha(k)}$. The remaining or unused probability is $1 - q_{\alpha(k)}$ and this is passed to the next token to the left, $t_{\alpha(k-1)}$. The probability $1 - q_{\alpha(k)}$ is scaled by the reliability and then the significance of $t_{\alpha(k-1)}$ to obtain $(1 - q_{\alpha(k)}) q_{\alpha(k-1)} p_{\alpha(k-1)}$, which is the contribution of $t_{\alpha(k-1)}$ toward the probability that the name is of class C_1. The remaining probability is now $\left(1 - q_{\alpha(k-1)}\right)\left(1 - q_{\alpha(k)}\right)$ and this is again passed to the next token to the left, etc. At the last token on the left the reliability is not used to scale because there are no further tokens to the left and only significance $p_{\alpha(1)}$ is used.

We want to choose all the parameters p_α and q_α to maximize the probability of the data. Thus we seek to maximize

$$F = \sum_{n \in T_1} \log\left(p\left(C_1 \mid n\right)\right) + \sum_{n \in T_2} \log\left(p\left(C2 \mid n\right)\right). \tag{6}$$

Because probabilities are restricted to be in the interval $[0,1]$, it is convenient to make a change of variables through the definitions

$$p_\alpha = \frac{e^{x_\alpha}}{1 + e^{x_\alpha}},\ q_\alpha = \frac{e^{y_\alpha}}{1 + e^{y_\alpha}}. \tag{7}$$

Then it is a simple exercise to show that

$$\frac{dp_\alpha}{dx_\alpha} = p_\alpha\left(1 - p_\alpha\right),\ \frac{dq_\alpha}{dy_\alpha} = q_\alpha\left(1 - q_\alpha\right). \tag{8}$$

From (5), (6), and (8) it is straightforward to compute the gradient of F as a function of x_α and y_α and because of (8) it is most naturally expressed in terms of p_α and q_α. Before we carry out the optimization one further step is important. Let B denote the subset of $\alpha \in A$ for which all the occurrences of t_α either occur in names in T_1 or all occurrences occur in names in T_2. For any such α we set $q_\alpha = 1$ and if all occurrences of t_α are in names in T_1 we set $p_\alpha = 1$, while if all occurrences are in names in T_2 we set $p_\alpha = 0$. These choices are optimal and because of the form of (8) it is easily seen that

$$\frac{\partial F}{\partial x_\alpha} = \frac{\partial F}{\partial y_\alpha} = 0 \tag{9}$$

for such an α. Thus we may ignore all the $\alpha \in B$ in our optimization process because the values of p_α and q_α are already set optimally. We therefore carry out optimization of F using the x_α, y_α, $\alpha \in A - B$. For the optimization we have had good success using a Limited Memory BFGS method (Nash et al., 1991).

When the optimization of F is complete we will have estimates for all the p_α and q_α, $\alpha \in A$. We still must deal with tokens t_β that are not included among the t_α. For this purpose we train variable order Markov Models MP_1 based on the weighted set of strings $\left\{\left(t_\alpha, p_\alpha\right)\right\}_{\alpha \in A}$ and MP_2 based on $\left\{\left(t_\alpha, 1 - p_\alpha\right)\right\}_{\alpha \in A}$. Likewise we train MQ_1 based on $\left\{\left(t_\alpha, q_\alpha\right)\right\}_{\alpha \in A}$ and MQ_2 based on $\left\{\left(t_\alpha, 1 - q_\alpha\right)\right\}_{\alpha \in A}$. Then if we allow $mp_i\left(t_\beta\right)$ to represent the prediction from model MP_i and $mq_i\left(t_\beta\right)$ that from model MQ_i, we set

$$p_\beta = \frac{mp_1(t_\beta)}{mp_1(t_\beta)+mp_2(t_\beta)},\; q_\beta = \frac{mq_1(t_\beta)}{mq_1(t_\beta)+mq_2(t_\beta)} \tag{10}$$

This allows us to apply the priority model to any name to predict its classification based on equation 5.

4 Results

We ran all three methods on the SemCat sets *gp1*, *gp2* and *gp3*. Results are shown in Table 2. For evaluation we applied the standard information retrieval measures precision, recall and F-measure.

$$precision = \frac{rel\_ret}{(rel\_ret + non-rel\_ret)}$$

$$recall = \frac{rel\_ret}{(rel\_ret + rel\_not\_ret)}$$

$$F-measure = \frac{2 * precision * recall}{(precision + recall)}$$

For name classification, *rel_ret* refers to true positive entities, *non-rel_ret* to false positive entities and *rel_ not_ret* to false negative entities.

Table 2. Three-fold cross validation results. P = Precision, R = Recall, F = F-measure. PCFG = Probabilistic Context-Free Grammar, LM = Bigram Model with Witten-Bell smoothing, PM = Priority Model.

Method	Run	P	R	F
PCFG-3	gp1	0.883	0.934	0.908
	gp2	0.882	0.937	0.909
	gp3	0.877	0.936	0.906
PCFG-8	gp1	0.939	0.966	0.952
	gp2	0.938	0.967	0.952
	gp3	0.939	0.966	0.952
LM	gp1	0.920	0.968	0.944
	gp2	0.923	0.968	0.945
	gp3	0.917	0.971	0.943
PM	gp1	0.949	0.968	0.958
	gp2	0.950	0.968	0.960
	gp3	0.950	0.967	0.958

5 Discussion

Using a variable order Markov model for strings improved the results for all methods (results not shown). The *gp1-3* results are similar within each method, yet it is clear that the overall performance of these methods is PM > PCFG-8 > LM > PCFG-3. The very large size of the database and the very uniform results obtained over the three independent random splits of the data support this conclusion.

The improvement of PCFG-8 over PCFG-3 can be attributed to the considerable ambiguity in this domain. Since there are many cases of term overlap in the training data, a grammar incorporating some of this ambiguity should outperform one that does not. In PCFG-8, additional production rules allow phrases beginning as CATPs to be overall NotCATPs, and vice versa.

The Priority Model outperformed all other methods using F-measure. This supports our impression that the right-most words in a name should be given higher priority when classifying names. A decrease in performance for the model is expected when applying this model to the named entity extraction (NER) task, since the model is based on terminology alone and not on the surrounding natural language text. In our classification experiments, there is no context, so disambiguation is not an issue. However, the application of our model to NER will require addressing this problem.

SemCat has not been tested for accuracy, but we retain a set of manually-assigned scores that attest to the reliability of each contributing list of terms. Table 2 indicates that good results can be obtained even with noisy training data.

6 Conclusion

In this paper, we have concentrated on the information inherent in gene and protein names versus other biomedical entities. We have demonstrated the utility of the SemCat database in training probabilistic methods for gene and protein entity classification. We have also introduced a new model for named entity prediction that prioritizes the contribution of words towards the right end of terms. The Priority Model shows promise in the domain of gene and protein name classification. We plan to apply the Priority Model, along with appropriate contextual and meta-level information, to gene and protein named entity recognition in future work. We intend to make SemCat freely available.

Acknowledgements

This research was supported in part by the Intramural Research Program of the NIH, National Library of Medicine.

References

T. L. Booth. 1969. Probabilistic representation of formal languages. In: *IEEE Conference Record of the 1969 Tenth Annual Symposium on Switching and Automata Theory*, 74-81.

Stanley F. Chen and Joshua T. Goodman. 1998. An empirical study of smoothing techniques for language modeling. *Technical Report TR-10-98*, Computer Science Group, Harvard University.

Eugene Charniak. 1993. *Statistical Language Learning*. The MIT Press, Cambridge, Massachusetts.

K. Bretonnel Cohen, Lynne Fox, Philip V. Ogren and Lawrence Hunter. 2005. Corpus design for biomedical natural language processing. *Proceedings of the ACL-ISMB Workshop on Linking Biological Literature, Ontologies and Databases*, 38-45.

The Gene Ontology Consortium. 2000. Gene Ontology: tool for the unification of biology, *Nat Genet.* 25: 25-29.

Henk Harkema, Robert Gaizauskas, Mark Hepple, Angus Roberts, Ian Roberts, Neil Davis and Yikun Guo. 2004. A large scale terminology resource for biomedical text processing. *Proc BioLINK 2004*, 53-60.

Vasileios Hatzivassiloglou, Pablo A. Duboué and Andrey Rzhetsky. 2001. Disambiguating proteins, genes, and RNA in text: a machine learning approach. *Bioinformatics* 17 Suppl 1:S97-106.

J.-D. Kim, Tomoko Ohta, Yuka Tateisi and Jun-ichi Tsujii. 2003. GENIA corpus--semantically annotated corpus for bio-textmining. *Bioinformatics* 19 Suppl 1:i180-2.

Donald A. Lindberg, Betsy L. Humphreys and Alexa T. McCray. 1993. The Unified Medical Language System. *Methods Inf Med* 32(4):281-91.

Hongfang Liu, Stephen B. Johnson, and Carol Friedman. 2002. Automatic resolution of ambiguous terms based on machine learning and conceptual relations in the UMLS. *J Am Med Inform Assoc* 9(6): 621–636.

Donna Maglott, Jim Ostell, Kim D. Pruitt and Tatiana Tatusova. 2005. Entrez Gene: gene-centered information at NCBI. *Nucleic Acids Res.* 33:D54-8.

Alexa T. McCray. 1989. The UMLS semantic network. In: Kingsland LC (ed). *Proc 13rd Annu Symp Comput Appl Med Care*. Washington, DC: IEEE Computer Society Press, 503-7.

Ryan McDonald and Fernando Pereira. 2005. Identifying gene and protein mentions in text using conditional random fields. *BMC Bioinformatics* 6 Supp 1:S6.

S. Nash and J. Nocedal. 1991. A numerical study of the limited memory BFGS method and the truncated-Newton method for large scale optimization, *SIAM J. Optimization*1(3): 358-372.

Goran Nenadic, Irena Spasic and Sophia Ananiadou. 2003. Terminology-driven mining of biomedical literature. *Bioinformatics* 19:8, 938-943.

Raf M. Podowski, John G. Cleary, Nicholas T. Goncharoff, Gregory Amoutzias and William S. Hayes. 2004. AZuRE, a scalable system for automated term disambiguation of gene and protein Names *IEEE Computer Society Bioinformatics Conference*, 415-424.

Lawrence H. Smith, Lorraine Tanabe, Thomas C. Rindflesch and W. John Wilbur. 2005. MedTag: A collection of biomedical annotations. *Proceedings of the ACL-ISMB Workshop on Linking Biological Literature, Ontologies and Databases*, 32-37.

Lorraine Tanabe, Natalie Xie, Lynne H. Thom, Wayne Matten and W. John Wilbur. 2005. GENETAG: a tagged corpus for gene/protein named entity recognition. *BMC Bioinformatics* 6 Suppl 1:S3.

I. Witten and T. Bell, 1991. The zero-frequency problem: Estimating the probabilities of novel events in adaptive text compression. *IEEE Transactions on Information Theory* 37(4).

Alexander Yeh, Alexander Morgan, Mark Colosimo and Lynette Hirschman. 2005. BioCreAtIvE Task 1A: gene mention finding evaluation. *BMC Bioinformatics* 6 Suppl 1:S2.

Hong Yu, Carol Friedman, Andrey Rhzetsky and Pauline Kra. 1999. Representing genomic knowledge in the UMLS semantic network. *Proc AMIA Symp.* 181-5.

Human Gene Name Normalization using Text Matching with Automatically Extracted Synonym Dictionaries

Haw-ren Fang
Department of Computer Science, University of Maryland
College Park, MD 20742, USA
hrfang@cs.umd.edu

Kevin Murphy and **Yang Jin** and **Jessica S. Kim** and **Peter S. White***
Division of Oncology, Children's Hospital of Philadelphia
Philadelphia, PA 19104, USA
{murphy,jin,kim,white}@genome.chop.edu

Abstract

The identification of genes in biomedical text typically consists of two stages: identifying gene mentions and normalization of gene names. We have created an automated process that takes the output of named entity recognition (NER) systems designed to identify genes and normalizes them to standard referents. The system identifies human gene synonyms from online databases to generate an extensive synonym lexicon. The lexicon is then compared to a list of candidate gene mentions using various string transformations that can be applied and chained in a flexible order, followed by exact string matching or approximate string matching.

Using a gold standard of MEDLINE abstracts manually tagged and normalized for mentions of human genes, a combined tagging and normalization system achieved 0.669 F-measure (0.718 precision and 0.626 recall) at the mention level, and 0.901 F-measure (0.957 precision and 0.857 recall) at the document level for documents used for tagger training.

1 Introduction

Gene and protein name identification and recognition in biomedical text are challenging problems. A recent competition, BioCreAtIvE, highlighted the two tasks inherent in gene recognition: identifying gene mentions in text (task 1A) (Yeh et al., 2005) and normalizing an identified gene list (task 1B) (Hirschman et al., 2005). This competition resulted in many novel and useful approaches, but the results clearly identified that more important work is necessary, especially for normalization, the subject of the current work.

Compared with gene NER, gene normalization is syntactically easier because identification of the textual boundaries of each mention is not required. However, gene normalization poses significant semantic challenges, as it requires detection of the actual gene intended, along with reporting of the gene in a standardized form (Crim et al., 2005). Several approaches have been proposed for gene normalization, including classification techniques (Crim et al., 2005; McDonald et al., 2004), rule-based systems (Hanisch et al., 2005), text matching with dictionaries (Cohen, 2005), and combinations of these approaches. Integrated systems for gene identification typically have three stages: identifying candidate mentions in text, identifying the semantic intent of each mention, and normalizing mentions by associating each mention with a unique gene identifier (Morgan et al., 2004). In our current work, we focus upon normalization, which is currently underexplored for human gene names. Our objective is to create systems for automatically identifying human gene mentions with high accuracy that can be used for practical tasks in biomedical literature retrieval and extraction. Our current approach relies on a manually created and tuned set of rules.

* To whom correspondence should be addressed.

Proceedings of the BioNLP Workshop on Linking Natural Language Processing and Biology at HLT-NAACL 06, pages 41–48,
New York City, June 2006.

2 Automatically Extracted Synonym Dictionaries

Even when restricted to human genes, biomedical researchers mention genes in a highly variable manner, with a minimum of adherence to the gene naming standard provided by the Human Gene Nomenclature Committee (HGNC). In addition, frequent variations in spelling and punctuation generate additional non-standard forms. Extracting gene synonyms automatically from online databases has several benefits (Cohen, 2005). First, online databases contain highly accurate annotations from expert curators, and thus serve as excellent information sources. Second, refreshing of specialized lexicons from online sources provides a means to obtain new information automatically and with no human intervention. We thus sought a way to rapidly collect as many human gene identifiers as possible. All the statistics used in this section are from online database holdings last extracted on February 20, 2006.

2.1 Building the Initial Dictionaries

Nineteen online websites and databases were initially surveyed to identify a set of resources that collectively contain a large proportion of all known human gene identifiers. After examination of the 19 resources with a limited but representative set of gene names, we determined that only four databases together contained all identifiers (excluding resource-specific identifiers used for internal tracking purposes) used by the 19 resources. We then built an automated retrieval agent to extract gene synonyms from these four online databases: The HGNC Genew database, Entrez Gene, Swiss-Prot, and Stanford SOURCE. The results were collected into a single dictionary. Each entry in the dictionary consists of a gene identifier and a corresponding official HGNC symbol. For data from HGNC, withdrawn entries were excluded. Retrieving gene synonyms from SOURCE required a list of gene identifiers to query SOURCE, which was compiled by the retrieval agent from the other sources (i.e., HGNC, Entrez Gene and Swiss-Prot). In total, there were 333,297 entries in the combined dictionary.

2.2 Rule-Based Filter for Purification

Examination of the initial dictionary showed that some entries did not fit our definition of a gene identifier, usually because they were peripheral (e.g., a GenBank sequence identifier) or were describing a gene class (e.g., an Enzyme Commission identifier or a term such as "tyrosine kinase"). A rule-based filter was imposed to prune these uninformative synonyms. The rules include removing identifiers under these conditions:

1. Follows the form of a GenBank or EC accession ID (e.g., 1-2 letters followed by 5-6 digits).
2. Contains at most 2 characters and 1 letter but not an official HGNC symbol (e.g., P1).
3. Matches a description in the OMIM morbid list[1] (e.g., Tangier disease).
4. Is a gene EC number.[2]
5. Ends with ', family ?', where ? is a capital letter or a digit.
6. Follows the form of a DNA clone (e.g., 1-4 digits followed by a single letter, followed by 1-2 digits).
7. Starts with 'similar to' (e.g., similar to zinc finger protein 533).

Our filter pruned 9,384 entries (2.82%).

2.3 Internal Update Across the Dictionaries

We used HGNC-designated human gene symbols as the unique identifiers. However, we found that certain gene symbols listed as "official" in the non-HGNC sources were not always current, and that other assigned symbols were not officially designated as such by HGNC. To remedy these issues, we treated HGNC as the most reliable source and Entrez Gene as the next most reliable, and then updated our dictionary as follows:

[1] ftp://ftp.ncbi.nih.gov/repository/OMIM/morbidmap

[2] EC numbers are removed because they often represent gene classes rather than specifi c instances.

- In the initial dictionary, some synonyms are associated with symbols that were later withdrawn by HGNC. Our retrieval agent extracted a list of 5,048 withdrawn symbols from HGNC, and then replaced any outdated symbols in the dictionary with the official ones. Sixty withdrawn symbols were found to be ambiguous, but we found none of them appearing as symbols in our dictionary.
- If a symbol used by Swiss-Prot or SOURCE was not found as a symbol in HGNC or Entrez Gene, but was a non-ambiguous synonym in HGNC or Entrez Gene, then we replaced it by the corresponding symbol of the non-ambiguous synonym.

Among the 323,913 remaining entries, 801 entries (0.25%) had symbols updated. After removing duplicate entries (42.19%), 187,267 distinct symbol-synonym pairs representing 33,463 unique genes were present. All tasks addressed in this section were performed automatically by the retrieval agent.

3 Exact String Matching

We initially invoked several string transformations for gene normalization, including:

1. Normalization of case.
2. Replacement of hyphens with spaces.
3. Removal of punctuation.
4. Removal of parenthesized materials.
5. Removal of stop words[3].
6. Stemming, where the Porter stemmer was employed (Porter, 1980).
7. Removal of all spaces.

The first four transformations are derived from (Cohen et al., 2002). Not all the rules we experimented with demonstrated good results for human gene name normalization. For example, we found that stemming is inappropriate for this task. To amend potential boundary errors of tagged mentions, or to match the variants of the synonyms, four mention reductions (Cohen et al., 2002) were also applied to the mentions or synonyms:

1. Removal of the first character.
2. Removal of the first word.
3. Removal of the last character.
4. Removal of the last word.

To provide utility, a system was built to allow for transformations and reductions to be invoked flexibly, including chaining of rules in various sequences, grouping of rules for simultaneous invocation, and application of transformations to either or both the candidate mention input and the dictionary. For example, the mention "alpha2C-adrenergic receptor" in PMID 8967963 matches synonym "Alpha-2C adrenergic receptor" of gene ADRA2C after normalizing case, replacing hyphens by spaces, and removing spaces. Each rule can be built into an invoked sequence deemed by evaluation to be optimal for a given application domain.

A *normalization step* is defined here as the process of finding string matches after a sequence of chained transformations, with optional reductions of the mentions or synonyms. We call a normalization step *safe* if it generally makes only minor changes to mentions. On the contrary, a normalization step is called *aggressive* if it often makes substantial changes. However, a normalization step safe for long mentions may not be safe for short ones. Hence, our system was designed to allow a user to set optional parameters factoring the minimal mention length and/or the minimal normalized mention length required to invoke a match.

A *normalization system* consists of multiple normalization steps in sequence. Transformations are applied sequentially and a match searched for; if no match is identified for a particular step, the algorithm proceeds to the next transformation. The normalization steps and the optional conditions are well-encoded in our program, which allows for a flexible system specified by the sequences of the step codes. Our general principle is to design a normalization system that invokes safe normalization steps first, and then gradually moves to more aggressive

[3]ftp://ftp.cs.cornell.edu/pub/smart/English.stop

ones. As the process lengthens, the precision decreases while the recall increases. The balance between precision and recall desired for a particular application can be defined by the user.

Specifically, given string s, we use $\mathcal{T}(s)$ to denote the transformed string. All the 7 transformation rules listed at the beginning of this subsection are *idempotent*, since $\mathcal{T}(\mathcal{T}(s)) = \mathcal{T}(s)$. Two transformations, denoted by $\mathcal{T}_1$ and $\mathcal{T}_2$, are called *commutative*, if $\mathcal{T}_1(\mathcal{T}_2(s)) = \mathcal{T}_2(\mathcal{T}_1(s))$. The first four transformations listed form a set of commutative rules. Knowledge of these properties helps design a normalization system.

Recall that NER systems, such as those required for BioCreAtIvE task 1B, consist of two stages. For our applications of interest, the normalization input is generated by a gene tagger (McDonald and Pereira, 2005), followed by the normalization system described here as the second stage. In the second stage, more synonyms do not necessarily imply better performance, because less frequently used or less informative synonyms may result in ambiguous matches, where a match is called *ambiguous* if it associates a mention with multiple gene identifiers. For example, from the Swiss-Prot dictionary we know the gene mention 'MDR1' in PMID 8880878 is a synonym uniquely representing the ABCB1 gene. However, if we include synonyms from HGNC, it results in an ambiguous match because the TBC1D9 gene also uses the synonym 'MDR1'.

We investigated the rules separately, designed the initial normalization procedure, and tuned our system at the end. To evaluate the efficacy of our compiled dictionary and its sources, we determined the accuracy of our system with all transformations and reductions invoked sequentially, and without any efforts to optimize the sequence (see section 6 for evaluation details). The goal in this experiment was to evaluate the effectiveness of each vocabulary source alone and in combination. Our experimental results at the mention level are summarized in Table 1. The best two-staged system achieved a precision of 0.725 and recall of 0.704 with an F-measure of 0.714, by using only HGNC and Swiss-Prot entries.

As errors can be derived from the tagger or the normalization alone or in combination, we also assessed the performance of our normalization program alone by directly normalizing the mentions in the gold standard file used for evaluation (i.e., assuming the tagger is perfect). Our normalization system achieved 0.824 F-measure (0.958 precision and 0.723 recall) in this evaluation.

Table 1: Results of Gene Normalization Using Exact String Matching

Steps	Recall	Precision	F-measure
(1) HGNC	0.762	0.511	0.611
(2) Entrez Gene	0.686	0.559	0.616
(3) Swiss-Prot	0.722	0.622	0.669
(4) SOURCE	0.743	0.431	0.545
(1)+(2)	0.684	0.564	0.618
(1)+(3)	0.725	0.704	0.714
(2)+(3)	0.665	0.697	0.681
(1)+(2)+(3)	0.667	0.702	0.684
(1)+(2)+(3)+(4)	0.646	0.707	0.675

4 Approximate String Matching

Approximate string matching techniques have been well-developed for entity identification. Given two strings, a *distance metric* generates a score that reflects their similarity. Various string distance metrics have been developed based upon edit-distance, string tokenization, or a hybrid of the two approaches (Cohen et al., 2003). Given a gene mention, we consider the synonym(s) with the highest score to be a match if the score is higher than a defined threshold. Our program also allows optional string transformations and provides a user-defined parameter for determining the minimal mention length for approximate string matching. The decision on the method chosen may be affected by several factors, such as the application domain, features of the strings representing the entity class, and the particular data sets used. For gene NER, various scoring methods have been favored (Crim et al., 2005; Cohen et al., 2003; Wellner et al., 2005).

Approximate string matching is usually considered more aggressive than exact string matching with transformations; hence, we applied it as the last step of our normalization sequence. To assess the usefulness of approximate string matching, we began with our best dictionary subset in Subsection 3 (i.e., using HGNC and SwissProt), and applied approximate string matching as an additional normalization step.

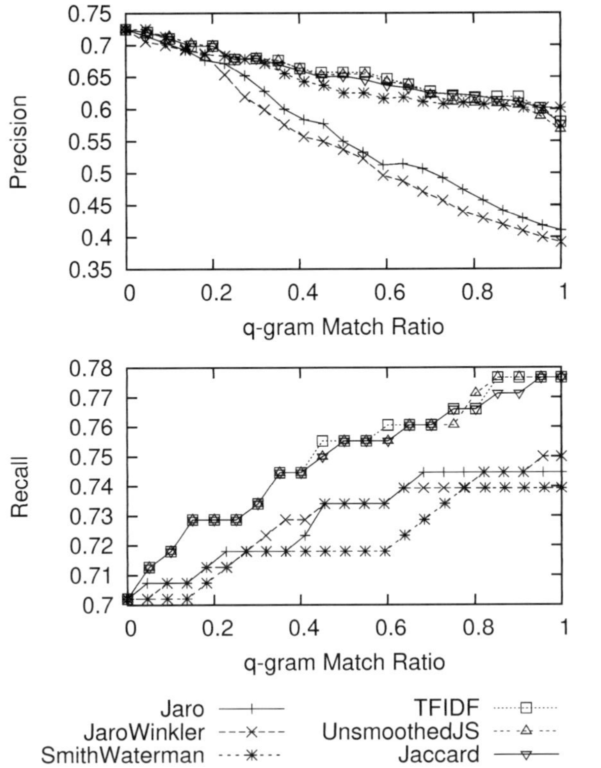

Figure 1: Performance of Approximate String Matching for Gene Normalization.

We selected six existing distance metrics that appeared to be useful for human gene normalization: Jaro, JaroWinkler, SmithWaterman, TFIDF, UnsmoothedJS, and Jaccard. Our experiment showed that TFIDF, UnsmoothedJS and Jaccard outperformed the others for human gene normalization in our system, as shown in Figure 1. By incorporating approximate string matching using either of these metrics into our system, overall performance was slightly improved to 0.718 F-measure (0.724 precision and 0.713 recall) when employing a high threshold (0.95). However, in most scenarios, approximate matching did not considerably improve recall and had a non-trivial detrimental effect upon precision.

5 Ambiguation Analysis

Gene identifier ambiguity is inherent in synonym dictionaries as well as being generated during normalization steps that transform mention strings.

5.1 Ambiguity in Synonym Dictionaries

If multiple gene identifiers share the same synonym, it results in ambiguity. Table 2 shows the level of ambiguity between and among the four sources of gene identifiers used by our dictionary. The rate of ambiguity ranges from 0.89% to 2.83%, which is a rate comparable with that of mouse (1.5%) and *Drosophila* (3.6%) identifiers (Hirschman et al., 2005).

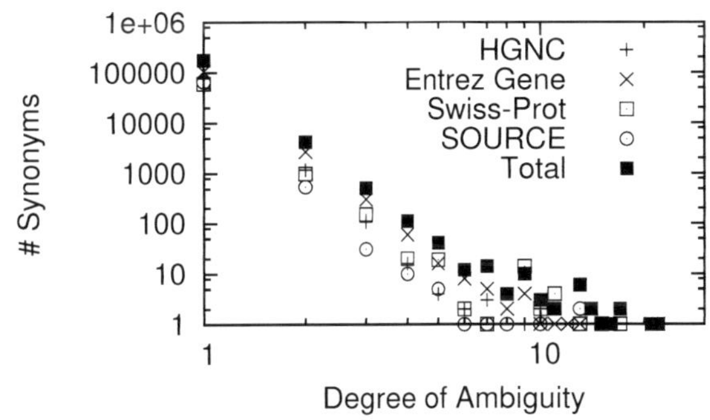

Figure 2: Distribution of ambiguous synonyms in the human gene dictionary.

Figure 2 is a log-log plot showing the distribution of ambiguous synonyms, where the degree is the number of gene identifiers that a synonym is associated with. Comparing Figure 2 with (Hirschman et al., 2005, Figure 3), we noted that on average, human gene synonyms are less ambiguous than those of the three model organisms.

Another type of ambiguity is caused by gene symbols or synonyms being common English words or other biological terms. Our dictionary contains 11 gene symbols identical to common stop words[4]: T, AS, DO, ET, IF, RD, TH, ASK, ITS, SHE and WAS.

5.2 Ambiguous Matches in Gene Normalization

We call a match *ambiguous* if it associates a mention with multiple gene identifiers. Although the

[4]ftp://ftp.cs.cornell.edu/pub/smart/English.stop

Table 2: Statistics for Dictionary Sources

Dictionary	# Symbols	# Synonyms	Ratio	Max. # of Synonyms per Gene	# with One Definition	Ambiguity Rate
HGNC	22,838	78,706	3.446	10	77,389	1.67%
Entrez Gene	33,007	109,127	3.306	22	106,034	2.83%
Swiss-Prot	12,470	61,743	4.951	17	60,536	1.95%
SOURCE	17,130	66,682	3.893	13	66,086	0.89%
Total	33,469	181,061	5.410	22	176,157	2.71%

normalization procedure may create ambiguity, if a mention matches multiple synonyms, it may not be strictly ambiguous. For example, the gene mention "M creatine kinase" in PMID 1690725 matches the synonyms "Creatine kinase M-type" and "Creatine kinase, M chain" in our dictionary using the TFIDF scoring method (with score 0.866). In this case, both synonyms are associated with the CKM gene, so the match is not ambiguous. However, even if a mention matches only one synonym, it can be ambiguous, because the synonym is possibly ambiguous.

Figure 3 shows the result of an experiment conducted upon 200,000 MEDLINE abstracts, where the degree of ambiguity is the number of gene identifiers that a mention is associated with. The maximum, average, and standard deviation of the ambiguity degrees are 20, 1.129 and 0.550, respectively. The overall ambiguity rate of all matched mentions was 8.16%, and the rate of ambiguity is less than 10% at each step. Successful disambiguation can increase the true positive match rate and therefore improve performance but is beyond the scope of the current investigation.

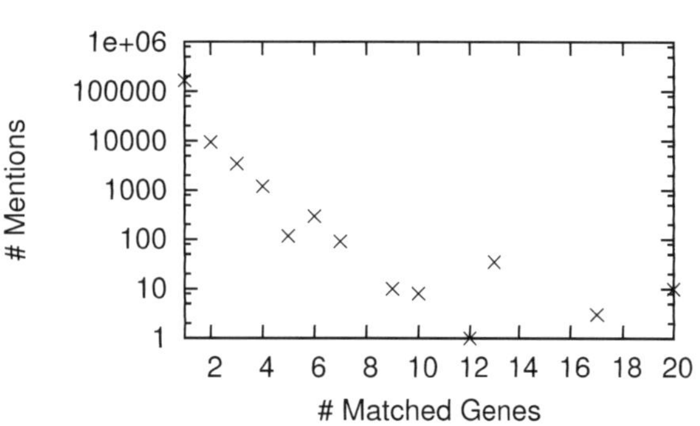

Figure 3: Distribution of Ambiguous Genes in 200,000 MEDLINE Abstracts.

6 Application and Evaluation of an Optimized Normalizer

Finally, we were interested in determining the effectiveness of an optimized system based upon the gene normalization system described above, and also coupled with a state-of-the-art gene tagger. To determine the optimal results of such a system, we created a corpus of 100 MEDLINE abstracts that together contained 1,094 gene mentions for 170 unique genes (also used in the evaluations above). These documents were a subset of those used to train the tagger, and thus measure optimal, rather than typical MEDLINE, performance (data for a generalized evaluation is forthcoming). This corpus was manually annotated to identify human genes, according to a precise definition of gene mentions that an NER gene system would be reasonably expected to tag and normalize correctly. Briefly, the definition included only human genes, excluded multi-protein complexes and antibodies, excluded chained mentions of genes (e.g., "HDAC1- and -2 genes"), and excluded gene classes that were not normalizable to a specific symbol (e.g., tyrosine kinase). Documents were dual-pass annotated in full and then adjudicated by a 3rd expert. Adjudication revealed a very high level of agreement between annotators.

To optimize the rule set for human gene normalization, we evaluated up to 200 cases randomly chosen from all MEDLINE files for each rule, where invocation of that specific rule alone resulted in a match. Most of the transformations worked perfectly or very well. Stemming and removal of the first or last word or character each demonstrated poor performance, as genes and gene classes were often incorrectly converted to other gene instances (e.g., "CAP" and "CAPS" are distinct genes). Removal of stop words generated a high rate of false positives. Rules were ranked according to their precision when invoked separately. A high-performing sequence was "0 01 02 03 06 016 026 036", with 0 referring to case-insensitivity, 1 being replacement of hyphens with spaces, 2 being removal of punctuation, 3 being removal of parenthesized materials, and 6 being removal of spaces; grouped digits indicate simultaneous invocation of each specified rule in the group. Table 3 indicates the cumulative accuracy achieved at each step[5]. A formalized determination of an optimal sequence is in progress. Approximate matching did not considerably improve recall and had a non-trivial detrimental effect upon precision.

Table 3: Results of Gene Normalization after Each Step of Exact String Matching

Steps	Recall	Precision	F-measure
0	0.628	0.698	0.661
01	0.649	0.701	0.674
02	0.654	0.699	0.676
03	0.665	0.702	0.683
06	0.665	0.702	0.683
016	0.718	0.685	0.701
026	0.718	0.685	0.701
036	0.718	0.685	0.701

The normalization sequence "0 01 02 03 06 016 026 036" was then utilized for two separate evaluations. First, we used the actual textual mentions of each gene from the gold standard files as input into our optimized normalization sequence, in order to determine the accuracy of the normalization process alone. We also used a previously developed CRF gene tagger (McDonald and Pereira, 2005) to tag the gold standard files, and then used the tagger's output as input for our normalization sequence. This second evaluation determined the accuracy of a combined NER system for human gene identification.

Depending upon the application, evaluation can be determined more significant at either at the mention level (redundantly), where each individual mention is evaluated independently for accuracy, or as in the case of BioCreAtIvE task 1B, at the document level (non-redundantly), where all mentions within a document are considered to be equivalent. For pure information extraction tasks, mention level accuracy is a relevant performance indicator. However, for applications such as information extraction-based information retrieval (e.g., the identification of documents mentioning a specific gene), document-level accuracy is a relevant gauge of system performance.

For normalization alone, at the mention level our optimized normalization system achieved 0.882 precision, 0.704 recall, and 0.783 F-measure. At the document level, the normalization results were 1.000 precision, 0.994 recall, and 0.997 F-measure.

For the combined NER system, the performance was 0.718 precision, 0.626 recall, and 0.669 F-measure at the mention level. At the document level, the NER system results were 0.957 precision, 0.857 recall, and 0.901 F-measure. The lower accuracy of the combined system was due to the fact that both the tagger and the normalizer introduce error rates that are multiplicative in combination.

7 Conclusions and Future Work

In this article we present a gene normalization system that is intended for use in human gene NER, but that can also be readily adapted to other biomedical normalization tasks. When optimized for human gene normalization, our system achieved 0.783 F-measure at the mention level.

Choosing the proper normalization steps depends on several factors, such as (for genes) the organism of interest, the entity class, the accuracy of identifying gene mentions, and the reliability of the underlying dictionary. While the results of our normalizer compare favorably with previous efforts, much future work can be done to further improve the performance of our system, including:

1. Performance of identifying gene mentions. Only approximately 50 percent of gene mentions identified by our tagger were normalizable. While this is mostly due to the fact that the tagger identifies gene classes that cannot be normalized to a gene instance, a significant subset of gene instance mentions are not being normalized.

2. Reliability of the dictionary. Though we have

[5]The last two steps did not generate new matches using our gold standard fi le and therefore the scores were unchanged. These rule sets may improve performance in other cases.

investigated a sizable number of gene identifier sources, the four representative sources used for compiling our gene dictionary are incomplete and often not precise for individual terms. Some text mentions were not normalizable due the the incompleteness of our dictionary, which limited the recall.

3. Disambiguation. A small portion (typically 7%-10%) of the matches were ambiguous. Successful development of disambiguation tools can improve the performance.

4. Machine-learning. It is likely possible that optimized rules can be used as probabilistic features for a machine-learning-based version of our normalizer.

Gene normalization has several potential applications, such as for biomedical information extraction, database curation, and as a prerequisite for relation extraction. Providing a proper synonym dictionary, our normalization program is amenable to generalizing to other organisms, and has already proven successful in our group for other entity normalization tasks. An interesting future study would be to determine accuracy for BioCreAtIvE data once mouse, Drosophila, and yeast vocabularies are incorporated into our system.

Acknowledgment

This work was supported in part by NSF grant EIA-0205448, funds from the David Lawrence Altschuler Chair in Genomics and Computational Biology, and the Penn Genomics Institute. The authors acknowledge Shannon Davis and Jeremy Lautman for gene dictionary assessment, Steven Carroll for gene tagger implementation and results, Penn BioIE annotators for annotation of the gold standard, and Monica D'arcy and members of the Penn BioIE team for helpful comments.

References

K. B. Cohen, A. E. Dolbey, G. K. Acquaah-Mensah, and L. Hunter. 2002. Contrast and variability in gene names. In *ACL Workshop on Natural Language Processing in the Biomedical Domain*, pages 14–20.

W. W. Cohen, P. Ravikumar, and S. E. Fienberg. 2003. A comparison of string distance metrices for name-matching tasks. In *Proceedings of IIWeb Workshop*.

A. M. Cohen. 2005. Unsupervised gene/protein entity normalization using automatically extracted dictionaries. In *Linking Biological Literature, Ontologies and Databases: Mining Biological Semantics, Proceedings of the BioLINK2005 Workshop*, pages 17–24. MI: Association for Computational Linguistics, Detroit.

J. Crim, R. McDonald, and F. Pereira. 2005. Automatically annotating documents with normalized gene lists. *BMC Bioinformatics*, 6(Suppl 1)(S13).

D. Hanisch, K. Fundel, H.-T. Mevissen, R. Zimmer, and J. Fluck. 2005. Prominer: Rule-based protein and gene entity recognition. *BMC Bioinformatics*, 6(Suppl 1)(S14).

L. Hirschman, M. Colosimo, A. Morgan, and A. Yeh. 2005. Overview of biocreative task 1b: Normalized gene lists. *BMC Bioinformatics*, 6(Suppl 1)(S11).

R. McDonald and F. Pereira. 2005. Identifying gene and protein mentions in text using conditional random fi elds. *BMC Bioinformatics*, 6(Suppl 1)(S6).

R. McDonald, R. S. Winters, M. Mandel, Y. Jin, P. S. White, and F. Pereira. 2004. An entity tagger for recognizing acquired genomic variations in cancer literature. *Journal of Bioinformatics*, 20(17):3249–3251.

A. A. Morgan, L. Hirschman, M. Colosimo, A. S. Yeh, and J. B. Colombe. 2004. Gene name identifi cation and normalization using a model organism database. *Journal of Biomedical Informatics*, 37(6):396–410.

M. F. Porter. 1980. An algorithm for suffi x stripping. *Program*, 14(3).

B Wellner, J. Castaño, and J. Pustejovsky. 2005. Adaptive string similarity metrics for biomedical reference resolution. In *Proceedings of the ACL-ISMB Workshop on Linking Biological Literature, Ontologies and Databases: Mining Biological Semantics*, pages 9–16, Detroit. Association for Computational Linguistics.

A. Yeh, A. Morgan, M. Colosimo, and L. Hirschman. 2005. Biocreative task 1a: Gene mention fi nding evaluation. *BMC Bioinformatics*, 6(Suppl 1)(S2).

Integrating Co-occurrence Statistics with Information Extraction for Robust Retrieval of Protein Interactions from Medline

Razvan Bunescu, Raymond Mooney
Department of Computer Sciences
University of Texas at Austin
1 University Station C0500
Austin, TX 78712
razvan@cs.utexas.edu
mooney@cs.utexas.edu

Arun Ramani, Edward Marcotte
Institute for Cellular and Molecular Biology
University of Texas at Austin
1 University Station A4800
Austin, TX 78712
arun@icmb.utexas.edu
marcotte@icmb.utexas.edu

Abstract

The task of mining relations from collections of documents is usually approached in two different ways. One type of systems do relation extraction from individual sentences, followed by an aggregation of the results over the entire collection. Other systems follow an entirely different approach, in which co-occurrence counts are used to determine whether the mentioning together of two entities is due to more than simple chance. We show that increased extraction performance can be obtained by combining the two approaches into an integrated relation extraction model.

1 Introduction

Information Extraction (IE) is a natural language processing task in which text documents are analyzed with the aim of finding mentions of relevant entities and important relationships between them. In many cases, the subtask of relation extraction reduces to deciding whether a sentence asserts a particular relationship between two entities, which is still a difficult, unsolved problem. There are however cases where the decision whether the two entities are in a relationship is made relative to an entire document, or a collection of documents. In the biomedical domain, for example, one may be interested in finding the pairs of human proteins that are said to be interacting in any of the Medline abstracts, where the answer is not required to specify which abstracts are actually describing the interaction. Assembling a ranked list of interacting proteins can be very useful to biologists - based on this list, they can make more informed decisions with respect to which genes to focus on in their research.

In this paper, we investigate methods that use multiple occurrences of the same pair of entities across a collection of documents in order to boost the performance of a relation extraction system. The proposed methods are evaluated on the task of finding pairs of human proteins whose interactions are reported in Medline abstracts. The majority of known human protein interactions are derived from individual, small-scale experiments reported in Medline. Some of these interactions have already been collected in the Reactome (Joshi-Tope et al., 2005), BIND (Bader et al., 2003), DIP (Xenarios et al., 2002), and HPRD (Peri et al., 2004) databases. The amount of human effort involved in creating and updating these databases is currently no match for the continuous growth of Medline. It is therefore very useful to have a method that automatically and reliably extracts interaction pairs from Medline.

Systems that do relation extraction from a collection of documents can be divided into two major categories. In one category are IE systems that first extract information from individual sentences, and then combine the results into corpus-level results (Craven, 1999; Skounakis and Craven, 2003). The second category corresponds to approaches that do not exploit much information from the context of individual occurrences. Instead, based on co-occurrence counts, various statistical

Proceedings of the BioNLP Workshop on Linking Natural Language Processing and Biology at HLT-NAACL 06, pages 49–56,
New York City, June 2006.

or information-theoretic tests are used to decide whether the two entities in a pair appear together more often than simple chance would predict (Lee et al., 2004; Ramani et al., 2005). We believe that a combination of the two approaches can inherit the advantages of each method and lead to improved relation extraction accuracy.

The following two sections describe the two orthogonal approaches to corpus-level relation extraction. A model that integrates the two approaches is then introduced in Section 4. This is followed by a description of the dataset used for evaluation in Section 5, and experimental results in Section 6.

2 Sentence-level relation extraction

Most systems that identify relations between entities mentioned in text documents consider only pair of entities that are mentioned in the same sentence (Ray and Craven, 2001; Zhao and Grishman, 2005; Bunescu and Mooney, 2005). To decide the existence and the type of a relationship, these systems generally use lexico-semantic clues inferred from the sentence context of the two entities. Much research has been focused recently on automatically identifying biologically relevant entities and their relationships such as protein-protein interactions or subcellular localizations. For example, the sentence "*TR6* specifically binds *Fas ligand*", states an interaction between the two proteins *TR6* and *Fas ligand.* One of the first systems for extracting interactions between proteins is described in (Blaschke and Valencia, 2001). There, sentences are matched deterministically against a set of manually developed patterns, where a pattern is a sequence of words or Part-of-Speech (POS) tags and two protein-name tokens. Between every two adjacent words is a number indicating the maximum number of words that can be skipped at that position. An example is: "*interaction of (3) <P> (3) with (3) <P>*". This approach is generalized in (Bunescu and Mooney, 2005), where subsequences of words (or POS tags) from the sentence are used as implicit features. Their weights are learned by training a customized subsequence kernel on a dataset of Medline abstracts annotated with proteins and their interactions.

A relation extraction system that works at the sentence-level and which outputs normalized confidence values for each extracted pair of entities can also be used for corpus-level relation extraction. A straightforward way to do this is to apply an aggregation operator over the confidence values inferred for all occurrences of a given pair of entities. More exactly, if p_1 and p_2 are two entities that occur in a total of n sentences $s_1, s_2, ..., s_n$ in the entire corpus C, then the confidence $P(R(p_1,p_2)|C)$ that they are in a particular relationship R is defined as:

$$P(R(p_1,p_2)|C) = \Gamma(\{P(R(p_1,p_2)|s_i)|i{=}1{:}n\})$$

Table 1 shows only four of the many possible choices for the aggregation operator Γ.

max	$\Gamma_{max} = \max_i P(R(p_1,p_2)\|s_i)$
noisy-or	$\Gamma_{nor} = 1 - \prod_i (1 - P(R(p_1,p_2)\|s_i))$
avg	$\Gamma_{avg} = \sum_i \frac{P(R(p_1,p_2)\|s_i)}{n}$
and	$\Gamma_{and} = \prod_i P(R(p_1,p_2)\|s_i)^{1/n}$

Table 1: Aggregation Operators.

Out of the four operators in Table 1, we believe that the *max* operator is the most appropriate for aggregating confidence values at the corpus-level. The question that needs to be answered is whether there is a sentence somewhere in the corpus that asserts the relationship R between entities p_1 and p_2. Using *avg* instead would answer a different question - whether $R(p_1,p_2)$ is true in most of the sentences containing p_1 and p_2. Also, the *and* operator would be most appropriate for finding whether $R(p_1,p_2)$ is true in all corresponding sentences in the corpus. The value of the *noisy-or* operator (Pearl, 1986) is too dependent on the number of occurrences, therefore it is less appropriate for a corpus where the occurrence counts vary from one entity pair to another (as confirmed in our experiments from Section 6). For examples, if the confidence threshold is set at 0.5, and the entity pair (p_1,p_2) occurs in 6 sentences or less, each with confidence 0.1, then $R(p_1,p_2)$ is false, according to the noisy-or operator. However, if (p_1,p_2) occur in more than 6 sentences, with the same confidence value of 0.1, then the corresponding noisy-or value exceeds 0.5, making $R(p_1,p_2)$ true.

3 Co-occurrence statistics

Given two entities with multiple mentions in a large corpus, another approach to detect whether a relationship holds between them is to use statistics over their occurrences in textual patterns that are indicative for that relation. Various measures such as pointwise mutual information (PMI) , chi-square (χ^2) or log-likelihood ratio (LLR) (Manning and Schütze, 1999) use the two entities' occurrence statistics to detect whether their co-occurrence is due to chance, or to an underlying relationship.

A recent example is the *co-citation* approach from (Ramani et al., 2005), which does not try to find specific assertions of interactions in text, but rather exploits the idea that if many different abstracts reference both protein p_1 and protein p_2, then p_1 and p_2 are likely to interact. Particularly, if the two proteins are co-cited significantly more often than one would expect if they were cited independently at random, then it is likely that they interact. The model used to compute the probability of random co-citation is based on the hypergeometric distribution (Lee et al., 2004; Jenssen et al., 2001). Thus, if N is the total number of abstracts, n of which cite the first protein, m cite the second protein, and k cite both, then the probability of co-citation under a random model is:

$$P(k|N,m,n) = \frac{\binom{n}{k}\binom{N-n}{m-k}}{\binom{N}{m}} \tag{1}$$

The approach that we take in this paper is to constrain the two proteins to be mentioned in the same sentence, based on the assumption that if there is a reason for two protein names to co-occur in the same sentence, then in most cases that is caused by their interaction. To compute the "degree of interaction" between two proteins p_1 and p_2, we use the information-theoretic measure of pointwise mutual information (Church and Hanks, 1990; Manning and Schütze, 1999), which is computed based on the following quantities:

1. N : the total number of protein pairs co-occurring in the same sentence in the corpus.

2. $P(p_1, p_2) \simeq n_{12}/N$: the probability that p_1 and p_2 co-occur in the same sentence; n_{12} = the number of sentences mentioning both p_1 and p_2.

3. $P(p_1, p) \simeq n_1/N$: the probability that p_1 co-occurs with any other protein in the same sentence; n_1 = the number of sentences mentioning p_1 and p.

4. $P(p_2, p) \simeq n_2/N$: the probability that p_2 co-occurs with any other protein in the same sentence; n_2 = the number of sentences mentioning p_2 and p.

The PMI is then defined as in Equation 2 below:

$$\begin{aligned} PMI(p_1, p_2) &= \log \frac{P(p_1, p_2)}{P(p_1, p) \cdot P(p_2, p)} \\ &\simeq \log N \frac{n_{12}}{n_1 \cdot n_2} \end{aligned} \tag{2}$$

Given that the PMI will be used only for ranking pairs of potentially interacting proteins, the constant factor N and the log operator can be ignored. For sake of simplicity, we use the simpler formula from Equation 3.

$$sPMI(p_1, p_2) = \frac{n_{12}}{n_1 \cdot n_2} \tag{3}$$

4 Integrated model

The $sPMI(p_1, p_2)$ formula can be rewritten as:

$$sPMI(p_1, p_2) = \frac{1}{n_1 \cdot n_2} \cdot \sum_{i=1}^{n_{12}} 1 \tag{4}$$

Let s_1, s_2, ..., $s_{n_{12}}$ be the sentence contexts corresponding to the n_{12} co-occurrences of p_1 and p_2, and assume that a sentence-level relation extractor is available, with the capability of computing normalized confidence values for all extractions. Then one way of using the extraction confidence is to have each co-occurrence weighted by its confidence, i.e. replace the constant 1 with the normalized scores $P(R(p_1, p_2)|s_i)$, as illustrated in Equation 5. This results in a new formula $wPMI$ (*weighted PMI*), which is equal with the product between $sPMI$ and the average aggregation operator Γ_{avg}.

$$\begin{aligned} wPMI(p_1, p_2) &= \frac{1}{n_1 \cdot n_2} \cdot \sum_{i=1}^{n_{12}} P(R(p_1, p_2)|s_i) \\ &= \frac{n_{12}}{n_1 \cdot n_2} \cdot \Gamma_{avg} \end{aligned} \tag{5}$$

The operator Γ_{avg} can be replaced with any other aggregation operator from Table 1. As argued in Section 2, we consider max to be the most appropriate operator for our task, therefore the integrated model is based on the weighted PMI product illustrated in Equation 6.

$$\begin{aligned} wPMI(p_1, p_2) &= \frac{n_{12}}{n_1 \cdot n_2} \cdot \Gamma_{max} \\ &= \frac{n_{12}}{n_1 \cdot n_2} \cdot \max_i P(R(p_1, p_2)|s_i) \end{aligned} \quad (6)$$

If a pair of entities p_1 and p_2 is ranked by $wPMI$ among the top pairs, this means that it is unlikely that p_1 and p_2 have co-occurred together in the entire corpus by chance, and at the same time there is at least one mention where the relation extractor decides with high confidence that $R(p_1, p_2) = 1$.

5 Evaluation Corpus

Contrasting the performance of the integrated model against the sentence-level extractor or the PMI-based ranking requires an evaluation dataset that provides two types of annotations:

1. The complete *list of interactions* reported in the corpus (Section 5.1).
2. Annotation of *mentions* of genes and proteins, together with their corresponding *gene identifiers* (Section 5.2).

We do not differentiate between genes and their protein products, mapping them to the same gene identifiers. Also, even though proteins may participate in different types of interactions, we are concerned only with detecting whether they interact in the general sense of the word.

5.1 Medline Abstracts and Interactions

In order to compile an evaluation corpus and an associated comprehensive list of interactions, we exploited information contained in the HPRD (Peri et al., 2004) database. Every interaction listed in HPRD is linked to a set of Medline articles where the corresponding experiment is reported. More exactly, each interaction is specified in the database as a tuple that contains the LocusLink (now EntrezGene) identifiers of all genes involved and the PubMed identifiers of the corresponding articles (as illustrated in Table 2).

Interaction (XML) (HPRD)

```
<interaction>
  <gene>2318</gene>
  <gene>58529</gene>
  <pubmed>10984498 11171996</pubmed>
</interaction>
```

Participant Genes (XML) (NCBI)

```
<gene id="2318">
  <name>FLNC</name>
  <description>filamin C, gamma</description>
  <synonyms>
    <synonym>ABPA</synonym>
    <synonym>ABPL</synonym>
    <synonym>FLN2</synonym>
    <synonym>ABP-280</synonym>
    <synonym>ABP280A</synonym>
  </synonyms>
  <proteins>
    <protein>gamma filamin</protein>
    <protein>filamin 2</protein>
    <protein>gamma-filamin</protein>
    <protein>ABP-L, gamma filamin</protein>
    <protein>actin-binding protein 280</protein>
    <protein>gamma actin-binding protein</protein>
    <protein>filamin C, gamma</protein>
  </proteins>
</gene>
<gene id="58529">
  <name>MYOZ1</name>
  <description>myozenin 1</description>
  <synonyms> ... </synonyms>
  <proteins> ... </proteins>
</gene>
```

Medline Abstract (XML) (NCBI)

```
<PMID>10984498</PMID>
<AbstractText>
We found that this protein binds to three other Z-disc proteins; therefore, we have named it FATZ, gamma-filamin, alpha-actinin and telethonin binding protein of the Z-disc.
</AbstractText>
```

Table 2: Interactions, Genes and Abstracts.

The evaluation corpus (henceforth referred to as the *HPRD corpus*) is created by collecting the Medline abstracts corresponding to interactions between human proteins, as specified in HPRD. In total, 5,617 abstracts are included in this corpus, with an associated list of 7,785 interactions. This list is comprehensive - the HPRD database is based on an annotation process in which the human annotators report all interactions described in a Medline article. On the other hand, the fact that only abstracts are included in the corpus (as opposed to including the full article) means that the list may contain interactions that are not actually reported in the HPRD corpus. Nevertheless, if the abstracts were annotated with gene mentions and corresponding GIDs, then a "quasi-exact" interaction list could be computed based on the following heuristic:

[H] *If two genes with identifiers* gid_1 *and* gid_2 *are mentioned in the same sentence in an abstract with PubMed identifier* $pmid$, *and if* gid_1 *and* gid_2 *are participants in an interaction that is linked to* $pmid$ *in HPRD, then consider that the abstract (and consequently the entire HPRD corpus) reports the interaction between* gid_1 *and* gid_2. ■

An application of the above heuristic is shown at the bottom of Table 2. The HPRD record at the top of the table specifies that the Medline article with ID 10984498 reports an interaction between the proteins *FATZ* (with ID 58529) and *gamma-filamin* (with ID 2318). The two protein names are mentioned in a sentence in the abstract for 10984498, therefore, by **[H]**, we consider that the HPRD corpus reports this interaction.

This is very similar to the procedure used in (Craven, 1999) for creating a "weakly-labeled" dataset of *subcellular-localization* relations. **[H]** is a strong heuristic – it is already known that the full article reports an interaction between the two genes. Finding the two genes collocated in the same sentence in the abstract is very likely to be due to the fact that the abstract discusses their interaction. The heuristic can be made even more accurate if a pair of genes is considered as interacting only if they co-occur in a (predefined) minimum number of sentences in the entire corpus – with the evaluation modified accordingly, as described later in Section 6.

5.2 Gene Name Annotation and Normalization

For the annotation of gene names and their normalization, we use a dictionary-based approach similar to (Cohen, 2005). NCBI[1] provides a comprehensive dictionary of human genes, where each gene is specified by its unique identifier, and qualified with an official name, a description, synonym names and one or more protein names, as illustrated in Table 2. All of these names, including the description, are considered as potential referential expressions for the gene entity. Each name string is reduced to a normal form by: replacing dashes with spaces, introducing spaces between sequences of letters and sequences of digits, replacing Greek letters with their Latin counterparts (capitalized), substituting Roman numerals with Arabic numerals, decapitalizing the first word if capitalized. All names are further tokenized, and checked against a dictionary of close to 100K English nouns. Names that are found in this dictionary are simply filtered out. We also ignore all ambiguous names (i.e. names corresponding to more than one gene identifier). The remaining non-ambiguous names are added to the final gene dictionary, which is implemented as a trie-like structure in order to allow a fast lookup of gene IDs based on the associated normalized sequences of tokens.

Each abstract from the HPRD corpus is tokenized and segmented in sentences using the OpenNLP[2] package. The resulting sentences are then annotated by traversing them from left to right and finding the longest token sequences whose normal forms match entries from the gene dictionary.

6 Experimental Evaluation

The main purpose of the experiments in this section is to compare the performance of the following four methods on the task of corpus-level relation extraction:

1. Sentence-level relation extraction followed by the application of an aggregation operator that assembles corpus-level results (**SSK.Max**).
2. Pointwise Mutual Information (**PMI**).
3. The integrated model, a product of the two base models (**PMI.SSK.Max**).
4. The hypergeometric co-citation method (**HG**).

7 Experimental Methodology

All abstracts, either from the HPRD corpus, or from the entire Medline, are annotated using the dictionary-based approach described in Section 5.2. The sentence-level extraction is done with the subsequence kernel (SSK) approach from (Bunescu and Mooney, 2005), which was shown to give good results on extracting interactions from biomedical abstracts. The subsequence kernel was trained on a set of 225 Medline abstracts which were manually

[1] URL: http://www.ncbi.nih.gov

[2] URL: http://opennlp.sourceforge.net

annotated with protein names and their interactions. It is known that PMI gives undue importance to low frequency events (Dunning, 1993), therefore the evaluation considers only pairs of genes that occur at least 5 times in the whole corpus.

When evaluating corpus-level extraction on HPRD, because the "quasi-exact" list of interactions is known, we report the precision-recall (PR) graphs, where the precision (P) and recall (R) are computed as follows:

$$P = \frac{\#\textit{true interactions extracted}}{\#\textit{total interaction extracted}}$$

$$R = \frac{\#\textit{true interactions extracted}}{\#\textit{true interactions}}$$

All pairs of proteins are ranked based on each scoring method, and precision recall points are computed by considering the top N pairs, where N varies from 1 to the total number of pairs.

When evaluating on the entire Medline, we used the shared protein function benchmark described in (Ramani et al., 2005). Given the set of interacting pairs recovered at each recall level, this benchmark calculates the extent to which interaction partners in a data set share functional annotation, a measure previously shown to correlate with the accuracy of functional genomics data sets (Lee et al., 2004). The KEGG (Kanehisa et al., 2004) and Gene Ontology (Ashburner et al., 2000) databases provide specific pathway and biological process annotations for approximately 7,500 human genes, assigning human genes into 155 KEGG pathways (at the lowest level of KEGG) and 1,356 GO pathways (at level 8 of the GO biological process annotation).

The scoring scheme for measuring interaction set accuracy is in the form of a log odds ratio of gene pairs sharing functional annotations. To evaluate a data set, a log likelihood ratio (LLR) is calculated as follows:

$$LLR = ln\frac{P(D|I)}{P(D|\neg I)} = ln\frac{P(I|D)P(\neg I)}{P(\neg I|D)P(I)} \quad (7)$$

where $P(D|I)$ and $P(D|\neg I)$ are the probability of observing the data D conditioned on the genes sharing benchmark associations (I) and not sharing benchmark associations ($\neg I$). In its expanded form (obtained by Bayes theorem), $P(I|D)$ and $P(\neg I|D)$ are estimated using the frequencies of interactions observed in the given data set D between annotated genes sharing benchmark associations and not sharing associations, respectively, while the priors $P(I)$ and $P(\neg I)$ are estimated based on the total frequencies of all benchmark genes sharing the same associations and not sharing associations, respectively. A score of zero indicates interaction partners in the data set being tested are no more likely than random to belong to the same pathway or to interact; higher scores indicate a more accurate data set.

8 Experimental Results

The results for the HPRD corpus-level extraction are shown in Figure 1. Overall, the integrated model has a more consistent performance, with a gain in precision mostly at recall levels past 40%. The SSK.Max and HG models both exhibit a sudden decrease in precision at around 5% recall level. While SSK.Max goes back to a higher precision level, the HG model begins to recover only late at 70% recall.

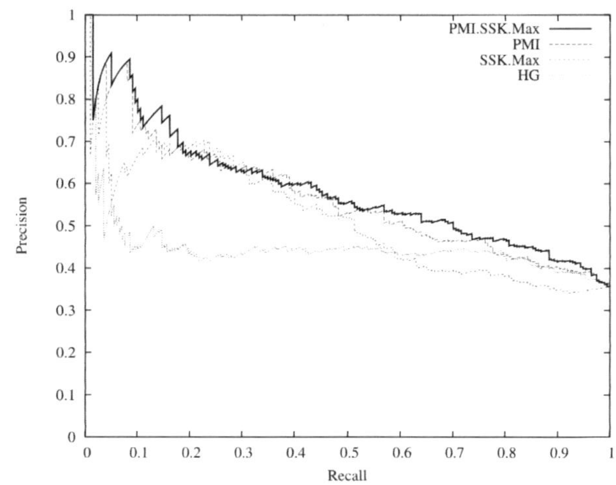

Figure 1: PR curves for corpus-level extraction.

A surprising result in this experiment is the behavior of the HG model, which is significantly outperformed by PMI, and which does only marginally better than a simple baseline that considers all pairs to be interacting.

We also compared the two methods on corpus-level extraction from the entire Medline, using the shared protein function benchmark. As before, we considered only protein pairs occurring in the same sentence, with a minimum frequency count of 5. The resulting 47,436 protein pairs were ranked according to their PMI and HG scores, with pairs that are most likely to be interacting being placed at the top. For each ranking, the LLR score was computed for the top N proteins, where N varied in increments of 1,000.

The comparative results for PMI and HG are shown in Figure 2, together with the scores for three human curated databases: HPRD, BIND and Reactome. On the top 18,000 protein pairs, PMI outperforms HG substantially, after which both converge to the same value for all the remaining pairs.

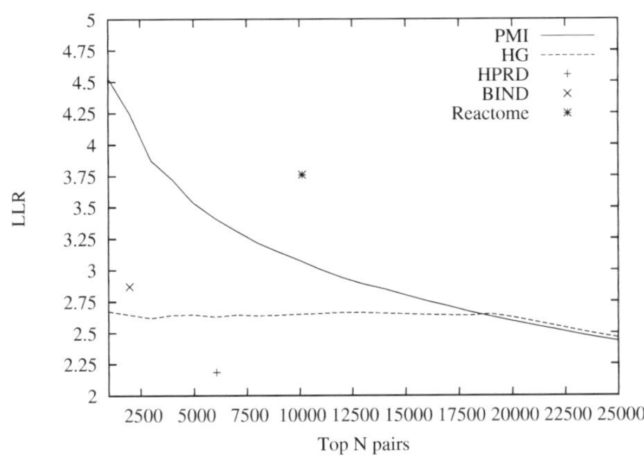

Figure 2: Functional annotation benchmark.

Figure 3 shows a comparison of the four aggregation operators on the same HPRD corpus, which confirms that, overall, *max* is most appropriate for integrating corpus-level results.

9 Future Work

The piece of related work that is closest to the aim of this paper is the Bayesian approach from (Skounakis and Craven, 2003). In their probabilistic model, co-occurrence statistics are taken into account by using a prior probability that a pair of proteins are interacting, given the number of co-occurrences in the corpus. However, they do not use the confidences of the sentence-level extractions. The GeneWays system from (Rzhetsky et al., 2004) takes a different approach, in which co-occurrence frequencies are simply used to re-rank the ouput from the relation extractor.

An interesting direction for future research is to

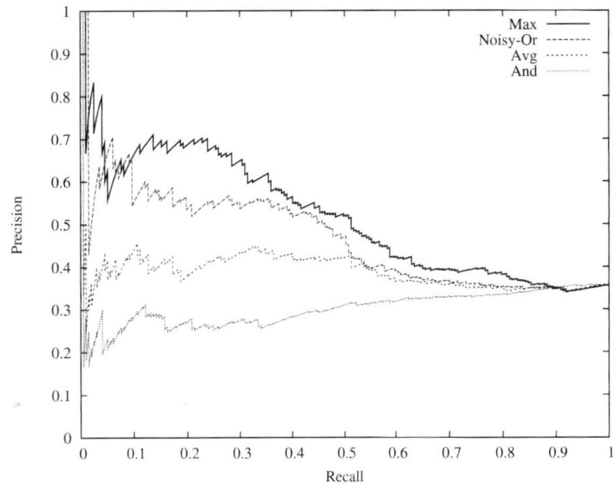

Figure 3: PR curves for aggregation operators.

design a model that takes into account both the extraction confidences and the co-occurrence statistics, without losing the probabilistic (or information-theoretic) interpretation. One could investigate ways of integrating the two orthogonal approaches to corpus-level extraction based on other statistical tests, such as chi-square and log-likelihood ratio.

The sentence-level extractor used in this paper was trained to recognize relation mentions *in isolation*. However, the trained model is later used, through the *max* aggregation operator, to recognize whether *multiple mentions* of the same pair of proteins indicate a relationship between them. This points to a fundamental mismatch between the training and testing phases of the model. We expect that better accuracy can be obtained by designing an approach that is using information from multiple occurrences of the same pair in both training and testing.

10 Conclusion

Extracting relations from a collection of documents can be approached in two fundamentally different ways. In one approach, an IE system extracts relation instances from corpus sentences, and then aggregates the local extractions into corpus-level results. In the second approach, statistical tests based on co-occurrence counts are used for deciding if a given pair of entities are mentioned together more often than chance would predict. We have described a method to integrate the two approaches, and given experimental results that confirmed our intuition that an integrated model would have a better performance.

11 Acknowledgements

This work was supported by grants from the N.S.F. (IIS-0325116, EIA-0219061), N.I.H. (GM06779-01), Welch (F1515), and a Packard Fellowship (E.M.M.).

References

M. Ashburner, C. A. Ball, J. A. Blake, D. Botstein, H. Butler, J. M. Cherry, A. P. Davis, K. Dolinski, S. S. Dwight, and J. T. et al. Eppig. 2000. Gene ontology: tool for the unification of biology. the gene ontology consortium. *Nature Genetics*, 25(1):25–29.

G. D. Bader, D. Betel, and C. W. Hogue. 2003. Bind: the biomolecular interaction network database. *Nucleic Acids Research*, 31(1):248–250.

C. Blaschke and A. Valencia. 2001. Can bibliographic pointers for known biological data be found automatically? protein interactions as a case study. *Comparative and Functional Genomics*, 2:196–206.

Razvan C. Bunescu and Raymond J. Mooney. 2005. Subsequence kernels for relation extraction. In *Proceedings of the Conference on Neural Information Processing Systems*, Vancouver, BC.

Kenneth W. Church and Patrick W. Hanks. 1990. Word association norms, mutual information and lexicography. *Computational Linguistics*, 16(1):22–29.

Aaron M. Cohen. 2005. Unsupervised gene/protein named entity normalization using automatically extracted dictionaries. In *Proceedings of the ACL-ISMB Workshop on Linking Biological Literature, Ontologies and Databases: Minining Biological Semantics*, pages 17–24, Detroit, MI.

Mark Craven. 1999. Learning to extract relations from MEDLINE. In *Papers from the Sixteenth National Conference on Artificial Intelligence (AAAI-99) Workshop on Machine Learning for Information Extraction*, pages 25–30, July.

Ted Dunning. 1993. Accurate methods for the statistics of surprise and coincidence. *Computational Linguistics*, 19(1):61–74.

T. K. Jenssen, A. Laegreid, J. Komorowski, and E. Hovig. 2001. A literature network of human genes for high-throughput analysis of gene expression. *Nature Genetics*, 28(1):21–28.

G. Joshi-Tope, M. Gillespie, I. Vastrik, P. D'Eustachio, E. Schmidt, B. de Bono, B. Jassal, G. R. Gopinath, G. R. Wu, L. Matthews, and et al. 2005. Reactome: a knowledgebase of biological pathways. *Nucleic Acids Research*, 33 Database Issue:D428–432.

M. Kanehisa, S. Goto, S. Kawashima, Y. Okuno, and M. Hattori. 2004. The KEGG resource for deciphering the genome. *Nucleic Acids Research*, 32 Database issue:D277–280.

I. Lee, S. V. Date, A. T. Adai, and E. M. Marcotte. 2004. A probabilistic functional network of yeast genes. *Science*, 306(5701):1555–1558.

Christopher D. Manning and Hinrich Schütze. 1999. *Foundations of Statistical Natural Language Processing*. MIT Press, Cambridge, MA.

Judea Pearl. 1986. Fusion, propagation, and structuring in belief networks. *Artificial Intelligence*, 29(3):241–288.

S. Peri, J. D. Navarro, T. Z. Kristiansen, R. Amanchy, V. Surendranath, B. Muthusamy, T. K. Gandhi, K. N. Chandrika, N. Deshpande, S. Suresh, and et al. 2004. Human protein reference database as a discovery resource for proteomics. *Nucleic Acids Research*, 32 Database issue:D497–501.

A. K. Ramani, R. C. Bunescu, R. J. Mooney, and E. M. Marcotte. 2005. Consolidating the set of know human protein-protein interactions in preparation for large-scale mapping of the human interactome. *Genome Biology*, 6(5):r40.

Soumya Ray and Mark Craven. 2001. Representing sentence structure in hidden Markov models for information extraction. In *Proceedings of the Seventeenth International Joint Conference on Artificial Intelligence (IJCAI-2001)*, pages 1273–1279, Seattle, WA.

A. Rzhetsky, T. Iossifov, I. Koike, M. Krauthammer, P. Kra, M. Morris, H. Yu, P.A. Duboue, W. Weng, W.J. Wilbur, V. Hatzivassiloglou, and C. Friedman. 2004. GeneWays: a system for extracting, analyzing, visualizing, and integrating molecular pathway data. *Journal of Biomedical Informatics*, 37:43–53.

Marios Skounakis and Mark Craven. 2003. Evidence combination in biomedical natural-language processing. In *Proceedings of the 3nd ACM SIGKDD Workshop on Data Mining in Bioinformatics (BIOKDD 2003)*, pages 25–32, Washington, DC.

I. Xenarios, L. Salwinski, X. J. Duan, P. Higney, S. M. Kim, and D. Eisenberg. 2002. DIP, the database of interacting proteins: a research tool for studying cellular networks of protein interactions. *Nucleic Acids Research*, 30(1):303–305.

Shubin Zhao and Ralph Grishman. 2005. Extracting relations with integrated information using kernel methods. In *Proceedings of the 43rd Annual Meeting of the Association for Computational Linguistics (ACL'05)*, pages 419–426, Ann Arbor, Michigan, June. Association for Computational Linguistics.

BIOSMILE: Adapting Semantic Role Labeling for Biomedical Verbs: An Exponential Model Coupled with Automatically Generated Template Features

Richard Tzong-Han Tsai[1,2], Wen-Chi Chou[1], Yu-Chun Lin[1,2], Cheng-Lung Sung[1], Wei Ku[1,3], Ying-Shan Su[1,4], Ting-Yi Sung[1] and Wen-Lian Hsu[1]

[1]Institute of Information Science, Academia Sinica

[2]Dept. of Computer Science and Information Engineering, National Taiwan University

[3]Institute of Molecular Medicine, National Taiwan University

[4]Dept. of Biochemical Science and Technology, National Taiwan University

{thtsai,jacky957,sbb,clsung,wilmaku,qnn,tsung,hsu}@iis.sinica.edu.tw

Abstract

In this paper, we construct a biomedical semantic role labeling (SRL) system that can be used to facilitate relation extraction. First, we construct a proposition bank on top of the popular biomedical GENIA treebank following the PropBank annotation scheme. We only annotate the predicate-argument structures (PAS's) of thirty frequently used biomedical predicates and their corresponding arguments. Second, we use our proposition bank to train a biomedical SRL system, which uses a maximum entropy (ME) model. Thirdly, we automatically generate argument-type templates which can be used to improve classification of biomedical argument types. Our experimental results show that a newswire SRL system that achieves an F-score of 86.29% in the newswire domain can maintain an F-score of 64.64% when ported to the biomedical domain. By using our annotated biomedical corpus, we can increase that F-score by 22.9%. Adding automatically generated template features further increases overall F-score by 0.47% and adjunct arguments (AM) F-score by 1.57%, respectively.

1 Introduction

The volume of biomedical literature available has experienced unprecedented growth in recent years. The ability to automatically process this literature would be an invaluable tool for both the design and interpretation of large-scale experiments. To this end, more and more information extraction (IE) systems using natural language processing (NLP) have been developed for use in the biomedical field. A key IE task in the biomedical field is extraction of relations, such as protein-protein and gene-gene interactions.

Currently, most biomedical relation-extraction systems fall under one of the following three approaches: cooccurence-based (Leroy et al., 2005), pattern-based (Huang et al., 2004), and machine-learning-based. All three, however, share the same limitation when extracting relations from complex natural language. They only extract the relation targets (e.g., proteins, genes) and the verbs representing those relations, overlooking the many adverbial and prepositional phrases and words that describe location, manner, timing, condition, and extent. The information in such phrases may be important for precise definition and clarification of complex biological relations.

The above problem can be tackled by using semantic role labeling (SRL) because it not only recognizes main roles, such as agents and objects, but also extracts adjunct roles such as location, manner,

Proceedings of the BioNLP Workshop on Linking Natural Language Processing and Biology at HLT-NAACL 06, pages 57–64, New York City, June 2006.

timing, condition, and extent. The goal of SRL is to group sequences of words together and classify them with semantic labels. In the newswire domain, Morarescu et al. (2005) have demonstrated that full-parsing and SRL can improve the performance of relation extraction, resulting in an F-score increase of 15% (from 67% to 82%). This significant result leads us to surmise that SRL may also have potential for relation extraction in the biomedical domain. Unfortunately, no SRL system for the biomedical domain exists.

In this paper, we aim to build such a biomedical SRL system. To achieve this goal we roughly implement the following three steps as proposed by Wattarujeekrit et al., (2004): (1) create semantic roles for each biomedical verb; (2) construct a biomedical corpus annotated with verbs and their corresponding semantic roles (following definitions created in (1) as a reference resource;) (3) build an automatic semantic interpretation model using the annotated text as a training corpus for machine learning. In the first step, we adopt the definitions found in PropBank (Palmer et al., 2005), defining our own framesets for verbs not in PropBank, such as "phosphorylate". In the second step, we first use an SRL system (Tsai et al., 2005) trained on the Wall Street Journal (WSJ) to automatically tag our corpus. We then have the results double-checked by human annotators. Finally, we add automatically-generated template features to our SRL system to identify adjunct (modifier) arguments, especially those highly relevant to the biomedical domain.

2 Biomedical Proposition Bank

As proposition banks are semantically annotated versions of a Penn-style treebank, they provide consistent semantic role labels across different syntactic realizations of the same verb (Palmer et al., 2005). The annotation captures predicate-argument structures based on the sense tags of polysemous verbs (called framesets) and semantic role labels for each argument of the verb. Figure 1 shows the annotation of semantic roles, exemplified by the following sentence: "IL4 and IL13 receptors activate STAT6, STAT3 and STAT5 proteins in the human B cells." The chosen predicate is the word "activate"; its arguments and their associated word groups are illustrated in the figure.

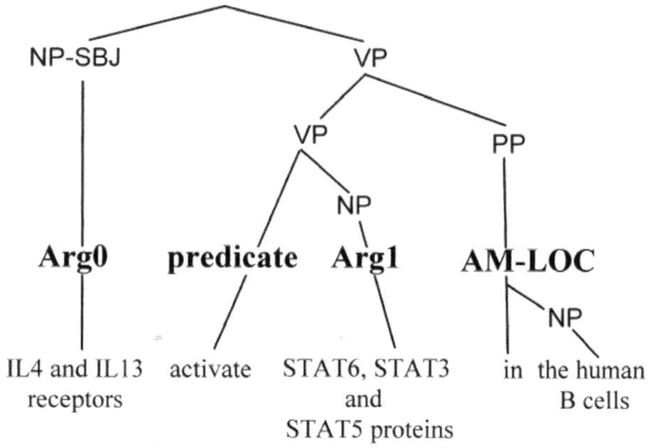

Figure 1. A Treebank Annotated with Semantic Role Labels

Since proposition banks are annotated on top of a Penn-style treebank, we selected a biomedical corpus that has a Penn-style treebank as our corpus. We chose the GENIA corpus (Kim et al., 2003), a collection of MEDLINE abstracts selected from the search results with the following keywords: human, blood cells, and transcription factors. In the GENIA corpus, the abstracts are encoded in XML format, where each abstract also contains a MEDLINE UID, and the title and content of the abstract. The text of the title and content is segmented into sentences, in which biological terms are annotated with their semantic classes. The GENIA corpus is also annotated with part-of-speech (POS) tags (Tateisi et al., 2004), and co-references (Yang et al., 2004).

The Penn-style treebank for GENIA, created by Tateisi et al. (2005), currently contains 500 abstracts. The annotation scheme of the GENIA Treebank (GTB), which basically follows the Penn Treebank II (PTB) scheme (Bies et al., 1995), is encoded in XML. However, in contrast to the WSJ corpus, GENIA lacks a proposition bank. We therefore use its 500 abstracts with GTB as our corpus. To develop our biomedical proposition bank, BioProp, we add the proposition bank annotation on top of the GTB annotation.

2.1 Important Argument Types

In the biomedical domain, relations are often dependent upon locative and temporal factors (Kholodenko, 2006). Therefore, locative (AM-LOC) and temporal modifiers (AM-TMP) are particularly important as they tell us where and when biomedical events take place. Additionally, negative modifiers (AM-NEG) are also vital to correctly extracting relations. Without AM-NEG, we may interpret a negative relation as a positive one or vice versa. In total, we use thirteen modifiers in our biomedical proposition bank.

2.2 Verb Selection

We select 30 frequently used verbs from the molecular biology domain given in Table 1.

express	trigger	encode
associate	repress	enhance
interact	signal	increase
suppress	activate	induce
prevent	alter	Inhibit
modulate	affect	Mediate
phosphorylate	bind	Mutated
transactivate	block	Reduce
transform	decrease	Regulate
differentiated	promote	Stimulate

Table 1. 30 Frequently Biomedical Verbs

Let us examine a representative verb, "activate". Its most frequent usage in molecular biology is the same as that in newswire. Generally speaking, "activate" means, "to start a process" or "to turn on." Many instances of this verb express the action of waking genes, proteins, or cells up. The following sentence shows a typical usage of the verb "activate."

[NF-kappaB $_{\text{Arg1}}$] is [not $_{\text{AM-NEG}}$] [activated $_{\text{predicate}}$] [upon tetracycline removal $_{\text{AM-TMP}}$] [in the NIH3T3 cell line $_{\text{AM-LOC}}$].

3 Semantic Role Labeling on BioProp

In this section, we introduce our BIOmedical SeMantIc roLe labEler, BIOSMILE. Like POS tagging, chunking, and named entity recognition, SRL can be formulated as a sentence tagging problem. A sentence can be represented by a sequence of words, a sequence of phrases, or a parsing tree; the basic units of a sentence are words, phrases, and constituents arranged in the above representations, respectively. Hacioglu et al. (2004) showed that tagging phrase by phrase (P-by-P) is better than word by word (W-by-W). Punyakanok et al., (2004) further showed that constituent-by-constituent (C-by-C) tagging is better than P-by-P. Therefore, we choose C-by-C tagging for SRL. The gold standard SRL corpus, PropBank, was designed as an additional layer of annotation on top of the syntactic structures of the Penn Treebank.

SRL can be broken into two steps. First, we must identify all the predicates. This can be easily accomplished by finding all instances of verbs of interest and checking their POS's.

Second, for each predicate, we need to label all arguments corresponding to the predicate. It is a complicated problem since the number of arguments and their positions vary depending on a verb's voice (active/passive) and sense, along with many other factors.

In this section, we first describe the maximum entropy model used for argument classification. Then, we illustrate basic features as well as specialized features such as biomedical named entities and argument templates.

3.1 Maximum Entropy Model

The maximum entropy model (ME) is a flexible statistical model that assigns an outcome for each instance based on the instance's history, which is all the conditioning data that enables one to assign probabilities to the space of all outcomes. In SRL, a history can be viewed as all the information related to the current token that is derivable from the training corpus. ME computes the probability, $p(o|h)$, for any o from the space of all possible outcomes, O, and for every h from the space of all possible histories, H.

The computation of $p(o|h)$ in ME depends on a set of binary features, which are helpful in making predictions about the outcome. For instance, the node in question ends in "cell", it is likely to be AM-LOC. Formally, we can represent this feature as follows:

$$f(h,o)=\begin{cases}1:\text{if current\_node\_ends\_in\_cell}(h)=\text{true}\\ \quad\text{and o = AM - LOC}\\ 0:\text{otherwise}\end{cases}$$

Here, current_node_ends_in_cell(h) is a binary function that returns a true value if the current node in the history, h, ends in "cell". Given a set of features and a training corpus, the ME estimation process produces a model in which every feature f_i has a weight α_i. Following Bies et al. (1995), we can compute the conditional probability as:

$$p(o\mid h)=\frac{1}{Z(h)}\prod_i \alpha_i^{f_i(h,o)}$$

$$Z(h)=\sum_o\prod_i \alpha_i^{f_i(h,o)}$$

The probability is calculated by multiplying the weights of the active features (i.e., those of f_i $(h,o) = 1$). α_i is estimated by a procedure called Generalized Iterative Scaling (GIS) (Darroch et al., 1972). The ME estimation technique guarantees that, for every feature, f_i, the expected value of α_i equals the empirical expectation of α_i in the training corpus. We use Zhang's MaxEnt toolkit and the L-BFGS (Nocedal et al., 1999) method of parameter estimation for our ME model.

BASIC FEATURES ● **Predicate** – The predicate lemma ● **Path** – The syntactic path through the parsing tree from the parse constituent be-ing classified to the predicate ● **Constituent type** ● **Position** – Whether the phrase is located before or after the predicate ● **Voice** – passive: if the predicate has a POS tag VBN, and its chunk is not a VP, or it is preceded by a form of "to be" or "to get" within its chunk; otherwise, it is active ● **Head word** – calculated using the head word table described by (Collins, 1999) ● **Head POS** – The POS of the Head Word ● **Sub-categorization** – The phrase structure rule that expands the predicate's parent node in the parsing tree ● **First and last Word and their POS tags** ● **Level** – The level in the parsing tree
PREDICATE FEATURES ● **Predicate's verb class** ● **Predicate POS tag** ● **Predicate frequency** ● **Predicate's context POS** ● **Number of predicates**
FULL PARSING FEATURES ● **Parent's, left sibling's, and right sibling's paths, constituent types, positions, head words and head POS tags** ● **Head of PP parent –** If the parent is a PP, then the head of this PP is also used as a feature
COMBINATION FEATURES ● **Predicate distance combination** ● **Predicate phrase type combination** ● **Head word and predicate combination** ● **Voice position combination**
OTHERS ● **Syntactic frame of predicate/NP** ● **Headword suffixes of lengths 2, 3, and 4** ● **Number of words in the phrase** ● **Context words & POS tags**

Table 2. The Features Used in the Baseline Argument Classification Model

3.2 Basic Features

Table 2 shows the features that are used in our baseline argument classification model. Their effectiveness has been previously shown by (Pradhan et al., 2004; Surdeanu et al., 2003; Xue et al., 2004). Detailed descriptions of these features can be found in (Tsai et al., 2005).

3.3 Named Entity Features

In the newswire domain, Surdeanu et al. (2003) used named entity (NE) features that indicate whether a constituent contains NEs, such as personal names, organization names, location names, time expressions, and quantities of money. Using these NE features, they increased their system's F-score by 2.12%. However, because NEs in the biomedical domain are quite different from newswire NEs, we create bio-specific NE features using the five primary NE categories found in the GENIA ontology[1]: protein, nucleotide, other organic compounds, source and others. Table 3 illustrates the definitions of these five categories. When a constituent exactly matches an NE, the corresponding NE feature is enabled.

NE	Definition
Protein	Proteins include protein groups, families, molecules, complexes, and substructures.
Nucleotide	A nucleic acid molecule or the compounds that consist of nucleic acids.
Other organic compounds	Organic compounds exclude protein and nucleotide.
Source	Sources are biological locations where substances are found and their reactions take place.
Others	The terms that are not categorized as sources or substances may be marked up, with

Table 3. Five GENIA Ontology NE Categories

3.4 Biomedical Template Features

Although a few NEs tend to belong almost exclusively to certain argument types (such as "...cell" being mainly AM-LOC), this information alone is not sufficient for argument-type classification. For one, most NEs appear in a variety of argument types. For another, many appear in more than one constituent (node in a parsing tree) in the same sentence. Take the sentence "IL4 and IL13 receptors activate STAT6, STAT3 and STAT5 proteins in the human B cells," for example. The NE "the human B cells" is found in two constituents ("the

[1] http://www-tsujii.is.s.u-tokyo.ac.jp/~genia/topics/Corpus/genia-ontology.html

human B cells" and "in the human B cells") as shown in figure 1. Yet only "in the human B cells" is an AM-LOC because here "human B cells" is preceded by the preposition "in" and the determiner "the". Another way to express this would be as a template—<prep> the <cell>." We believe such templates composed of NEs, real words, and POS tags may be helpful in identifying constituents' argument types. In this section, we first describe our template generation algorithm, and then explain how we use the generated templates to improve SRL performance.

Template Generation (TG)

Our template generation (TG) algorithm extracts general patterns for all argument types using the local alignment algorithm. We begin by pairing all arguments belonging to the same type according to their similarity. Closely matching pairs are then aligned word by word and a template that fits both is created. Each slot in the template is given constraint information in the form of either a word, NE type, or POS. The hierarchy of this constraint information is word > NE type > POS. If the arguments share nothing in common for a given slot, the TG algorithm will put a wildcard in that position. Figure 2 shows an aligned pair arguments. For this pair, the TG algorithm generated the template "AP-1 CC PTN" (PTN: protein name) because in the first position, both arguments have "AP-1;" in the second position, they have the same POS "CC;" and in the third position, they share a common NE type, "PTN." The complete TG algorithm is described in Algorithm 1.

AP-1/PTN/NN and/O/CC NF-AT/PTN/NN
AP-1/PTN/NN or/O/CC NFIL-2A/PTN/NN

Figure 2. Aligned Argument Pair

Applying Generated Templates

The generated templates may match exactly or partially with constituents. According to our observations, the former is more useful for argument classification. For example, constituents that perfectly match the template "IN a * <cell>" are overwhelmingly AM-LOCs. Therefore, we only accept exact template matches. That is, if a constituent exactly matches a template t, then the feature corresponding to t will be enabled.

Algorithm 1 Template Generation

Input: Sentences set $S = \{s_1, \ldots, s_n\}$,
Output: A set of template $T = \{t_1, \ldots, t_k\}$.

$T = \{\}$;
for each sentence s_i from s_1 to s_{n-1} **do**
  for each sentence s_j from s_i to s_n **do**
    perform ***alignment*** on s_i and s_j, then
      pair arguments according to similarity;
    generate common template $\boldsymbol{t}$ from argument pairs;
    $T \leftarrow T \cup \boldsymbol{t}$;
  end;
end;
return T;

4 Experiments

4.1 Datasets

In this paper, we extracted all our datasets from two corpora, the Wall Street Journal (WSJ) corpus and the BioProp, which respectively represent the newswire and biomedical domains. The Wall Street Journal corpus has 39,892 sentences, and 950,028 words. It contains full-parsing information, first annotated by Marcus et al. (1997), and is the most famous treebank (WSJ treebank). In addition to these syntactic structures, it was also annotated with predicate-argument structures (WSJ proposition bank) by Palmer et al. (2005).

In biomedical domain, there is one available treebank for GENIA, created by Yuka Tateshi et al. (2005), who has so far added full-parsing information to 500 abstracts. In contrast to WSJ, however, GENIA lacks any proposition bank.

Since predicate-argument annotation is essential for training and evaluating statistical SRL systems, to make up for GENIA's lack of a proposition bank, we constructed BioProp. Two biologists with masters degrees in our laboratory undertook the annotation task after receiving computational linguistic training for approximately three months.

We adopted a semi-automatic strategy to annotate BioProp. First, we used the PropBank to train a statistical SRL system which achieves an F-score of over 86% on section 24 of the PropBank. Next, we used this SRL system to annotate the GENIA treebank automatically. Table 4 shows the amounts of all adjunct argument types (AMs) in BioProp. The detail description of can be found in (Babko-Malaya, 2005).

Type	Description	#	Type	Description	#
NEG	negation marker	103	ADV	general purpose	307
LOC	location	389	PNC	purpose	3
TMP	time	145	CAU	cause	15
MNR	manner	489	DIR	direction	22
EXT	extent	23	DIS	discourse connectives	179
			MOD	modal verb	121

Table 4. Subtypes of the AM Modifier Tag

4.2 Experiment Design

Experiment 1: Portability

Ideally, an SRL system should be adaptable to the task of information extraction in various domains with minimal effort. That is, we should be able to port it from one domain to another. In this experiment, we evaluate the cross-domain portability of our SRL system. We use Sections 2 to 21 of the PropBank to train our SRL system. Then, we use our system to annotate Section 24 of the PropBank (denoted by Exp 1a) and all of BioProp (denoted by Exp 1b).

Experiment 2: The Necessity of BioProp

To compare the effects of using biomedical training data vs. using newswire data, we train our SRL system on 30 randomly selected training sets from BioProp (g_1,.., g_{30}) and 30 from PropBank (w_1,.., w_{30}), each having 1200 training PAS's. We then test our system on 30 400-PAS test sets from BioProp, with g_1 and w_1 being tested on test set 1, g_2 and w_2 on set 2, and so on. Then we add up the scores for w_1-w_{30} and g_1-g_{30}, and compare their averages.

Experiment 3: The Effect of Using Biomedical-Specific Features

In order to improve SRL performance, we add domain specific features. In Experiment 3, we investigate the effects of adding biomedical NE features and argument template features composed of words, NEs, and POSs. The dataset selection procedure is the same as in Experiment 2.

5 Results and Discussion

All experimental results are summarized in Table 5. For argument classification, we report the precision (P), recall (R) and F-scores (F). The details are illustrated in the following paragraphs.

Configuration	Training	Test	P	R	F
Exp 1a	PropBank	PropBank	90.47	82.48	86.29
Exp 1b	PropBank	BioProp	75.28	56.64	64.64
Exp 2a	PropBank	BioProp	74.78	56.25	64.20
Exp 2b	BioProp	BioProp	88.65	85.61	87.10
Exp 3a	BioProp	BioProp	88.67	85.59	87.11
Exp 3b	BioProp	BioProp	89.13	86.07	87.57

Table 5. Summary of All Experiments

Role	Exp 1a			Exp 1b			+/-(%)
	P	R	F	P	R	F	
Overall	90.47	82.48	86.29	75.28	56.64	64.64	-21.65
ArgX	91.46	86.39	88.85	78.92	67.82	72.95	-15.90
Arg0	86.36	78.01	81.97	85.56	64.41	73.49	-8.48
Arg1	95.52	92.11	93.78	82.56	75.75	79.01	-14.77
Arg2	87.19	84.53	85.84	32.76	31.59	32.16	-53.68
AM	86.76	70.02	77.50	62.70	32.98	43.22	-34.28
-ADV	73.44	52.32	61.11	39.27	26.34	31.53	-29.58
-DIS	81.71	48.18	60.62	67.12	48.18	56.09	-4.53
-LOC	89.19	57.02	69.57	68.54	2.67	5.14	-64.43
-MNR	67.93	57.86	62.49	46.55	22.97	30.76	-31.73
-MOD	99.42	92.5	95.84	99.05	88.01	93.2	-2.64
-NEG	100	91.21	95.40	99.61	80.13	88.81	-6.59
-TMP	88.15	72.83	79.76	70.97	60.36	65.24	-14.52

Table 6. Performance of Exp 1a and Exp 1b

Experiment 1

Table 6 shows the results of Experiment 1. The SRL system trained on the WSJ corpus obtains an F-score of 64.64% when used in the biomedical domain. Compared to traditional rule-based or template-based approaches, our approach suffers acceptable decrease in overall performance when recognizing ArgX arguments. However, Table 6 also shows significant decreases in F-scores from other argument types. AM-LOC drops 64.43% and AM-MNR falls 31.73%. This may be due to the fact that the head words in PropBank are quite different from those in BioProp. Therefore, to achieve better performance, we believe it will be necessary to annotate biomedical corpora for training biomedical SRL systems.

Experiment 2

Table 7 shows the results of Experiment 2. When tested on BioProp, BIOSMILE (Exp 2b) outperforms the newswire SRL system (Exp 2a) by 22.9% since the two systems are trained on different domains. This result is statistically significant.

Furthermore, Table 7 shows that BIOSMILE outperforms the newswire SRL system in most argument types, especially Arg0, Arg2, AM-ADV, AM-LOC, AM-MNR.

Role	Exp 2a			Exp 2b			+/-(%)
	P	R	F	P	R	F	
Overall	74.78	56.25	64.20	88.65	85.61	87.10	22.90
ArgX	78.40	67.32	72.44	91.96	89.73	90.83	18.39
Arg0	85.55	64.40	73.48	92.24	90.59	91.41	17.93
Arg1	81.41	75.11	78.13	92.54	90.49	91.50	13.37
Arg2	34.42	31.56	32.93	86.89	81.35	84.03	51.10
AM	61.96	32.38	42.53	81.27	76.72	78.93	36.40
-ADV	36.00	23.26	28.26	64.02	52.12	57.46	29.20
-DIS	69.55	51.29	59.04	82.71	75.60	79.00	19.96
-LOC	75.51	3.23	6.20	80.05	85.00	82.45	76.25
-MNR	44.67	21.66	29.17	83.44	82.23	82.83	53.66
-MOD	99.38	88.89	93.84	98.00	95.28	96.62	2.78
-NEG	99.80	79.55	88.53	97.82	94.81	96.29	7.76
-TMP	67.95	60.40	63.95	80.96	61.82	70.11	6.16

Table 7. Performance of Exp 2a and Exp 2b

The performance of Arg0 and Arg2 in our system increases considerably because biomedical verbs can be successfully identified by BIOSMILE but not by the newswire SRL system. For AM-LOC, the newswire SRL system scored as low as 76.25% lower than BIOSMILE. This is likely due to the reason that in the biomedical domain, many biomedical nouns, e.g., organisms and cells, function as locations, while in the newswire domain, they do not. In newswire, the word "cell" seldom appears. However, in biomedical texts, cells represent the location of many biological reactions, and, therefore, if a constituent node on a parsing tree contains "cell", this node is very likely an AM-LOC. If we use only newswire texts, the SRL system will not learn to recognize this pattern. In the biomedical domain, arguments of manner (AM-MNR) usually describe how to conduct an experiment or how an interaction arises or occurs, while in newswire they are extremely broad in scope. Without adequate biomedical domain training corpora, systems will easily confuse adverbs of manner (AM-MNR), which are differentiated from general adverbials in semantic role labeling, with general adverbials (AM-ADV). In addition, the performance of the referential arguments of Arg0, Arg1, and Arg2 increases significantly.

Experiment 3

Table 8 shows the results of Experiment 3. The performance does not significantly improve after adding NE features. We originally expected that NE features would improve recognition of AM arguments such as AM-LOC. However, they failed to ameliorate the results since in the biomedical domain most NEs are just matched parts of a constituent. This results in fewer exact matches. Furthermore, in matched cases, NE information alone is insufficient to distinguish argument types. For example, even if a constituent exactly matches a protein name, we still cannot be sure whether it belongs to the subject (Arg0) or object (Arg1). Therefore, NE features were not as effective as we had expected.

Role	NE (Exp 3a)			Template (Exp 3b)			+/-(%)
	P	R	F	P	R	F	
Overall	88.67	85.59	87.11	89.13	86.07	87.57	0.46
ArgX	91.99	89.70	90.83	91.89	89.73	90.80	-0.03
Arg0	92.41	90.57	91.48	92.19	90.59	91.38	-0.1
Arg1	92.47	90.45	91.45	92.42	90.44	91.42	-0.03
Arg2	86.93	81.3	84.02	87.08	81.66	84.28	0.26
AM	81.30	76.75	78.96	82.96	78.18	80.50	1.54
-ADV	64.11	52.23	57.56	65.66	55.60	60.21	2.65
-DIS	82.51	75.42	78.81	83.00	75.79	79.23	0.42
-LOC	80.07	85.09	82.50	84.24	85.48	84.86	2.36
-MNR	83.50	82.19	82.84	84.56	84.14	84.35	1.51
-MOD	98.14	95.28	96.69	98.00	95.28	96.62	-0.07
-NEG	97.66	94.81	96.21	97.82	94.81	96.29	0.08
-TMP	81.14	62.06	70.33	83.10	63.95	72.28	1.95

Table 8. Performance of Exp 3a and Exp 3b

6 Conclusions and Future Work

In Experiment 3b, we used the argument templates as features. Since ArgX's F-score is close to 90%, adding the template features does not improve its score. However, AM's F-score increases by 1.54%. For AM-ADV, AM-LOC, and AM-TMP, the increase is greater because the automatically generated templates effectively extract these AMs.

In Figure 3, we compare the performance of argument classification models with and without argument template features. The overall F-score improves only slightly. However, the F-scores of main adjunct arguments increase significantly.

The contribution of this paper is threefold. First, we construct a biomedical proposition bank, BioProp, on top of the popular biomedical GENIA treebank following the PropBank annotation scheme. We employ semi-automatic annotation using an SRL system trained on PropBank, thereby significantly reducing annotation effort. Second, we create BIOSMILE, a biomedical SRL system, which uses BioProp as its training corpus. Thirdly, we develop a method to automatically generate templates that can boost overall performance, especially on location, manner, adverb, and temporal arguments. In the future, we will expand BioProp to include more verbs and will also integrate an automatic parser into BIOSMILE.

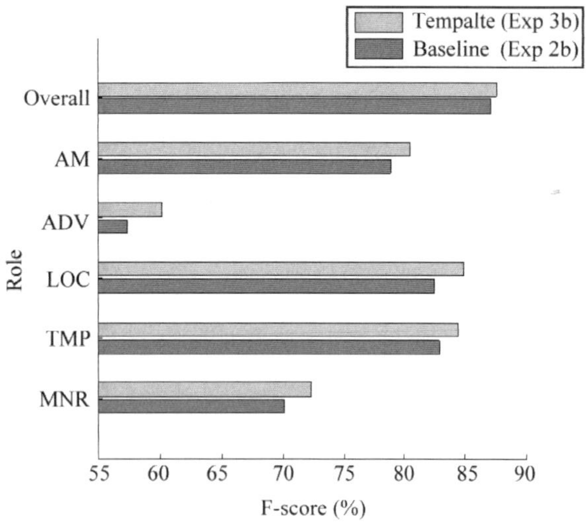

Figure 3. Improvement of Template Features Overall and on Several Adjunct Types

Acknowledgement

We would like to thank Dr. Nianwen Xue for his instruction of using the WordFreak annotation tool. This research was supported in part by the National Science Council under grant NSC94-2752-E-001-001 and the thematic program of Academia Sinica under grant AS94B003. Editing services were provided by Dorion Berg.

References

Babko-Malaya, O. (2005). *Propbank Annotation Guidelines*.

Bies, A., Ferguson, M., Katz, K., MacIntyre, R., Tredinnick, V., Kim, G., et al. (1995). *Bracketing Guidelines for Treebank II Style Penn Treebank Project*

Collins, M. J. (1999). *Head-driven Statistical Models for Natural Language Parsing*. Unpublished Ph.D. thesis, University of Pennsylvania.

Darroch, J. N., & Ratcliff, D. (1972). Generalized Iterative Scaling for Log-Linear Models. *The Annals of Mathematical Statistics*.

Hacioglu, K., Pradhan, S., Ward, W., Martin, J. H., & Jurafsky, D. (2004). *Semantic Role Labeling by Tagging Syntactic Chunks*. Paper presented at the CONLL-04.

Huang, M., Zhu, X., Hao, Y., Payan, D. G., Qu, K., & Li, M. (2004). Discovering patterns to extract protein-protein interactions from full texts. *Bioinformatics, 20*(18), 3604-3612.

Kholodenko, B. N. (2006). Cell-signalling dynamics in time and space. *Nat Rev Mol Cell Biol, 7*(3), 165-176.

Kim, J. D., Ohta, T., Tateisi, Y., & Tsujii, J. (2003). GENIA corpus--semantically annotated corpus for bio-textmining. *Bioinformatics, 19 Suppl 1*, i180-182.

Leroy, G., Chen, H., & Genescene. (2005). An ontology-enhanced integration of linguistic and co-occurrence based relations in biomedical texts. *Journal of the American Society for Information Science and Technology, 56*(5), 457-468.

Marcus, M. P., Santorini, B., & Marcinkiewicz, M. A. (1997). Building a large annotated corpus of English: the Penn Treebank. *Computational Linguistics, 19*.

Morarescu, P., Bejan, C., & Harabagiu, S. (2005). *Shallow Semantics for Relation Extraction*. Paper presented at the IJCAI-05.

Nocedal, J., & Wright, S. J. (1999). *Numerical Optimization*: Springer.

Palmer, M., Gildea, D., & Kingsbury, P. (2005). The proposition bank: an annotated corpus of semantic roles. *Computational Linguistics, 31*(1).

Pradhan, S., Hacioglu, K., Kruglery, V., Ward, W., Martin, J. H., & Jurafsky, D. (2004). Support vector learning for semantic argument classification. *Journal of Machine Learning*

Punyakanok, V., Roth, D., Yih, W., & Zimak, D. (2004). *Semantic Role Labeling via Integer Linear Programming Inference*. Paper presented at the COLING-04.

Surdeanu, M., Harabagiu, S. M., Williams, J., & Aarseth, P. (2003). *Using Predicate-Argument Structures for Information Extraction*. Paper presented at the ACL-03.

Tateisi, Y., & Tsujii, J. (2004). *Part-of-Speech Annotation of Biology Research Abstracts*. Paper presented at the LREC-04.

Tateisi, Y., Yakushiji, A., Ohta, T., & Tsujii, J. (2005). *Syntax Annotation for the GENIA corpus*.

Tsai, T.-H., Wu, C.-W., Lin, Y.-C., & Hsu, W.-L. (2005). *Exploiting Full Parsing Information to Label Semantic Roles Using an Ensemble of ME and SVM via Integer Linear Programming.* . Paper presented at the CoNLL-05.

Wattarujeekrit, T., Shah, P. K., & Collier, N. (2004). PASBio: predicate-argument structures for event extraction in molecular biology. *BMC Bioinformatics, 5*, 155.

Xue, N., & Palmer, M. (2004). *Calibrating Features for Semantic Role Labeling*. Paper presented at the EMNLP-04.

Yang, X., Zhou, G., Su, J., & Tan., C. (2004). *Improving Noun Phrase Coreference Resolution by Matching Strings*. Paper presented at the IJCNLP-04.

Generative Content Models for Structural Analysis of Medical Abstracts

Jimmy Lin[1,2], **Damianos Karakos**[3], **Dina Demner-Fushman**[2], **and Sanjeev Khudanpur**[3]
[1]College of Information Studies
[2]Institute for Advanced Computer Studies
University of Maryland
College Park, MD 20742, USA
jimmylin@umd.edu, demner@cs.umd.edu
[3]Center for Language and
Speech Processing
Johns Hopkins University
Baltimore, MD 21218, USA
(damianos, khudanpur)@jhu.edu

Abstract

The ability to accurately model the content structure of text is important for many natural language processing applications. This paper describes experiments with generative models for analyzing the discourse structure of medical abstracts, which generally follow the pattern of "introduction", "methods", "results", and "conclusions". We demonstrate that Hidden Markov Models are capable of accurately capturing the structure of such texts, and can achieve classification accuracy comparable to that of discriminative techniques. In addition, generative approaches provide advantages that may make them preferable to discriminative techniques such as Support Vector Machines under certain conditions. Our work makes two contributions: at the application level, we report good performance on an interesting task in an important domain; more generally, our results contribute to an ongoing discussion regarding the tradeoffs between generative and discriminative techniques.

1 Introduction

Certain types of text follow a predictable structure, the knowledge of which would be useful in many natural language processing applications. As an example, scientific abstracts across many different fields generally follow the pattern of "introduction", "methods", "results", and "conclusions" (Salanger-Meyer, 1990; Swales, 1990; Orăsan, 2001). The ability to explicitly identify these sections in unstructured text could play an important role in applications such as document summarization (Teufel and Moens, 2000), information retrieval (Tbahriti et al., 2005), information extraction (Mizuta et al., 2005), and question answering. Although there is a trend towards analysis of full article texts, we believe that abstracts still provide a tremendous amount of information, and much value can still be extracted from them. For example, Gay et al. (2005) experimented with abstracts and full article texts in the task of automatically generating index term recommendations and discovered that using full article texts yields at most a 7.4% improvement in F-score. Demner-Fushman et al. (2005) found a correlation between the quality and strength of clinical conclusions in the full article texts and abstracts.

This paper presents experiments with generative content models for analyzing the discourse structure of medical abstracts, which has been confirmed to follow the four-section pattern discussed above (Salanger-Meyer, 1990). For a variety of reasons, medicine is an interesting domain of research. The need for information systems to support physicians at the point of care has been well studied (Covell et al., 1985; Gorman et al., 1994; Ely et al., 2005). Retrieval techniques can have a large impact on how physicians access and leverage clinical evidence. Information that satisfies physicians' needs can be found in the MEDLINE database maintained by the U.S. National Library of Medicine

Proceedings of the BioNLP Workshop on Linking Natural Language Processing and Biology at HLT-NAACL 06, pages 65–72,
New York City, June 2006.

(NLM), which also serves as a readily available corpus of abstracts for our experiments. Furthermore, the availability of rich ontological resources, in the form of the Unified Medical Language System (UMLS) (Lindberg et al., 1993), and the availability of software that leverages this knowledge—MetaMap (Aronson, 2001) for concept identification and SemRep (Rindflesch and Fiszman, 2003) for relation extraction—provide a foundation for studying the role of semantics in various tasks.

McKnight and Srinivasan (2003) have previously examined the task of categorizing sentences in medical abstracts using supervised discriminative machine learning techniques. Building on the work of Ruch et al. (2003) in the same domain, we present a generative approach that attempts to directly model the discourse structure of MEDLINE abstracts using Hidden Markov Models (HMMs); cf. (Barzilay and Lee, 2004). Although our results were not obtained from the same exact collection as those used by authors of these two previous studies, comparable experiments suggest that our techniques are competitive in terms of performance, and may offer additional advantages as well.

Discriminative approaches (especially SVMs) have been shown to be very effective for many supervised classification tasks; see, for example, (Joachims, 1998; Ng and Jordan, 2001). However, their high computational complexity (quadratic in the number of training samples) renders them prohibitive for massive data processing. Under certain conditions, generative approaches with linear complexity are preferable, even if their performance is lower than that which can be achieved through discriminative training. Since HMMs are very well-suited to modeling sequences, our discourse modeling task lends itself naturally to this particular generative approach. In fact, we demonstrate that HMMs are competitive with SVMs, with the added advantage of lower computational complexity. In addition, generative models can be directly applied to tackle certain classes of problems, such as sentence ordering, in ways that discriminative approaches cannot readily. In the context of machine learning, we see our work as contributing to the ongoing debate between generative and discriminative approaches—we provide a case study in an interesting domain that begins to explore some of these tradeoffs.

2 Methods

2.1 Corpus and Data Preparation

Our experiments involved MEDLINE, the bibliographical database of biomedical articles maintained by the U.S. National Library of Medicine (NLM). We used the subset of MEDLINE that was extracted for the TREC 2004 Genomics Track, consisting of citations from 1994 to 2003. In total, 4,591,008 records (abstract text and associated metadata) were extracted using the Date Completed (DCOM) field for all references in the range of 19940101 to 20031231.

Viewing structural modeling of medical abstracts as a sentence classification task, we leveraged the existence of so-called structured abstracts (see Figure 1 for an example) in order to obtain the appropriate section label for each sentence. The use of section headings is a device recommended by the Ad Hoc Working Group for Critical Appraisal of the Medical Literature (1987) to help humans assess the reliability and content of a publication and to facilitate the indexing and retrieval processes. Although structured abstracts loosely adhere to the introduction, methods, results, and conclusions format, the exact choice of section headings varies from abstract to abstract and from journal to journal. In our test collection, we observed a total of 2688 unique section headings in structured abstracts—these were manually mapped to the four broad classes of "introduction", "methods", "results", and "conclusions". All sentences falling under a section heading were assigned the label of its appropriately-mapped heading (naturally, the actual section headings were removed in our test collection). As a concrete example, in the abstract shown in Figure 1, the "OBJECTIVE" section would be mapped to "introduction", the "RESEARCH DESIGN AND METHODS" section to "methods". The "RESULTS" and "CONCLUSIONS" sections map directly to our own labels. In total, 308,055 structured abstracts were extracted and prepared in this manner, serving as the complete dataset. In addition, we created a reduced collection of 27,075 abstracts consisting of only Randomized Controlled Trials (RCTs), which represent definitive sources of evidence highly-valued in the clinical decision-making process.

Separately, we manually annotated 49 unstruc-

Integrating medical management with diabetes self-management training: a randomized control trial of the Diabetes Outpatient Intensive Treatment program.
OBJECTIVE– This study evaluated the Diabetes Outpatient Intensive Treatment (DOIT) program, a multiday group education and skills training experience combined with daily medical management, followed by case management over 6 months. Using a randomized control design, the study explored how DOIT affected glycemic control and self-care behaviors over a short term. The impact of two additional factors on clinical outcomes were also examined (frequency of case management contacts and whether or not insulin was started during the program). RESEARCH DESIGN AND METHODS– Patients with type 1 and type 2 diabetes in poor glycemic control (A1c ¿8.5%) were randomly assigned to DOIT or a second condition, entitled EDUPOST, which was standard diabetes care with the addition of quarterly educational mailings. A total of 167 patients (78 EDUPOST, 89 DOIT) completed all baseline measures, including A1c and a questionnaire assessing diabetes-related self-care behaviors. At 6 months, 117 patients (52 EDUPOST, 65 DOIT) returned to complete a follow-up A1c and the identical self-care questionnaire. RESULTS– At follow-up, DOIT evidenced a significantly greater drop in A1c than EDUPOST. DOIT patients also reported significantly more frequent blood glucose monitoring and greater attention to carbohydrate and fat contents (ACFC) of food compared with EDUPOST patients. An increase in ACFC over the 6-month period was associated with improved glycemic control among DOIT patients. Also, the frequency of nurse case manager follow-up contacts was positively linked to better A1c outcomes. The addition of insulin did not appear to be a significant contributor to glycemic change. CONCLUSIONS– DOIT appears to be effective in promoting better diabetes care and positively influencing glycemia and diabetes-related self-care behaviors. However, it demands significant time, commitment, and careful coordination with many health care professionals. The role of the nurse case manager in providing ongoing follow-up contact seems important.

Figure 1: Sample structured abstract from MEDLINE.

tured abstracts of randomized controlled trials retrieved to answer a question about the management of elevated low-density lipoprotein cholesterol (LDL-C). We submitted a PubMed query ("elevated LDL-C") and restricted results to English abstracts of RCTs, gathering 49 unstructured abstracts from 26 journals. Each sentence was annotated with its section label by the third author, who is a medical doctor—this collection served as our blind held-out testset. Note that the annotation process preceded our experiments, which helped to guard against annotator-introduced bias. Of 49 abstracts, 35 contained all four sections (which we refer to as "complete"), while 14 abstracts were missing one or more sections (which we refer to as "partial").

Two different types of experiments were conducted: the first consisted of cross-validation on the structured abstracts; the second consisted of training on the structured abstracts and testing on the unstructured abstracts. We hypothesized that structured and unstructured abstracts share the same underlying discourse patterns, and that content models trained with one can be applied to the other.

2.2 Generative Models of Content

Following Ruch et al. (2003) and Barzilay and Lee (2004), we employed Hidden Markov Models to model the discourse structure of MEDLINE abstracts. The four states in our HMMs correspond to the information that characterizes each section ("introduction", "methods", "results", and "conclusions") and state transitions capture the discourse flow from section to section.

Using the SRI language modeling toolkit, we first computed bigram language models for each of the four sections using Kneser-Ney discounting and Katz backoff. All words in the training set were downcased, all numbers were converted into a generic symbol, and all singleton unigrams and bigrams were removed. Using these results, each sentence was converted into a four dimensional vector, where each component represents the log probability, divided by the number of words, of the sentence under each of the four language models.

We then built a four-state Hidden Markov Model that outputs these four-dimensional vectors. The transition probability matrix of the HMM was initialized with uniform probabilities over a fully connected graph. The output probabilities were modeled as four-dimensional Gaussians mixtures with diagonal covariance matrices. Using the section labels, the HMM was trained using the HTK toolkit (Young et al., 2002), which efficiently performs the forward-backward algorithm and Baum-Welch estimation. For testing, we performed a Viterbi (maximum likelihood) estimation of the label of each test sentence/vector (also using the HTK toolkit).

In an attempt to further boost performance, we employed Linear Discriminant Analysis (LDA) to find a linear projection of the four-dimensional vectors that maximizes the separation of the Gaussians (corresponding to the HMM states). Venables and Ripley (1994) describe an efficient algorithm (of linear complexity in the number of training sentences) for computing the LDA transform matrix, which entails computing the within- and between-covariance matrices of the classes, and using Singular Value Decomposition (SVD) to compute the eigenvectors of the new space. Each sentence/vector is then multiplied by this matrix, and new HMM models are re-computed from the projected data.

An important aspect of our work is modeling content structure using generative techniques. To assess the impact of taking discourse transitions into account, we compare our fully trained model to one that does not take advantage of the Markov assumption—i.e., it assumes that the labels are independently and identically distributed.

To facilitate comparison with previous work, we also experimented with binary classifiers specifically tuned to each section. This was done by creating a two-state HMM: one state corresponds to the label we want to detect, and the other state corresponds to all the other labels. We built four such classifiers, one for each section, and trained them in the same manner as above.

3 Results

We report results on three distinct sets of experiments: (1) ten-fold cross-validation (90/10 split) on all structured abstracts from the TREC 2004 MEDLINE corpus, (2) ten-fold cross-validation (90/10 split) on the RCT subset of structured abstracts from the TREC 2004 MEDLINE corpus, (3) training on the RCT subset of the TREC 2004 MEDLINE corpus and testing on the 49 hand-annotated held-out testset.

The results of our first set of experiments are shown in Tables 1(a) and 1(b). Table 1(a) reports the classification error in assigning a unique label to every sentence, drawn from the set {"introduction", "methods", "results", "conclusions"}. For this task, we compare the performance of three separate models: one that does not make the Markov assumption, the basic four-state HMM, and the improved four-state HMM with LDA. As expected, explicitly modeling the discourse transitions significantly reduces the error rate. Applying LDA further enhances classification performance. Table 1(b) reports accuracy, precision, recall, and F-measure for four separate binary classifiers specifically trained for each of the sections (one per row in the table). We only display results with our best model, namely HMM with LDA.

Model	*Error*
non-HMM	.220
HMM	.148
HMM + LDA	.118

(a)

Section	*Acc*	*Prec*	*Rec*	*F*
Introduction	.957	.930	.840	.885
Methods	.921	.810	.875	.843
Results	.921	.898	.898	.898
Conclusions	.963	.898	.896	.897

(b)

Table 1: Ten-fold cross-validation results on all structured abstracts from the TREC 2004 MEDLINE corpus: multi-way classification on complete abstract structure (a) and by-section binary classification (b).

The results of our second set of experiments (with RCTs only) are shown in Tables 2(a) and 2(b). Table 2(a) reports the multi-way classification error rate; once again, applying the Markov assumption to model discourse transitions improves performance, and using LDA further reduces error rate. Table 2(b) reports accuracy, precision, recall, and F-measure for four separate binary classifiers (HMM with LDA) specifically trained for each of the sections (one per row in the table). The table also presents the closest comparable experimental results reported by McKnight and Srinivasan (2003).[1] McKnight and Srinivasan (henceforth, M&S) created a test collection consisting of 37,151 RCTs from approximately 12 million MEDLINE abstracts dated between 1976 and 2001. This collection has

[1] After contacting the authors, we were unable to obtain the same exact dataset that they used for their experiments.

Model	*Error*
non-HMM	.238
HMM	.212
HMM + LDA	.209

(a)

	Present study				*McKnight and Srinivasan*			
Section	*Acc*	*Prec*	*Rec*	*F*	*Acc*	*Prec*	*Rec*	*F*
Introduction	.931	.898	.715	.807	.967	.920	.970	.945
Methods	.904	.812	.847	.830	.895	.810	.830	.820
Results	.902	.902	.831	.867	.860	.810	.830	.820
Conclusions	.929	.772	.790	.781	.970	.880	.910	.820

(b)

Table 2: Ten-fold cross-validation results on the structured RCT subset of the TREC 2004 MEDLINE corpus: multi-way classification (a) and binary classification (b). Table (b) also reproduces the results from McKnight and Srinivasan (2003) for a comparable task on a different RCT-subset of structured abstracts.

Model	*Complete*	*Partial*
non-HMM	.247	.371
HMM	.226	.314
HMM + LDA	.217	.279

(a)

	Complete				*Partial*				*McKnight and Srinivasan*			
Section	*Acc*	*Prec*	*Rec*	*F*	*Acc*	*Prec*	*Rec*	*F*	*Acc*	*Prec*	*Rec*	*F*
Introduction	.923	.739	.723	.731	.867	.368	.636	.502	.896	.630	.450	.524
Methods	.905	.841	.793	.817	.859	.958	.589	.774	.897	.880	.730	.799
Results	.899	.913	.857	.885	.892	.942	.830	.886	.872	.840	.880	.861
Conclusions	.911	.639	.847	.743	.884	.361	.995	.678	.941	.830	.750	.785

(b)

Table 3: Training on the structured RCT subset of the TREC 2004 MEDLINE corpus, testing on corpus of hand-annotated abstracts: multi-way classification (a) and binary classification (b). Unstructured abstracts with all four sections (complete), and with missing sections (partial) are shown. Table (b) again reproduces the results from McKnight and Srinivasan (2003) for a comparable task on a different subset of 206 unstructured abstracts.

significantly more training examples than our corpus of 27,075 abstracts, which could be a source of performance differences. Furthermore, details regarding their procedure for mapping structured abstract headings to one of the four general labels was not discussed in their paper. Nevertheless, our HMM-based approach is at least competitive with SVMs, perhaps better in some cases.

The results of our third set of experiments (training on RCTs and testing on a held-out testset of hand-annotated abstracts) is shown in Tables 3(a) and 3(b). Mirroring the presentation format above, Table 3(a) shows the classification error for the four-way label assignment problem. We noticed that some unstructured abstracts are qualitatively different from structured abstracts in that some sections are missing. For example, some unstructured abstracts lack an introduction, and instead dive straight into methods; other unstructured abstracts lack a conclusion. As a result, classification error is higher in this experiment than in the cross-validation experiments. We report performance figures for 35 abstracts that contained all four sections ("complete") and for 14 abstracts that had one or more missing sections ("partial"). Table 3(b) reports accuracy, precision, recall, and F-measure for four separate binary classifiers (HMM with LDA) specifically trained for each section (one per row in the table). The table also presents the closest comparable experimental results reported by M&S—over 206 hand-annotated unstructured abstracts. Interestingly, M&S did not specifically note missing sections in their testset.

4 Discussion

An interesting aspect of our generative approach is that we model HMM outputs as Gaussian vectors (log probabilities of observing entire sentences based on our language models), as opposed to sequences of terms, as done in (Barzilay and Lee, 2004). This technique provides two important advantages. First, Gaussian modeling adds an extra degree of freedom during training, by capturing second-order statistics. This is not possible when modeling word sequences, where only the probability of a sentence is actually used in the HMM training. Second, using continuous distributions allows us to leverage a variety of tools (e.g., LDA) that have been shown to be successful in other fields, such as speech recognition (Evermann et al., 2004).

Table 2(b) represents the closest head-to-head comparison between our generative approach (HMM with LDA) and state-of-the-art results reported by M&S using SVMs. In some ways, the results reported by M&S have an advantage because they use significantly more training examples. Yet, we can see that generative techniques for the modeling of content structure are at least competitive—we even outperform SVMs on detecting "methods" and "results". Moreover, the fact that the training and testing of HMMs have *linear* complexity (as opposed to the quadratic complexity of SVMs) makes our approach a very attractive alternative, given the amount of training data that is available for such experiments.

Although exploration of the tradeoffs between generative and discriminative machine learning techniques is one of the aims of this work, our ultimate goal, however, is to build clinical systems that provide timely access to information essential to the patient treatment process. In truth, our cross-validation experiments do not correspond to any meaningful naturally-occurring task—structured abstracts are, after all, already appropriately labeled. The true utility of content models is to structure abstracts that have no structure to begin with. Thus, our exploratory experiments in applying content models trained with structured RCTs on unstructured RCTs is a closer approximation of an extrinsically-valid measure of performance. Such a component would serve as the first stage of a clinical question answering system (Demner-Fushman and Lin, 2005) or summarization system (McKeown et al., 2003). We chose to focus on randomized controlled trials because they represent the standard benchmark by which all other clinical studies are measured.

Table 3(b) shows the effectiveness of our trained content models on abstracts that had no explicit structure to begin with. We can see that although classification accuracy is lower than that from our cross-validation experiments, performance is quite respectable. Thus, our hypothesis that unstructured abstracts are not qualitatively different from structured abstracts appears to be mostly valid.

5 Related Work

Although not the first to employ a generative approach to directly model content, the seminal work of Barzilay and Lee (2004) is a noteworthy point of reference and comparison. However, our study differs in several important respects. Barzilay and Lee employed an unsupervised approach to building topic sequence models for the newswire text genre using clustering techniques. In contrast, because the discourse structure of medical abstracts is well-defined and training data is relatively easy to obtain, we were able to apply a supervised approach. Whereas Barzilay and Lee evaluated their work in the context of document summarization, the four-part structure of medical abstracts allows us to conduct meaningful intrinsic evaluations and focus on the sentence classification task. Nevertheless, their work bolsters our claims regarding the usefulness of generative models in extrinsic tasks, which we do not describe here.

Although this study falls under the general topic of discourse modeling, our work differs from previous attempts to characterize text in terms of domain-independent rhetorical elements (McKeown, 1985; Marcu and Echihabi, 2002). Our task is closer to the work of Teufel and Moens (2000), who looked at the problem of intellectual attribution in scientific texts.

6 Conclusion

We believe that there are two contributions as a result of our work. From the perspective of machine learning, the assignment of sequentially-occurring labels represents an underexplored problem with respect to the generative vs. discriminative debate—previous work has mostly focused on stateless classification tasks. This paper demonstrates that Hidden Markov Models are capable of capturing discourse transitions from section to section, and are at least competitive with Support Vector Machines from a purely performance point of view.

The other contribution of our work is that it contributes to building advanced clinical information systems. From an application point of view, the ability to assign structure to otherwise unstructured text represents a key capability that may assist in question answering, document summarization, and other natural language processing applications.

Much research in computational linguistics has focused on corpora comprised of newswire articles. We would like to point out that clinical texts provide another attractive genre in which to conduct experiments. Such texts are easy to acquire, and the availability of domain ontologies provides new opportunities for knowledge-rich approaches to shine. Although we have only experimented with lexical features in this study, the door is wide open for follow-on studies based on semantic features.

7 Acknowledgments

The first author would like to thank Esther and Kiri for their loving support.

References

Ad Hoc Working Group for Critical Appraisal of the Medical Literature. 1987. A proposal for more informative abstracts of clinical articles. *Annals of Internal Medicine*, 106:595–604.

Alan R. Aronson. 2001. Effective mapping of biomedical text to the UMLS Metathesaurus: The MetaMap program. In *Proceeding of the 2001 Annual Symposium of the American Medical Informatics Association (AMIA 2001)*, pages 17–21.

Regina Barzilay and Lillian Lee. 2004. Catching the drift: Probabilistic content models, with applications to generation and summarization. In *Proceedings of the 2004 Human Language Technology Conference and the North American Chapter of the Association for Computational Linguistics Annual Meeting (HLT/NAACL 2004).*

David G. Covell, Gwen C. Uman, and Phil R. Manning. 1985. Information needs in office practice: Are they being met? *Annals of Internal Medicine*, 103(4):596–599, October.

Dina Demner-Fushman and Jimmy Lin. 2005. Knowledge extraction for clinical question answering: Preliminary results. In *Proceedings of the AAAI-05 Workshop on Question Answering in Restricted Domains.*

Dina Demner-Fushman, Susan E. Hauser, and George R. Thoma. 2005. The role of title, metadata and abstract in identifying clinically relevant journal articles. In *Proceeding of the 2005 Annual Symposium of the American Medical Informatics Association (AMIA 2005)*, pages 191–195.

John W. Ely, Jerome A. Osheroff, M. Lee Chambliss, Mark H. Ebell, and Marcy E. Rosenbaum. 2005. Answering physicians' clinical questions: Obstacles and potential solutions. *Journal of the American Medical Informatics Association*, 12(2):217–224, March-April.

Gunnar Evermann, H. Y. Chan, Mark J. F. Gales, Thomas Hain, Xunying Liu, David Mrva, Lan Wang, and Phil Woodland. 2004. Development of the 2003 CU-HTK Conversational Telephone Speech Transcription System. In *Proceedings of the 2004 International Conference on Acoustics, Speech and Signal Processing (ICASSP04)*.

Clifford W. Gay, Mehmet Kayaalp, and Alan R. Aronson. 2005. Semi-automatic indexing of full text biomedical articles. In *Proceeding of the 2005 Annual Symposium of the American Medical Informatics Association (AMIA 2005)*, pages 271–275.

Paul N. Gorman, Joan S. Ash, and Leslie W. Wykoff. 1994. Can primary care physicians' questions be answered using the medical journal literature? *Bulletin of the Medical Library Association*, 82(2):140–146, April.

Thorsten Joachims. 1998. Text categorization with Support Vector Machines: Learning with many relevant features. In *Proceedings of the European Conference on Machine Learning (ECML 1998)*.

Donald A. Lindberg, Betsy L. Humphreys, and Alexa T. McCray. 1993. The Unified Medical Language System. *Methods of Information in Medicine*, 32(4):281–291, August.

Daniel Marcu and Abdessamad Echihabi. 2002. An unsupervised approach to recognizing discourse relations. In *Proceedings of the 40th Annual Meeting of the Association for Computational Linguistics (ACL 2002)*.

Kathleen McKeown, Noemie Elhadad, and Vasileios Hatzivassiloglou. 2003. Leveraging a common representation for personalized search and summarization in a medical digital library. In *Proceedings of the 3rd ACM/IEEE Joint Conference on Digital Libraries (JCDL 2003)*.

Kathleen R. McKeown. 1985. *Text Generation: Using Discourse Strategies and Focus Constraints to Generate Natural Language Text*. Cambridge University Press, Cambridge, England.

Larry McKnight and Padmini Srinivasan. 2003. Categorization of sentence types in medical abstracts. In *Proceeding of the 2003 Annual Symposium of the American Medical Informatics Association (AMIA 2003)*.

Yoko Mizuta, Anna Korhonen, Tony Mullen, and Nigel Collier. 2005. Zone analysis in biology articles as a basis for information extraction. *International Journal of Medical Informatics*, in press.

Andrew Y. Ng and Michael Jordan. 2001. On discriminative vs. generative classifiers: A comparison of logistic regression and naive Bayes. In *Advances in Neural Information Processing Systems 14*.

Constantin Orăsan. 2001. Patterns in scientific abstracts. In *Proceedings of the 2001 Corpus Linguistics Conference*.

Thomas C. Rindflesch and Marcelo Fiszman. 2003. The interaction of domain knowledge and linguistic structure in natural language processing: Interpreting hypernymic propositions in biomedical text. *Journal of Biomedical Informatics*, 36(6):462–477, December.

Patrick Ruch, Christine Chichester, Gilles Cohen, Giovanni Coray, Frédéric Ehrler, Hatem Ghorbel, Henning Müller, and Vincenzo Pallotta. 2003. Report on the TREC 2003 experiment: Genomic track. In *Proceedings of the Twelfth Text REtrieval Conference (TREC 2003)*.

Françoise Salanger-Meyer. 1990. Discoursal movements in medical English abstracts and their linguistic exponents: A genre analysis study. *INTERFACE: Journal of Applied Linguistics*, 4(2):107–124.

John M. Swales. 1990. *Genre Analysis: English in Academic and Research Settings*. Cambridge University Press, Cambridge, England.

Imad Tbahriti, Christine Chichester, Frédérique Lisacek, and Patrick Ruch. 2005. Using argumentation to retrieve articles with similar citations: An inquiry into improving related articles search in the MEDLINE digital library. *International Journal of Medical Informatics*, in press.

Simone Teufel and Marc Moens. 2000. What's yours and what's mine: Determining intellectual attribution in scientific text. In *Proceedings of the Joint SIGDAT Conference on Empirical Methods in Natural Language Processing and Very Large Corpora (EMNLP/VLC-2000)*.

William N. Venables and Brian D. Ripley. 1994. *Modern Applied Statistics with S-Plus*. Springer-Verlag.

Steve Young, Gunnar Evermann, Thomas Hain, Dan Kershaw, Gareth Moore, Julian Odell, Dave Ollason, Dan Povey, Valtcho Valtchev, and Phil Woodland. 2002. *The HTK Book*. Cambridge University Press.

Exploring Text and Image Features to Classify Images in Bioscience Literature

Barry Rafkind
DVMM Group
Columbia University
New York, NY 10027
Barryr @ee.columbia.edu

Minsuk Lee
Department of Health Sciences
University of Wisconsin-Milwaukee
Milwaukee, WI 53201
Minsuk.Lee @gmail.com

Shih-Fu Chang
DVMM Group
Columbia University
New York, NY 10027
Sfchang @ee.columbia.edu

Hong Yu
Department of Health Sciences
University of Wisconsin-Milwaukee
Milwaukee, WI 53201
Hong.Yu @uwm.edu

Abstract

A picture is worth a thousand words. Biomedical researchers tend to incorporate a significant number of images (i.e., figures or tables) in their publications to report experimental results, to present research models, and to display examples of biomedical objects. Unfortunately, this wealth of information remains virtually inaccessible without automatic systems to organize these images. We explored supervised machine-learning systems using Support Vector Machines to automatically classify images into six representative categories based on text, image, and the fusion of both. Our experiments show a significant improvement in the average F-score of the fusion classifier (73.66%) as compared with classifiers just based on image (50.74%) or text features (68.54%).

1 Introduction

A picture is worth a thousand words. Biomedical researchers tend to incorporate a significant number of figures and tables in their publications to report experimental results, to present research models, and to display examples of biomedical objects (e.g., cell, tissue, organ and other images). For example, we have found an average of 5.2 images per biological article in the journal Proceedings of the *National Academy of Sciences* (PNAS). We discovered that 43% of the articles in the medical journal *The Lancet* contain biomedical images. Physicians may want to access biomedical images reported in literature for the purpose of clinical education or to assist clinical diagnoses. For example, a physician may want to obtain images that illustrate the disease stage of infants with Retinopathy of Prematurity for the purpose of clinical diagnosis, or to request a picture of erythema chronicum migrans, a spreading annular rash that appears at the site of tick-bite in Lyme disease. Biologists may want to identify the experimental results or images that support specific biological phenomenon. For example, Figure 1 shows that a transplanted progeny of a single multipotent stem cell can generate sebaceous glands.

Organizing bioscience images is not a new task. Related work includes the building of domain-specific image databases. For example, the Protein Data Bank (PDB) [1] (Sussman et al., 1998) stores 3-D images of macromolecular structure data. WebPath [2] is a medical web-based resource that has been created by physicians to include over 4,700 gross and microscopic medical images. Text-based image search systems like Google ignore image content. The SLIF (Subcellular Location Image Finder) system (Murphy et al., 2001; Kou et al., 2003) searches protein images reported in literature. Other work has explored joint text-image features in classifying protein subcellular location images (Murphy et al., 2004). The existing systems, however, have not explored approaches that automatically classify general bioscience images into generic categories.

[1] http://www.rcsb.org/pdb/
[2] http://www-medlib.med.utah.edu/WebPath/webpath.html

Proceedings of the BioNLP Workshop on Linking Natural Language Processing and Biology at HLT-NAACL 06, pages 73–80,
New York City, June 2006.

Classifying images into generic categories is an important task that can benefit many other natural language processing and image processing tasks. For example, image retrieval and question answering systems may return "Image-of-Thing" images (e.g., Figure 1), not the other types (e.g., Figure 2~5), to illustrate erythema chronicum migrans. Biologists may examine "Gel" images (e.g., Figure 2), rather than "Model" (e.g., Figure 4) to access specific biological evidence for molecular interactions. Furthermore, a generic category may ease the task of identifying specific images that may be sub-categories of the generic category. For example, a biologist may want to obtain an image of a protein structure prediction, which might be a subcategory of "Model" (Figure 4), rather than an image of x-ray crystallography that can be readily obtained from the PDB database.

This paper represents the first study that defines a generic bioscience image taxonomy, and explores automatic image classification based on the fusion of text and image classifiers.

Gel-Image consists of gel images such as Northern (for DNA), Southern (for RNA), and Western (for protein). Figure 2 shows an example.

Graph consists of bar charts, column charts, line charts, plots and other graphs that are drawn either by authors or by a computer (e.g., results of patch clamping). Figure 3 shows an example.

Image-of-Thing refers to images of cells, cell components, tissues, organs, or species. Figure 1 shows an example.

Mix refers to an image (e.g., Figure 5) that incorporates two or more other categories of images.

Model: A model may demonstrate a biological process, molecular docking, or an experimental design. We include as Model any structure (e.g., chemical, molecular, or cellular) that is illustrated by a drawing. We also include gene or protein sequences and sequence alignments, as well as phylogenetic trees in this category. Figure 4 shows one example.

Table refers to a set of data arranged in rows and columns.

Table 1. Bioscience Image Taxonomy

2 Image Taxonomy

We downloaded from PubMed Central a total of 17,000 PNAS full-text articles (years 1995-2004), which contain a total of 88,225 images. We manually examined the images and defined an image taxonomy (as shown in Table 1) based on feedback from physicians. The categories were chosen to maintain balance between coherence of content in each category and the complexity of the taxonomy. For example, we keep images of biological objects (e.g., cells, tissues, organs etc) in one single category in this experiment to avoid over decomposition of categories and insufficient data in individual categories. Therefore we stress principled approaches for feature extraction and classifier design. The same fusion classification framework can be applied to cases where each category is further refined to include subclasses.

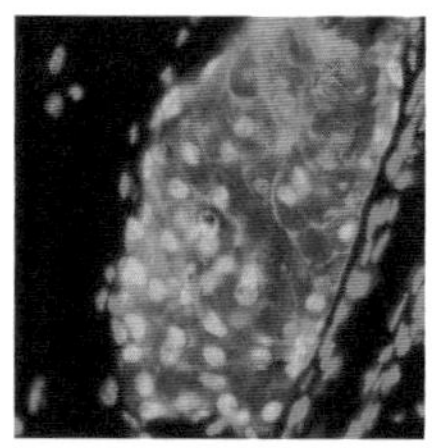

Figure 1. Image of_Thing[3]

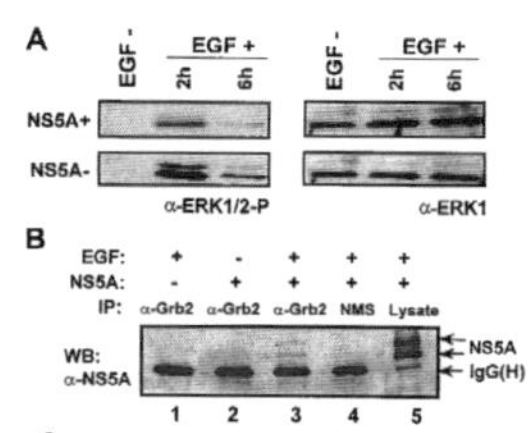

Figure 2. Gel image[4]

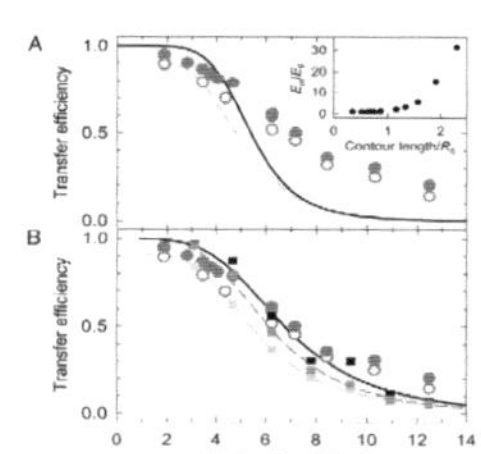

Figure 3. Graph image[5]

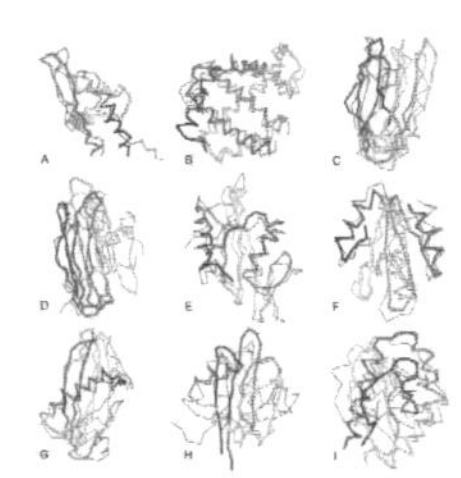

Figure 4. Model image[6]

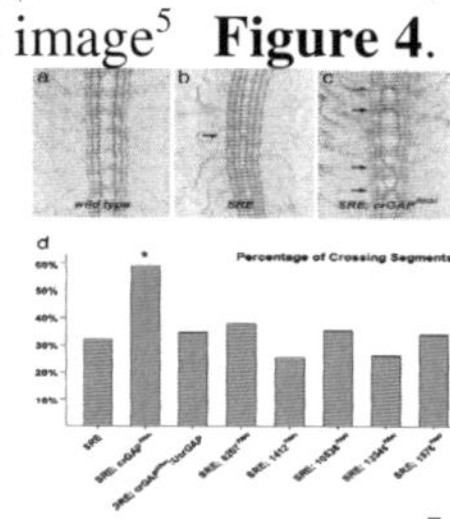

Figure 5. Mix image[7]

[3] This image appears in the cover page of PNAS 102 (41): 14477 – 14936.
[4] The image appears in the article (pmid=10318918)
[5] The image appears in the article (pmid=15699337)
[6] The image appears in the article (pmid=11504922)
[7] The image appears in the article (pmid=15755809)

3 Image Classification

We explored supervised machine-learning methods to automatically classify images according to our image taxonomy (Table 1). Since it is straightforward to distinguish table separately by applying surface cues (e.g., "Table" and "Figure"), we have decided to exclude it from our experiments.

3.1 Support Vector Machines

We explored supervised machine-learning systems using Support Vector Machines (SVMs) which have shown to out-perform many other supervised machine-learning systems for text categorization tasks (Joachims, 1998). We applied the freely available machine learning MATLAB package *The Spider* to train our SVM systems (Sable and Weston, 2005; MATLAB). *The Spider* implements many learning algorithms including a multi-class SVM classifier which was used to learn our discriminative classifiers as described below in section 3.4.

A fundamental concept in SVM theory is the projection of the original data into a high-dimensional space in which separating hyperplanes can be found. Rather than actually doing this projection, kernel functions are selected that efficiently compute the inner products between data in the high-dimensional space. Slack variables are introduced to handle non-separable cases and this requires an upper bound variable, C.

Our experiments considered three popular kernel function families over five different variants and five different values of C. The kernel function implementations are explained in the software documentation. We considered kernel functions in the forms of polynomial, radial basis function, and Gaussian. The adjustable parameter for polynomial functions is the order of the polynomial. For radial basis function and Gaussian functions, sigma is the adjustable parameter. A grid search was performed over the adjustable parameter for values 1 to 5 and for values of C equal to [10^0, 10^1, 10^2, 10^3, 10^4].

3.2 Text Features

Previous work in the context of newswire image classification show that text features in image captions are efficient for image categorization (Sable, 2000, 2002, 2003). We hypothesize that image captions provide certain lexical cues that efficiently represent image content. For example, the words "diameter", "gene-expression", "histogram", "lane", "model", "stained", "western", etc are strong indicators for image classes and therefore can be used to classify an image into categories. The features we explored are bag-of-words and n-grams from the image captions after processing the caption text by the Word Vector Tool (Wurst).

3.3 Image Features

We also investigated image features for the tasks of image classification. We started with four types of image features that include intensity histogram features, edge-direction histogram features, edge-based axis features, and the number of 8-connected regions in the binary-valued image obtained from thresholding the intensity.

The intensity histogram was created by quantizing the gray-scale intensity values into the range 0-255 and then making a 256-bin histogram for these values. The histogram was then normalized by dividing all values by the total sum. For the purpose of entropy calculations, all zero values in the histogram are set to one. From this adjusted, normalized histogram, we calculated the total entropy as the sum of the products of the entries with their logarithms. Additionally, the mean, 2nd moment, and 3rd moment are derived. The combination of the total entropy, mean, 2nd, and 3rd moments constitute a robust and concise representation of the image intensity.

Edge-Direction Histogram (Jain and Vailaya, 1996) features may help distinguish images with predominantly straight lines such as those found in graphs, diagrams, or charts from other images with more variation in edge orientation. The EDH begins by convolving the gray-scale image with both 3x3 Sobel edge operators (Jain, 1989). One operator finds vertical gradients while the other finds horizontal gradients. The inverse tangent of the ratio of the vertical to horizontal gradient yields continuous orientation values in the range of –pi to +pi. These values are subsequently converted into degrees in the range of 0 to 179 degrees (we consider 180 and 0 degrees to be equal). A histogram is counted over these 180 degrees. Zero values in the histogram are set to one in order to anticipate entropy calculations and then the modified histogram is normalized to sum to one. Finally, the total entropy, mean, 2nd and 3rd moments are extracted to summarize the EDH.

The edge-based axis features are meant to help identify images containing graphs or charts. First, Sobel edges are extracted above a sensitivity threshold of 0.10 from the gray-scale image. This yields a binary-valued intensity image with 1's occurring in locations of all edges that exceed the threshold and 0's occurring otherwise. Next, the vertical and horizontal sums of this intensity image are taken yielding two vectors, one for each axis. Zero values are set to one to anticipate the entropy calculations. Each vector is then normalized by dividing each element by its total sum. Finally, we find the total entropy, mean, 2nd , and 3rd moments to represent each axis for a total of eight axis features.

The last image feature under consideration was the number of 8-connected regions in the binary-valued, thresholded Sobel edge image as described above for the axis features. An 8-connected region is a group of edge pixels for which each member touches another member vertically, horizontally, or diagonally in the eight adjacent pixel positions surrounding it. The justification for this feature is that the number of solid regions in an image may help separate classes.

A preliminary comparison of various combinations of these image features showed that the intensity histogram features used alone yielded the best classification accuracy of approximately 54% with a quadratic kernel SVM using an upper slack limit of C = 10^4.

3.4 Fusion

We integrated both image and text features for the purpose of image classification. Multi-class SVM's were trained separately on the image features and the text features. A multi-class SVM attempts to learn the boundaries of maximal margin in feature space that distinguishes each class from the rest. Once the optimal image and text classifiers were found, they were used to process a separate set of images in the fusion set. We extracted the margins from each data point to the boundary in feature space.

Thus, for a five-class classifier, each data point would have five associated margins. To make a fair comparison between the image-based classifier and the text-based classifier, the margins for each data point were normalized to have unit magnitude. So, the set of five margins for the image classifier constitutes a vector that then gets normalized by dividing each element by its L2 norm. The same is done for the vector of margins taken from the text classifier. Finally, both normalized vectors are concatenated to form a 10-dimensional fusion vector. To fuse the margin results from both classifiers, these normalized margins were used to train another multi-class SVM.

A grid search through parameter space with cross validation identified near-optimal parameter settings for the SVM classifiers. See Figure 6 for our system flowchart.

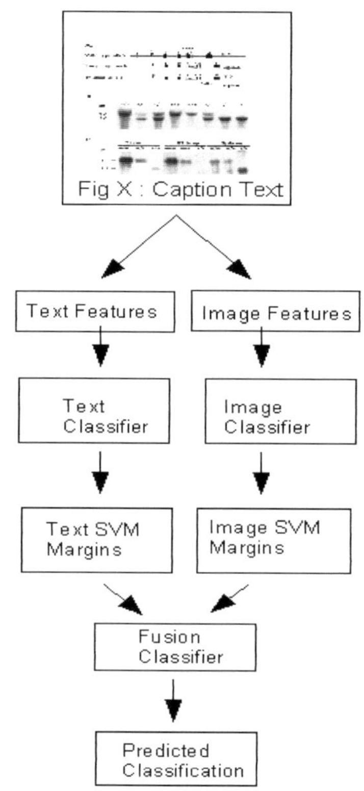

Figure 6. System Flow-chart

3.5 Training, Fusion, and Testing Data

We randomly selected a subset of 554 figure images from the total downloaded image pool. One author of this paper is a biologist who annotated figures under five classes; namely, *Gel_Image* (102), *Graph* (179), *Image_of_Thing* (64), *Mix* (106), and *Model* (103).

These images were split up such that for each category, roughly a half was used for training, a quarter for fusion, and a quarter for testing (see Figure 7). The training set was used to train classifiers for the image-based and text-based features. The fusion set was used to train a classifier on top of the results of the image-based and text-based classifiers. The testing set was used to evaluate the final classification system.

For each division of data, 10 folds were generated. Thus within the training and fusion data sets, there are 10 folds which each have a randomized partitioning into 90% for training and 10% for testing. The testing data set did not need to be partitioned into folds since all of it was used to test the final classification system. (See Figure 8).

In the 10-fold cross-validation process, a classifier is trained on the training partition and then measured for accuracy (or error rate) on the testing partition. Of the 10 resulting algorithms, the one which performs the best is chosen (or just one which ties for the best accuracy).

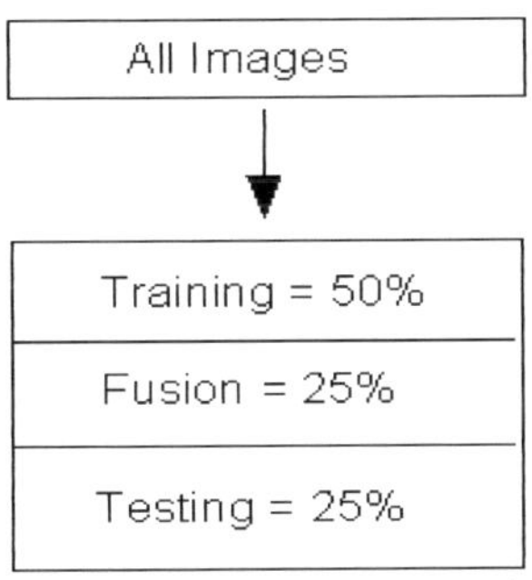

Figure 7. Image-set Divisions

3.6 Evaluation Metrics

We report the widely used recall, precision, and F-score (also known as F-measure) as the evaluation metrics for image classification. Recall is the total number of true positive predictions divided by the total number of true positives in the set (true pos + false neg). Precision is the fraction of the number of true positive predictions divided by the total number of positive predictions (true pos + false pos). F-score is the harmonic mean of recall and precision equal to (C. J. van Rijsbergen, 1979):

$$2 * precision * recall / (precision + recall)$$

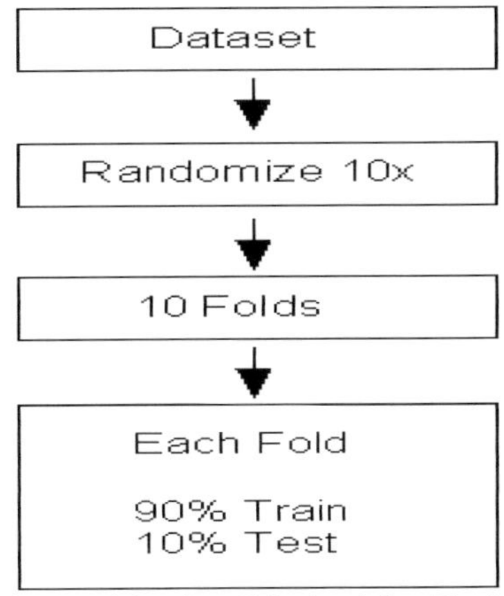

Figure 8. Partitioning Method for Training and Fusion Datasets

4 Experimental Results

Table 2 shows the Confusion Matrix for the image feature classifier obtained from the testing part of the training data. The actual categories are listed vertically and predicted categories are listed horizontally. For instance, of 26 actual GEL images, 18 were correctly classified as GEL, 4 were misclassified as GRAPH, 2 as IMAGE_OF_THING, 0 as MIX, and 2 as MODEL.

Actual	Predicted Categories				
	Gel	Graph	Thing	Mix	Model
Gel	18	4	2	0	2
Graph	3	39	0	1	1
Img_Thing	1	1	12	2	0
Mix	4	17	0	3	3
Model	8	13	0	1	3

Table 2. Confusion Matrix for Image Feature Classifier

A near-optimal parameter setting for the classifier based on image features alone used a polynomial kernel of order 2 and an upper slack limit of C = 10^4. Table 3 shows the performance of image classification with image features. True Positives, False Positives, False Negatives, Precision = TP/(TP+FP), Recall = TP/(TP+FN), and F-score = 2 * Precision * Recall / (Precision + Recall). According to the F-score scores, this classifier does best on distinguishing IMAGE_OF_THING images. The overall accuracy = sum of true positives / total number of images = (18+39+12+3+3)/138 = 75/138 = 54%. This can be compared with the baseline of (3+39+1+1)/138 = 32% if all images were classified as the most popular category, GRAPH. Clearly, the image-based classifier does best at recognizing IMAGE_OF_THING figures.

Category	TP	FP	FN	Prec.	Recall	Fscore
Gel	18	16	8	0.529	0.692	0.600
Graph	39	35	5	0.527	0.886	0.661
Img_Thing	12	2	4	0.857	0.750	0.800
Mix	3	4	10	0.429	0.231	0.300
Model	3	6	22	0.333	0.120	0.176

Table 3. Precision, Recall, F-score for Image Classifier

Actual	Predicted Categories				
	Gel	Graph	Thing	Mix	Model
Gel	22	2	0	2	0
Graph	4	36	0	4	0
Img_Thing	0	3	11	1	1
Mix	3	9	1	12	2
Model	3	5	0	3	14

Table 4. Confusion Matrix for Caption Text Classifier

Category	TP	FP	FN	Prec	Recall	Fscore
Gel	22	10	4	0.688	0.845	0.758
Graph	36	19	8	0.655	0.818	0.727
Img_Thing	11	1	5	0.917	0.688	0.786
Mix	12	10	15	0.545	0.444	0.489
Model	14	3	11	0.824	0.560	0.667

Table 5. Precision, Recall, F-score for Caption Text Classifier

The text-based classifier excels in finding GEL, GRAPH, and IMAGE_OF_THING images. It achieves an accuracy of (22+36+11+12+14)/138 = 95/138 = 69%.

A near-optimal parameter setting for the fusion classifier based on both image features and text features used a linear kernel with C = 10. The corresponding Confusion matrix follows in Table 6.

Actual	Predicted Categories				
	Gel	Graph	Thing	Mix	Model
Gel	23	0	0	3	0
Graph	2	37	1	2	2
Img_Thing	0	1	15	0	0
Mix	2	7	1	14	3
Model	3	5	0	4	13

Table 6. Confusion Matrix for Fusion Classifier

Category	TP	FP	FN	Prec.	Recall	Fscore
Gel	23	7	3	0.767	0.885	0.822
Graph	37	13	7	0.740	0.841	0.787
Img_Thing	15	2	1	0.882	0.938	0.909
Mix	14	9	13	0.609	0.519	0.560
Model	13	5	12	0.722	0.520	0.605

Table 7. Precision, Recall, F-score for Fusion Classifier

From Table 7, it is apparent that the fusion classifier does best on IMAGE_OF_THING and also performs well on GEL and GRAPH. These are substantial improvements over the classifiers that were based on image or text feature alone. Average F-scores and accuracies are summarized below in Table 8.

The overall accuracy for the fusion classifier = sum of true positives / total number of image = (23+37+15+14+13)/138 = 102/138 = 74%. This can be compared with the baseline of 44/138 = 32% if all images were classified as the most popular category, GRAPH.

Classifier	Average F-score	Accuracy
Image	50.74%	54%
Caption Text	68.54%	69%
Fusion	73.66%	74%

Table 8. Comparison of Average F-scores and Accuracy among all three Classifiers

5 Discussion

It is not surprising that the most difficult category to classify is Mix. This was due to the fact that Mix images incorporate multiple categories of other image types. Frequently, one other image type that appears in a Mix image dominates the image features and leads to its misclassification as the other image type. For example, Figure 9 shows that a Mix image was misclassified as Gel_Image.

This mistake is forgivable because the image does contain sub-images of gel-images, even though the entire figure is actually a mix of gel-images and diagrams. This type of result highlights the overlap between classifications and the difficulty in defining exclusive categories.

For both misclassifications, it is not easy to state exactly why they were classified wrongly based on their image or text features. This lack of intuitive understanding of discriminative behavior of SVM classifiers is a valid criticism of the technique. Although generative machine learning methods (such as Bayesian techniques or Graphical Models) offer more intuitive models for explaining success or failure, discriminative models like SVM are adopted here due to their higher performance and ease of use.

Figure 10 shows an example of a MIX figure that was mislabeled by the image classifier as GRAPH and as GEL_IMAGE by the text classifier. However, it was correctly labeled by the fusion classifier. This example illustrates the value of the fusion classifier for being able to improve upon its component classifiers.

6 Conclusions

From the comparisons in Table 8, we see that fusing the results of classifiers based on text and image features yields approximately 5% improvement over the text -based classifier alone with respect to both average F-score and Accuracy. In fact, the F-score improved for all categories except for MODEL which experienced a 6% drop. The natural conclusion is that the fusion classifier combines the classification performance from the text and image classifiers in a complementary fashion that unites the strengths of both.

7 Future Work

To enhance the performance of the text features, one may restrict the vocabulary to functionally important biological words. For example, "phosphorylation" and "3-D" are important words that might sufficiently separate "protein function" from "protein structure".

Further experimentation on a larger image set would give us even greater confidence in our results. It would also expand the diversity within each category, which would hopefully lead to better generalization performance of our classifiers.

Other possible extensions of this work include investigating different machine learning approaches besides SVMs and other fusion methods. Additionally, different sets of image and text features can be explored as well as other taxonomies.

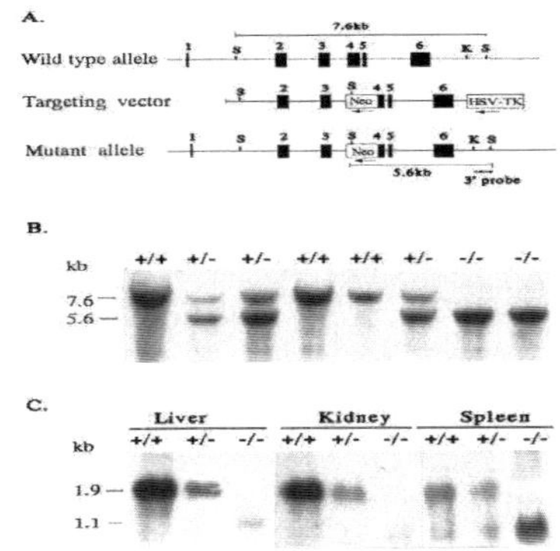

Caption: "The 2.6-kb HincII XhoI fragment containing approximately half of exon 4 and exon 5 and 6 was subcloned between the Neo gene and thymidine kinase (Fig. 1 A). The location of the genomic probe used to screen for homologous recombination is shown in Fig. 1 A. Gene Targeting in Embryonic Stem (ES) Cells and Generation of Mutant Mice. Genomic DNA of resistant clones was digested with SacI and hybridized with the 3 0.9-kb KpnI SacI external probe (Fig. 1 A). Chimeric male offspring were bred to C57BL/6J females and the agouti F1 offspring were tested for transmission of the disrupted allele by Southern blot analysis of SacI-digested genomic DNA by using the 3 external probe (Fig. 1 A and B). A 360-bp region, including the first 134 bp of the 275-bp exon 4, was deleted and replaced with the PGKneo cassette in the reverse orientation (Fig. 1 A). After selection with G418 and gangciclovir, doubly resistant clones were screened for homologous recombination by Southern blotting and hybridization with a 3 external probe (Fig. 1 A). Offspring were genotyped by Southern blotting of genomic tail DNA and hybridized with a 3 external probe (Fig. 1 B). To confirm that HFE / mice do not express the HFE gene product, we performed Northern blot analyses "

Figure 9. Above, caption text and image of a MIX figure mis-classified as GEL_IMAGE by the Fusion Classifier

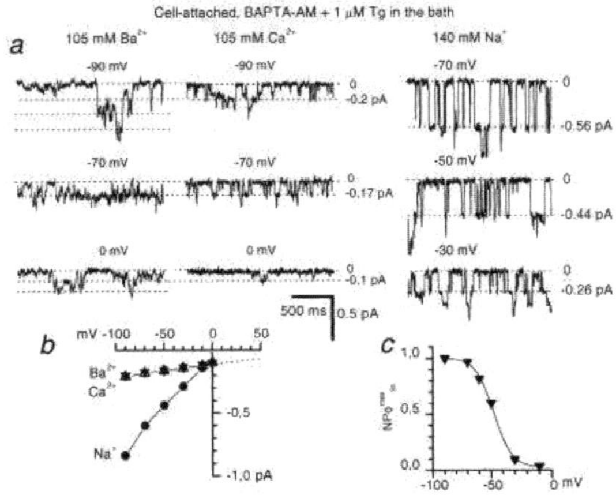

"Conductance properties of store-operated channels in A431 cells. (a) Store-operated channels in A431 cells, activated by the mixture of 100 mM BAPTA-AM and 1 mM Tg in the bath solution, were recorded in c/a mode with 105 mM Ba2+ (Left), 105 mM Ca2+ (Center), and 140 mM Na+ (Right) in the pipette solution at membrane potential as indicated. (b) Fit to the unitary current-voltage relationship of store-operated channels with Ba2+ (n = 46), Ca2+ (n = 4), Na+ (n = 3) yielded slope single-channel conductance of 1 pS for Ca2+ and Ba2+ and 6 pS for Na+. (c) Open channel probability of store-operated channels (NPomax30) expressed as a function of membrane potential. Data from six independent experiments in c/a mode with 105 mM Ba2+ as a current carrier were averaged at each membrane potential. (b and c) The average values are shown as mean ± SEM, unless the size of the error bars is smaller than the size of the symbols."

Figure 10. Above, caption text and image of a MIX figure incorrectly labeled as GRAPH by Image Classifier and GEL_IMAGE by the Text Classifier

Acknowledgements

We thank three anonymous reviewers for their valuable comments. Hong Yu and Minsuk Lee acknowledge the support of JDRF 6-2005-835.

References

Anil K. Jain and A. Vailaya., August 1996, *Image retrieval using color and shape*. Pattern Recognition, 29:1233–1244

Anil K. Jain, Fundamentals of Digital Image Processing, Prentice Hall, 1989

C. J. van Rijsbergen. *Information Retrieval*. Butterworths, London, second edition, 1979.

Joachims T, 1998, *Text categorization with support vector machines: Learning with many relevant features.* Presented at Proceedings of ECML-98, 10th European Conference on Machine Learning

Kou, Z., W.W. Cohen and R.F. Murphy. 2003. *Extracting Information from Text and Images for Location Protemics*, pp. 2-9. *In* ACM SIGKDD Workshop on Data Mining in Bioinformatics (BIOKDD).

Murphy, R.F., M. Velliste, J. Yao, and P.G. 2001. *Searching Online Journals for Fluorescence Microscope Images depicting Protein Subcellular Location Patterns*, pp. 119-128. *In* IEEE International Symposium on Bio-Informatics and Biomedical Engineering (BIBE).

Murphy, R.F., Kou, Z., Hua, J., Joffe, M., and Cohen, W. 2004. *Extracting and structuring subcellular location information from on-line journal articles: the subcellular location image finder.* In Proceedings of the IASTED International Conference on Knowledge Sharing and Collaborative Engineering (KSCE2004), St. Thomas, US Virgin Islands, pp. 109-114.

Sable, C. and V. Hatzivassiloglou. 2000. *Text-based approaches for non-tropical image categorization.* International Journal on Digital Libraries. *3*:261-275.

Sable, C., K. McKeown and K. Church. 2002. *NLP found helpful (at least for one text categorization task). In* Proceedings of Empirical Methods in Natural Language Processing (EMNLP). Philadelphia, PA

Sable, C. 2003. *Robust Statistical Techniques for the Categorization of Images Using Associated Text. In* Computer Science. Columbia University, New York.

Sussman J.L., Lin D., Jiang J., Manning N.O., Prilusky J., Ritter O., Abola E.E. (1998) Protein Data Bank (PDB): Database of Three-Dimensional Structural Information of Biological Macromolecules. Acta Crystallogr D Biol Crystallogr 54:1078-1084

MATLAB ™. The Mathworks Inc., http://www.mathworks.com/

Weston, J., A. Elisseeff, G. BakIr, F. Sinz. Jan. 26th, 2005. The SPIDER: object-orientated machine learning library. Version 6. MATLAB Package. http://www.kyb.tuebingen.mpg.de/bs/people/spider/

Wurst, M., Word Vector Tool, Univeristät Dortmund, http://www-ai.cs.uni-dortmund.de/SOFTWARE/WVTOOL/index.html

Procter and Gamble Keynote Speech: Mining biomedical texts for disease-related pathways

Andrey Rzhetsky

Columbia University
andrey.rzhetsky@dbmi.columbia.edu

Abstract

I will describe my collaborators' and my own effort to compile large models of molecular pathways in complex human disorders.

The talk will address a number of interrelated questions:

How to extract facts from texts at a large scale?

How to assess the quality of the extracted facts?

How to identify sets of conflicting or unreliable facts and to generate an internally consistent model?

How to use the resulting pathway model for automated generation of biological hypotheses?

Proceedings of the BioNLP Workshop on Linking Natural Language Processing and Biology at HLT-NAACL 06, page 81,
New York City, June 2006.

Postnominal Prepositional Phrase Attachment in Proteomics

Jonathan Schuman and **Sabine Bergler**
The CLaC Laboratory
Department of Computer Science and Software Engineering
Concordia University, Montreal, Canada
{j_schuma,bergler}@cs.concordia.ca

Abstract

We present a small set of attachment heuristics for postnominal PPs occurring in full-text articles related to enzymes. A detailed analysis of the results suggests their utility for extraction of relations expressed by nominalizations (often with several attached PPs). The system achieves 82% accuracy on a manually annotated test corpus of over 3000 PPs from varied biomedical texts.

1 Introduction

The biomedical sciences suffer from an overwhelming volume of information that is growing at explosive rates. Most of this information is found only in the form of published literature. Given the large volume, it is becoming increasingly difficult for researchers to find relevant information. Accordingly, there is much to be gained from the development of robust and reliable tools to automate this task.

Current systems in this domain focus primarily on abstracts. Though the salient points of an article are present in the abstract, much detailed information is entirely absent and can be found only in the full text (Shatkay and Feldman, 2003; Corney et al., 2004). Optimal conditions for enzymatic activity, details of experimental procedures, and useful observations that are tangential to the main point of the article are just a few examples of such information.

Full-text articles in enzymology are characterized by many complex noun phrases (NPs), usually with chains of several prepositional phrases (PPs). Nominalized relations are particularly frequent, with arguments and adjuncts mentioned in attached PPs. Thus, the tasks of automated search, retrieval, and extraction in this domain stand to benefit significantly from efforts in semantic interpretation of NPs and PPs.

There are currently no publicly available biomedical corpora suitable for this task. (See (Cohen et al., 2005) for an overview of currently available biomedical corpora.) Therefore, statistical approaches that rely on extensive training data are essentially not feasible. Instead, we approach the task through careful analysis of the data and development of heuristics. In this paper, we report on a rule-based postnominal PP attachment system developed as a first step toward a more general NP semantics for proteomics.

2 Background

Leroy *et al.* (2002; 2003) note the importance of noun phrases and prepositions in the capture of relational information in biomedical texts, citing the particular significance of the prepositions *by*, *of*, and *in*. Their parser can extract many different relations using few rules by relying on closed-class words (e.g. prepositions) instead of restricting patterns with specific predefined verbs and entities. This bottom-up approach achieves high precision (90%) and a claimed (though unquantified) high recall. However, they side-step the issue of prepositional attachment ambiguity altogether. Also, their system is targeted specifically and only toward relations. While relations do cover a considerable portion of the most relevant information in biomedical texts, there is also much relevant lower frequency information (particularly in enzymology) such as the conditions under which these relations are expressed.

Proceedings of the BioNLP Workshop on Linking Natural Language Processing and Biology at HLT-NAACL 06, pages 82–89,
New York City, June 2006.

Hahn *et al.* (2002) point out that PPs are crucial for semantic interpretation of biomedical texts due to the wide variety of conceptual relations they introduce. They note that this is reflected in their training and test data, extracted from findings reports in histopathology, where prepositions account for about 10% of all words and more than 25% of the text is contained in PPs. The coverage of PPs in our development and test data, comprised of varied texts in proteomics, is even higher with 26% of the text occurring in postnominal PPs alone.

Little research in the biomedical domain addresses the problem of PP attachment proper. This is partly due to the number of systems that process text using named-entity-based templates, disregarding PPs. In fact, the only recent BioNLP system found in the literature that makes any mention of PP attachment is Medstract (Pustejovsky et al., 2002), an automated information extraction system for Medline abstracts. The shallow parsing module used in Medstract performs "limited" prepositional attachment—only *of* prepositions are attached.

There are, of course, several PP attachment systems for other domains. Volk (2001) addresses PP attachment using the frequency of co-occurrence of a PP's preposition, object NP, and possible attachment points, calculated from query results of a web-based search engine. This system was evaluated on sentences from a weekly computer magazine, scoring 74% accuracy for both VP and NP attachment. Brill & Resnik (1994) put transformation-based learning with added word-class information from WordNet to the task of PP attachment. Their system achieves 81.8% accuracy on sentences from the Penn Treebank Wall Street Journal corpus.

The main concerns of both these systems differ from the requirements for successful PP attachment in proteomics. The main attachment ambiguity in these general texts is between VP and NP attachment, where there are few NPs to choose from for a given PP. In contrast, proteomics texts, where NPs are the main information carriers, contain many NPs with long sequences of postnominal PPs. Consequently, the possible attachment points for a given PP are more numerous. By "postnominal", we denote PPs following an NP, where the attachment point may be within the NP but may also precede it. In focusing on postnominal PPs, we exclude here PPs that trivially attach to the VP for lack of NP attachment points and focus on the subset of PPs with the highest degree of attachment ambiguity.

3 Approach

For this exploratory study we compiled two manually annotated corpora[1], a smaller, targeted development corpus consisting of sentences referring to enzymes in five articles, and a larger test corpus consisting of the full text of nine articles drawn from a wider set of topics. This bias in the data was set deliberately to test whether NPs referring to enzymes follow a distinct pattern. Our results suggest that the compiled heuristics are in fact not specific to enzymes, but work with comparable performance for a much wider set of NPs.

As our goal is semantic interpretation of NPs, only postnominal PPs were considered. A large number of these follow a very simple attachment principle—right association.

Right association (Kimball, 1973), or late closure, describes a preference for parses that result in the parse tree with the most right branches. Simply stated, right association assumes that new constituents are part of the closest possible constituent that is under construction. In the case of postnominal PPs, right association attaches each PP to the NP that immediately precedes it. An example where this strategy does fairly well is given below.

> *The effect of hydrolysis of the hemicelluloses in the milled wood lignin on the molecular mass distribution was then examined...*

Notice that, except for the last PP, attachment to the preceding NP is correct. The last PP, *on the molecular mass distribution*, modifies the head NP *effect*.

Another frequent pattern in our corpus is given below with a corresponding text fragment. In this pattern, the entire NP consists of one reaction fully described by several PPs that all attach to a nominalization in the head NP. Attachment according to this pattern is in direct opposition to right association.

```
<ACTION> <PREPOSITION> <PRODUCT>
         <PREPOSITION> <SUBSTRATE>
         <PREPOSITION> <ENZYME>
         <PREPOSITION> <MEASUREMENT>
```

[1]There was a single annotator for both corpora, who was also the developer of the heuristics.

...the release of reducing sugars from carboxymethylcellulose by cellulase at 37 °C, pH 4.8...

In general, the attachment behavior of a large percentage of PPs in the examined literature can be characterized by either right association or attachment to a nominalization. The preposition of a PP seems to be the main criterion for determining which attachment principle to apply. A few prepositions were observed to follow right association almost exclusively, while others show a strong affinity toward nominalizations, defaulting to right association only when no nominalization is available.

These observations were implemented as attachment heuristics for the most frequently occurring PPs, as distinguished by their prepositions (see Table 1 for frequency data). These rules, as outlined below, account for 90% of all postnominal PPs in the corpus. The remaining 10%, for which no clear pattern could be found, are attached using right association.

	Devel. Corpus			Test Corpus		
Prep	Freq	Syst	Base	Freq	Syst	Base
of	50.0	99.0	99.0	53.4	98.2	98.2
in	11.9	74.8	55.6	11.7	67.0	54.6
from	8.3	87.0	87.0	3.67	71.8	71.8
for	4.5	81.1	81.0	5.1	56.1	56.0
with	4.5	83.8	75.7	4.7	70.8	65.2
between	4.2	68.6	68.6	1.2	84.2	84.2
at	3.3	81.5	18.5	4.0	68.3	40.7
on	3.1	84.6	57.7	2.1	80.0	53.9
by	2.5	95.2	23.8	2.4	76.7	45.2
to	2.3	63.2	63.2	5.0	51.6	51.6
as	1.8	66.7	46.7	0.7	40.9	36.4

Table 1: Frequency of prepositions with corresponding PP attachment accuracy for the implemented heuristics and the baseline (right association) on development and test set.

Right Association (of, from, for)

PPs headed by *of*, *from*, and *for* attach almost exclusively according to right association. In particular, no violation of right association by *of* PPs has been found. The system, therefore, attaches any PP from this class to the NP immediately preceding it.

Strong Nominalization Affinity (by, at)

In contrast, *by* and *at* PPs attach almost exclusively to nominalizations. Only rarely have they been observed to attach to non-nominalization NPs. In most cases where no nominalizations are present in the NP, a PP of this class actually attaches to a preceding VP. Typical nominalization and VP attachments found in the corpus are exemplified in the following two sentences.

...the formation of stalk cells by culB⁻ pkaR⁻ cells decreased about threefold...

...xylooligosaccharides were not detected in hydrolytic products from corn cell walls by TLC analysis.

This attachment preference is implemented in the system as the heuristic for strong nominalization affinity. Given a PP from this class, the system first attempts attachment to the closest nominalization to the left. If no such NP is found, the PP is assumed to attach to a VP.

Weak Nominalization Affinity (in, with, as)

In, *with*, and *as* PPs show similar affinity toward nominalizations. In fact, initially, these PPs were attached with the strong affinity heuristic. However, after further observation it became apparent that these PPs do often attach to non-nominalization NPs. A typical example for each of these possibilities is given as follows.

...incubation of the substrate pullulan with protein fractions.

The major form of beta-amylase in Arabidopsis...

Here, the system first attempts nominalization attachment. If no nominalizations are present in the NP, instead of defaulting to VP attachment, the PP is attached to the closest NP to its left that is not the object of an *of* PP. This behavior is intuitively consistent since *in* PPs are usually adjuncts to the main NP (which is usually an entity if not a nominalization) and are unlikely to modify any of the NP's modifiers.

"Effect on"

The final heuristic encodes the frequent attachment of *on* PPs with NPs indicating effect, influence, impact, etc. While this relationship seems intuitive and likely to occur in varied texts, it may be disproportionally frequent in proteomics texts. Nonetheless, the heuristic does have a strong basis in the examined literature. An example is provided below.

> ... *the effects of reduced β-amylase activity on seed formation and germination...*

The system checks NPs preceding an *on* PP for the closest occurrence of an "effect" NP. If no such NPs are found, right association is used.

4 System Overview

There are three main phases of processing that must occur before the PP attachment heuristics can be applied. These include preprocessing and two stages of NP chunking. Upon completion of these three phases, the PP attachment module is executed.

The preprocessing phase consists of standard tokenization and part-of-speech tagging, as well as named entity recognition (and other term lookup) using gazetteer lists and simple transducers. Recognition is currently limited to enzymes, organisms, chemicals, (enzymological) activities, and measurements. A comprehensive enzyme list including synonyms was compiled from BRENDA[2] and some limited organism lists[3], including common abbreviations, were augmented based on organisms found in the development corpus. For recognition of substrates and products, some of the chemical entity lists from BioRAT (Corney et al., 2004) are used. Activity lists from BioRAT, with several enzyme-specific additions, are also used.

The next phase of processing uses a chunker reported in (Bergler et al., 2003) and further developed for a related project. NP chunking is performed in two stages, using two separate context-free grammars and an Earley-type chart parser. No domain-specific information is used in either of the grammars; recognized entities and terms are used only for improved tokenization. The first stage chunks base NPs, without attachments. Here, the parser input is segmented into smaller sentence fragments to reduce ambiguity and processing time. The fragments are delimited by verbs, prepositions, and sentence boundaries, since none of these can occur within a base NP. In the second chunking stage, entire sentences are parsed to extract NPs containing conjunctions and PP attachments. At this stage, no attempt is made to determine the proper attachment structure of the PPs or to exclude postnominal PPs that should actually be attached to a preceding VP—any PP that follows an NP has the potential to attach somewhere in the NP.

The final phase of processing is performed by the PP attachment module. Here, each postnominal PP is examined and attached according to the rule for its preposition. Only base NPs within the same NP are considered as possible attachment points. For the strong nominalization affinity heuristic, if no nominalization is found, the PP is assumed to attach to the closest preceding VP. For both nominalization affinity heuristics, the UMLS SPECIALIST Lexicon[4] is used to determine whether the head noun of each possible attachment point is a nominalization.

5 Results & Analysis

The development corpus was compiled from five articles retrieved from PubMed Central[5] (PMC). The articles were the top-ranked results returned from five separate queries[6] using BioKI:Enzymes, a literature navigation tool (Bergler et al., 2006). Sentences containing enzymes were extracted and the remaining sentences were discarded. In total, 476 sentences yielding 830 postnominal PPs were manually annotated as the development corpus.

Attachment accuracy on the development corpus is 88%. The accuracy and coverage of each rule is summarized in Table 2 and discussed in the following sections. Also, as a reference point for performance comparison, the system was tested using only the right association heuristic resulting in a baseline accuracy of 80%. The system performance is contrasted with the baseline and summarized for each preposition in Table 1.

	Devel. Corpus		Test Corpus	
Heuristic	Freq	Accuracy	Freq	Accuracy
Right Association	62.8	96.2	62.1	93.3
Weak NA	18.2	76.2	17.1	67.0
Strong NA	5.8	87.5	6.4	71.4
"Effect on"	3.1	84.6	2.1	80.0
Default (RA)	10.1	60.7	12.3	49.5

Table 2: Coverage and accuracy of each heuristic.

[2] http://www.brenda.uni-koeln.de

[3] Compiled for a related project.

[4] http://www.nlm.nih.gov/research/umls/

[5] http://www.pubmedcentral.com

[6] Amylase, CGTase, pullulanase, ferulic acid esterase, and cellwallase were used as the PMC search terms and a list of different enzymes was used for scoring.

To measure heuristic performance, the PP attachment heuristics were scored on manual NP and PP annotations. Thus all reported accuracy numbers reflect performance of the heuristics alone, isolated from possible chunking errors. The PP attachment module is, however, designed for input from the chunker and does not handle constructs which the chunker does not provide (e.g. PP conjunctions and non-simple parenthetical NPs).

5.1 Right Association

The application of right association for PPs headed by *of*, *for*, and *from* resulted in correct attachment in 96.2% of their occurrences in the development corpus. Because this class of PPs is processed using the baseline heuristic without any refinements, it has no effect on overall system accuracy as compared to overall baseline accuracy. However, it does provide a clear delineation of the subset of PPs for which right association is a sufficient and optimal solution for attachment. Given the coverage of this class of PPs (62.8% of the corpus), it also provides an explanation for the relatively high baseline performance.

Of PPs are attached with 99% accuracy. All errors involve attachment of PP conjunctions, such as "*. . . a search of the literature and of the GenBank database. . .* ", or attachment to NPs containing non-simple parenthetical statements, such as "*The synergy degree (the activities of XynA and cellulase cellulosome mixtures divided by the corresponding theoretical activities) of cellulase. . .* ". Sentences of these forms are not accounted for in the NP chunker, around which the PP attachment system was designed. Both scenarios reflect shortcomings in the NP grammars, not in the heuristic.

For and *from* PPs are attached with 81% and 87% accuracy, respectively. The majority of the error here corresponds to PPs that should be attached to a VP. For example, attachment errors occurred both in the sentence "*. . . this was followed by exoglucanases liberating cellobiose from these nicks. . .* " and in the sentence "*. . . the reactions were stopped by placing the microtubes in boiling water for 2 to 3 min.*"

5.2 Strong Nominalization Affinity

The heuristic for strong nominalization affinity deals with only two types of PPs, those headed by the prepositions *by* and *at*, both of which occur with relatively low frequency in the development corpus. Accordingly, the heuristic's impact on the overall accuracy of the system is rather small. However, it affords the largest increase in accuracy for the PPs of its class. The heuristic correctly determines attachment with 87.5% accuracy.

While these PPs account for a small portion of the corpus, they play a critical role in describing enzymological information. Specifically, *by* PPs are most often used in the description of relationships between entities, as in the NP "*degradation of xylan networks between cellulose microfibrils by xylanases*", while *at* PPs often quantitatively indicate the condition under which observed behavior or experiments take place, as in the NP "*Incubation of the enzyme at 40 °C and pH 9.0*".

The heuristic provides a strong performance increase over the baseline, correctly attaching 95.2% of *by* PPs in contrast to 23.8% with the baseline. In fact, only a single error occurred in attaching *by* PPs in the development corpus and the sentence in question, given below, appears to be ungrammatical in all of its possible interpretations.

> *The TLC pattern of liberated cellooligosaccharides by mixtures of XynA cellulosomes and cellulase cellulosomes was similar to that caused by cellulase cellulosomes alone.*

A few other errors (e.g. typos, omission of words, and grammatically incorrect or ambiguous constructs) were observed in the development corpus. The extent of such errors and the degree to which they affect the results (either negatively or positively) is unknown. However, such errors are inescapable and any automated system is susceptible to their effects.

Although no errors in *by* PP attachment were found in the development corpus, aside from the given problematic sentence, one that would be processed erroneously by the system was found manually in the GENIA Treebank[7]. It is given below to demonstrate a boundary case for this heuristic.

> *. . . modulation of activity in B cells by human T-cell leukemia virus type I tax gene. . .*

Here, the system would attach the *by* PP to the closest nominalization *activity*, when in fact, the cor-

[7]http://www-tsujii.is.s.u-tokyo.ac.jp/GENIA/

rect attachment is to the nominalization *modulation*. This error scenario is relevant to all of the PPs with nominalization affinity. A possible solution is to separate general nominalizations, such as *activity* and *action*, from more specific ones, such as *modulation*, and to favor the latter type whenever possible. An experiment toward this end, with emphasis on *in* PPs, was performed with promising results. It is discussed in the following section.

For *at* PPs, 81.5% accuracy was achieved, as compared to 18.5% with the baseline. The higher degree of error with *at* PPs is indicative of their more varied usage, requiring more contextual information for correct attachment. An example of typical variation is given in the following two sentences, both of which contain *at* PPs that the system incorrectly attached to the nominalization *activity*.

> *The amylase exhibited maximal activity at pH 8.7 and 55 °C in the presence of 2.5 M NaCl.*

> *...Bacillus sp. strain IMD370 produced alkaline α-amylases with maxima for activity at pH 10.0.*

While both sentences report observed conditions for maximal enzyme activity using similar language, the attachment of the *at* PPs differs between them. In the first sentence, the activity was *exhibited at* the given pH and temperature (VP attachment), but in the second sentence, the enzyme was not necessarily *produced at* the given pH (NP attachment)—production may have occurred under different conditions from those reported for the activity maxima.

For errors of this nature, it seems that employing semantic information about the preceding VP and possibly also the head NP would lead to more accurate attachment. There are, however, other similar errors where even the addition of such information does not immediately suggest the proper attachment.

5.3 Weak Nominalization Affinity

The weak nominalization affinity heuristic covers a large portion of the development corpus (18.2%). Overall system improvement over baseline attachment accuracy can be achieved through successful attachment of this class of PPs, particularly *in* and *with* PPs, which are the second and fourth most frequently used PPs in the development corpus, respectively. Unfortunately, the usage of these PPs is also perhaps the hardest to characterize. The heuristic achieves only 76.2% accuracy. Though noticeably better than right association alone, it is apparent that the behavior of this class of PPs cannot be entirely characterized by nominalization affinity.

Accuracy of *in* PP attachment increased by 19.2% from the baseline with this heuristic. A significant source of attachment error is the problem of multiple nominalizations in the same NP. As mentioned above, splitting nominalizations into general and specific classes may solve this problem. To explore this conjecture, the most common (particularly with *in* PPs) general nominalization, *activity*, was ignored when searching for nominalization attachment points. This resulted in a 3% increase in the accuracy for *in* PPs with no adverse effects on any of the other PPs with nominalization affinity.

Despite further anticipated improvements from similar changes, attachment of *in* PPs stands to benefit the most from additional semantic information in the form of rules that encode containment semantics (i.e. which types of things can be contained in other types of things). Possible containment rules exist for the few semantic categories that are already implemented; enzymes, for instance, can be contained in organisms, but organisms are rarely contained in anything (though organisms can be said to be contained in their species, the relationship is rarely expressed as containment). Further analysis and more semantic categories are needed to formulate more generally applicable rules.

With and *as* PPs are attached with 83.8% and 66.7% accuracy, respectively. All of the errors for these PPs involve incorrect attachment to an NP when the correct attachment is to a VP. Presented below are two sentences that provide examples of the particular difficulty of resolving these errors.

> *The xylanase A ...was expressed by E. coli with a C-terminal His tag from the vector pET-29b...*

> *The pullulanase-type activity was identified as ZPU1 and the isoamylase-type activity as SU1.*

In the first sentence, the *with* PP describes the method by which xylanase A was expressed; it does not restrict the organism in which the expression occurred. This distinction requires understanding the semantic relationship between C-terminal His tags, protein (or enzyme) expression, and E. coli. Namely, that His tags (polyhistidine-tags) are amino acid motifs used for purification of proteins, specifically proteins expressed in E. coli. Such information could only be obtained from a highly domain-specific knowledge source. In the second sentence, the verb to which the *as* PP attaches is omitted. Accordingly, even if the semantics of verbs were used to help determine attachment, the system would need to recognize the ellipsis for correct attachment.

5.4 "Effect on" Heuristic

The attachment accuracy for *on* PPs is 84.6% using the "effect on" heuristic, a noticeable improvement over the 57.7% accuracy of the baseline. The few attachment errors for *on* PPs were varied and revealed no regularities suggesting future improvements.

5.5 Unclassified PPs

The remaining PPs, for which no heurisitics were implemented, represent 10% of the development corpus. The system attaches these PPs using right association, with accuracy of 60.7%. Most frequent are PPs headed by *between*, which are attached with 68.6% accuracy. A significant improvement is expected from a heuristic that attaches these PPs based on observations of semantic features in the corpus. Namely, that most of the NPs to which *between* PPs attach can be categorized as binary relations (e.g. bond, linkage, difference, synergy). This relational feature can be expressed in the head noun or in a prenominal modifier. In fact, more than 25% of *between* PPs in the development corpus attach to the NP *synergistic effects* (or some similar alternative), where *between* shows affinity toward the adjective *synergistic*, not the head noun *effects*, which does not attract *between* PP attachment on its own.

6 Evaluation on Varied Texts

To assess the general applicability of the heuristics to varied texts, the system was evaluated on a test corpus of an additional nine articles[8] from PMC. The entire text, except the abstract and introduction, of each article was manually annotated, resulting in 1603 sentences with 3079 postnominal PPs. The system's overall attachment accuracy on this test data is 82%, comparable to that for the development enzymology data. The accuracy and coverage of each rule for the test data, as contrasted with the development set, is given in Table 2. The baseline heuristic achieved an accuracy of 77.5%. A comparative performance breakdown by preposition is given in Table 1.

Overall, changes in the coverage and accuracy of the heuristics are much less pronounced than expected from the increase in size and variance of both subject matter and writing style between the development and test data. The only significant change in rule coverage is a slight increase in the number of unclassified PPs to 12.3%. These PPs are also more varied and the right-associative default heuristic is less applicable (49.5% accuracy in the test data vs. 60.7% in the development data). The largest contribution to this additional error stems from a doubling of the frequency of *to* PPs in the test corpus. Preliminary analysis of the corresponding errors suggests that these PPs would be much better suited to the strong nominalization affinity heuristic than the right association default. The error incurred over all unclassified PPs accounts for 1.4% of the accuracy difference between the development and test data. The larger number of these PPs also explains the smaller overall difference between the system and baseline performance.

For PPs were observed to have more frequent VP attachment in the test data. In particular, *for* PPs with object NPs specifying a duration (or other measurement), as exemplified below, attach almost exclusively to VPs and nominalizations.

The sample was spun in a microfuge for 10 min...

This behavior is also apparent in the development data, though in much smaller numbers. Applying the strong nominalization affinity heuristic to these PPs resulted in an increase of *for* PP attachment accuracy in the test corpus to 75.8% and an overall increase in accuracy of 1.0%.

A similar pattern was observed for *at* PPs, where the pattern `<CHEMICAL> at <CONCENTRATION>` accounts for 25.6% of all *at* PP attachment errors and the majority of the performance decrease for the strong nominalization affinity heuristic between the two data sets. The remainder of the performance decrease for this heuristic is attributed to gaps in the

[8] PMC query terms: metabolism, biosynthesis, proteolysis, peptidyltransferase, hexokinase, epimerase, laccase, ligase, dehydrogenase.

UMLS SPECIALIST Lexicon. For instance, the underlined head nouns in the following examples are not marked as nominalizations in the lexicon.

> *The double mutant inhibited misreading by paromomycin ...*
>
> *... the formation of stalk cells by culB$^-$ pkaR$^-$ cells...*

In our test corpus, these errors were only apparent in *by* PP attachment, but can potentially affect all nominalization-based attachment.

Aside from the cases mentioned in this section, attachment trends in the test corpus are quite similar to those observed in the development corpus. Given the diversity in the test data, both in terms of subject matter (between articles) and writing style (between sections), the results suggest the suitability of our heuristics to proteomics texts in general.

7 Conclusion

The next step for BioNLP is to process the full text of scientific articles, where heavy NPs with potentially long chains of PP attachments are frequent. This study has investigated the attachment behavior of postnominal PPs in enzyme-related texts and evaluated a small set of simple attachment heuristics on a test set of over 3000 PPs from a collection of more varied texts in proteomics. The heuristics cover all prepositions, even infrequent ones, that nonetheless convey important information. This approach requires only NP chunked input and a nominalization dictionary, all readily available from on-line resources. The heuristics are thus useful for shallow approaches and their accuracy of 82% puts them in a position to reliably improve both, proper recognition of entities and their properties and bottom-up recognition of relationships between entities expressed in nominalizations.

References

Sabine Bergler, René Witte, Michelle Khalifé, Zhuoyan Li, and Frank Rudzicz. 2003. Using knowledge-poor coreference resolution for text summarization. In *On-line Proceedings of the Workshop on Text Summarization, Document Understanding Conference (DUC 2003)*, Edmonton, Canada, May.

Sabine Bergler, Jonathan Schuman, Julien Dubuc, and Alexandr Lebedev. 2006. BioKI:Enzymes - an adaptable system to locate low-frequency information in full-text proteomics articles. Poster abstract in *Proceedings of the HLT-NAACL Workshop on Linking Natural Language Processing and Biology (BioNLP'06)*, New York, NY, June.

Eric Brill and Philip Resnik. 1994. A rule-based approach to prepositional phrase attachment disambiguation. In *Proceedings of the 15th International Conference on Computational Linguistics (COLING-94)*.

Kevin Bretonnel Cohen, Lynne Fox, Philip V. Ogren, and Lawrence Hunter. 2005. Corpus design for biomedical natural language processing. In *Proceedings of the ACL-ISMB Workshop on Linking Biological Literature, Ontologies and Databases (BioLINK)*, pages 38–45, Detroit, MI, June. Association for Computational Linguistics.

David P.A. Corney, Bernard F. Buxton, William B. Langdon, and David T. Jones. 2004. BioRAT: extracting biological information from full-length papers. *Bioinformatics*, 20(17):3206–3213.

Udo Hahn, Martin Romacker, and Stefan Schulz. 2002. Creating knowledge repositories from biomedical reports: the MEDSYNDIKATE text mining system. In *Proceedings of the 7th Pacific Symposium on Biocomputing*, pages 338–49, Hawaii, USA.

John Kimball. 1973. Seven principles of surface structure parsing in natural language. *Cognition*, 2:15–47.

Gondy Leroy and Hsinchun Chen. 2002. Filling preposition-based templates to capture information from medical abstracts. In *Proceedings of the 7th Pacific Symposium on Biocomputing*, pages 350–361, Hawaii, USA.

Gondy Leroy, Hsinchun Chen, and Jesse D. Martinez. 2003. A shallow parser based on closed-class words to capture relations in biomedical text. *Journal of Biomedical Informatics*, 36:145–158, June.

James Pustejovsky, José Castaño, Roser Sauri, Anna Rumshisky, Jason Zhang, and Wei Luo. 2002. Medstract: Creating large-scale information servers for biomedical libraries. In *ACL 2002 Workshop on Natural Language Processing in the Biomedical Domain*, Philadelphia, PA.

Hagit Shatkay and Ronen Feldman. 2003. Mining the biomedical literature in the genomic era: An overview. *Journal of Computational Biology*, 10(6):821–855.

Martin Volk. 2001. Exploiting the WWW as a corpus to resolve PP attachment ambiguities. In Paul Rayson, Andrew Wilson, Tony McEnery, Andrew Hardie, and Shereen Khoja, editors, *Proceedings of Corpus Linguistics*, pages 601–606, Lancaster, England, March.

BioKI:Enzymes — an adaptable system to locate low-frequency information in full-text proteomics articles

Sabine Bergler, Jonathan Schuman, Julien Dubuc, Alexandr Lebedev
The CLaC Laboratory
Department of Computer Science and Software Engineering
Concordia University, 1455 de Maisonneuve Blvd West, Montreal, Quebec, H3G 1M8
bioki@cs.concordia.ca

1 Goals

BioKI:Enzymes is a literature navigation system that uses a two-step process. First, full-text articles are retrieved from PubMed Central (PMC). Then, for each article, the most relevant passages are identified according to a set of user selected keywords, and the articles are ranked according to the pertinence of the representative passages.

In contrast to most existing systems in information retrieval (IR) and information extraction (IE) for bioinformatics, BioKI:Enzymes processes full-text articles, not abstracts. Full-text articles[1] permit to highlight low-frequency information—i.e. information that is not redundant, that does not necessarily occur in many articles, and within each article, may be expressed only once (most likely in the body of the article, not the abstract). It contrasts thus with GoPubMed (Doms and Schroeder, 2005), a clustering system that retrieves abstracts using PMC search and clusters them according to terms from the Gene Ontology (GO).

Scientists face two major obstacles in using IR and IE technology: how to select the best keywords for an intended search and how to assess the validity and relevance of the extracted information.

To address the latter problem, BioKI provides convenient access to different degrees of context by allowing the user to view the information in three different formats. At the most abstract level, the ranked list of articles provides the first five lines of the most pertinent text segment selected by BioKI (similar to the snippets provided by Google). Clicking on the article link will open a new window with a side-by-side view of the full-text article as retrieved through PMC on the left and the different text segments[2], ordered by their relevance to the user selected keywords, on the right. The user has thus the possibility to assess the information in the context of the text segment first, and in the original, if desired.

2 Keyword-based Ranking

To address the problem of finding the best keywords, BioKI:Enzymes explores different approaches. For research in enzymology, our users specified a standard pattern of information retrieval, which is reflected in the user interface.

Enzymes are proteins that catalyze reactions differently in different environments (pH and temperature). Enzymes are characterized by the substrate they act on and by the product of their catalysis. Accordingly, a keyphrase pattern has entities (that tended to recur) prespecified for selection in four categories: enzymes, their activities (such as *carbohydrate degrading*), their qualities (such as *maximum activity*), and measurements (such as *pH*). The provided word lists are not exhaustive and BioKI:Enzymes expects the user to specify new terms (which are not required to conceptually fit the category). The word lists are convenient for selecting alternate spellings that might be hard to enter (α-*amylase*) and for setting up keyphrase templates in a *profile*, which can be stored under a name and later reused. Completion of the keyword lists is provided through stemming and the equivalent treatment of Greek characters and their different transliterations.

The interface presents the user with a search window, which has two distinct fields, one to specify

[1] Only articles that are available in HTML format can currently be processed.

[2] We use TextTiler (Hearst, 1997) to segment the article.

Proceedings of the BioNLP Workshop on Linking Natural Language Processing and Biology at HLT-NAACL 06, pages 91–92,
New York City, June 2006.

the search terms for the PMC search, the other to specify the (more fine-grained) keywords the system uses to select the most relevant passages in the texts and to rank the texts based on this choice. The BioKI specific keywords can be chosen from the four categories of keyword lists mentioned above or entered. What distinguishes BioKI:Enzymes is the direct control the user has over the weight of the keywords in the ranking and the general mode of considering the keywords. Each of the four keyword categories has a weight associated with it. In addition, bonus scores can be assigned for keywords that co-occur at a distance less than a user-defined threshold. The two modes of ranking are a basic "and", where the weight and threshold settings are ignored and the text segment that has the most specified keywords closest together will be ranked highest. This is the mode of choice for a targeted search for specific information, like "pH optima" in a PMC subcorpus for *amylase*.

The other mode is a basic "or", with additional points for the co-occurrence of keywords within the same text segment. Here, the co-occurrence bonus is given for terms from the four different lists, not for terms from the same list. While the search space is much too big for a scientist to control all these degrees of freedom without support, our initial experiments have shown that we could control the ranking behavior with repeated refinements of the weight settings, and even simulate the behavior of an "and" by judicious weight selection.

3 Assessment and Future Work

The evaluation of a ranking of full-text articles, for which there are no Gold standards as of yet, is difficult and begins in the anecdotal. Our experts did not explore the changes in ranking based on different weight settings, but found the "and" to be just what they wanted from the system. We will experiment with different weight distribution patterns to see whether a small size of different weight settings can be specified for predictable behavior and whether this will have better acceptance.

The strength of BioKI lies in its adaptability to user queries. In this it contrasts with template-based IE systems like BioRAT (Corney et al., 2004), which extracts information from full-length articles, but uses handcoded templates to do so. Since BioKI is not specific to an information need, but is meant to give more control to the user and thus facilitate access to any type of PMC search results, it is important that the same PMC search results can be reordered by successively refining the selected BioKI keywords until more desirable texts appear at the top. This behavior is modeled after frequent behavior using search engines such as Google, where often the first search serves to better select keywords for a subsequent, better targeted search. This reranking based on keyword refinement can be done almost instantaneously (20 sec for 480 keyphrases on 161 articles), since the downloaded texts from PMC are cached, and since the system spends most of its runtime downloading and storing the articles from PMC. This is currently a feasibility study, targeted to eventually become a Web service. Performance still needs to be improved (3:14 min for 1 keyphrase on 161 articles, including downloading), but the quality of the ranking and variable context views might still entice users to wait for them.

In conclusion, it is feasible to develop a highly user-adaptable passage highlighting system over full-text articles that focuses on low-frequency information. This adaptability is provided both through increased user control of the ranking parameters and through presentation of results in different contexts which at the same time justify the ranking and authenticate keyword occurrences in their source text.

Acknowledgments

The first prototype of BioKI was implemented by Evan Desai. We thank our domain experts Justin Powlowski, Emma Masters, and Regis-Olivier Benech. Work funded by Genome Quebec.

References

D. P. A. Corney, B.F. Buxton, W.B. Langdon, and D.T. Jones. 2004. BioRAT: Extracting biological information from full-length papers. *Bioinformatics*, 20(17):3206–3213.

Andreas Doms and Michael Schroeder. 2005. GoPubMed: exploring PubMed with the Gene Ontology. *Nucleic Acids Research*, 33:W783—W786. Web Server issue.

M.A. Hearst. 1997. Texttiling: Segmenting text into multi-paragraph subtopic passages. *Computational Linguistics*, 23(1):34–64.

A Graph-Search Framework for GeneId Ranking (Extended Abstract)

William W. Cohen
Machine Learning Department
Carnegie Mellon University
Pittsburgh PA 15213
wcohen@cs.cmu.edu

1 Introduction

One step in the curation process is *geneId finding*—the task of finding the database identifier of every gene discussed in an article. GeneId-finding was studied experimentally in the BioCreatIvE challenge (Hirschman et al., 2005), which developed testbed problems for each of three model organisms (yeast, mice, and fruitflies). Here we consider *geneId ranking*, a relaxation of geneId-finding in which the system provides a ranked list of genes that might be discussed by the document. We show how multiple named entity recognition (NER) methods can be combined into a single high-performance geneId-ranking system.

2 Methods and Results

We focused on the mouse dataset, which was the hardest for the BioCreatIvE participants. This dataset consists of several parts. The *gene synonym list* consists of 183,142 synonyms for 52,594 genes; the *training data* consists of 100 mouse-relevant Medline abstracts, associated with the MGI geneId's for those genes that are mentioned in the abstract; the *evaluation data* consists of an additional 50 mouse-relevant Medline abstracts, also associated with the MGI geneId's as above; the *test data* consists of an additional 250 mouse-relevant Medline abstracts, again associated with MGI geneId's; finally the *historical data* consists of 5000 mouse-relevant Medline abstracts, each of which is associated with the MGI geneId's for all genes which are (a) associated with the article according to the MGI database, and (b) mentioned in the abstract, as determined by an automated procedure based on the gene synonym list.[1] We also annotated the evaluation-data for NER evaluation.

We used two closely related gene-protein NER systems in our experiments, both trained using Minorthird (Min, 2004) on the YAPEX corpus (Franzén et al., 2002). The *likely-protein extractor* was designed to have high precision and lower recall, and the *possible-protein extractor* was designed to have high recall and lower precision. As shown in Table 1, the likely-protein extractor performs well on the YAPEX test set, but neither system performs well on the mouse evaluation data—here, they perform only comparably to exact matching against the synonym dictionary. This performance drop is typical when learning-based NER systems are tested on data from a statistical distribution different from their training set.

As a baseline for geneId-ranking, we used a string similarity metric called *soft TFIDF*, as implemented in the SecondString open-source software package (Cohen and Ravikumar, 2003), and soft-matched extracted gene names against the synonym list. Table 2 shows the *mean average precision* on the evaluation data. Note that the geneId ranker based on possible-protein performs statistically significantly better[2] than the one based on likely-protein, even though possible-protein has a lower F score.

To combine these two NER systems, we represent all information as a labeled directed graph which in-

[1] The training data and evaluation data are subsets of the BioCreatIvE "devtest" set. The historical data was called "training data" in the BioCreatIvE publications. The test data is the same as the blind test set used in BioCreatIvE.

[2] With $z = 3.1$, $p > 0.995$ using a two-tailed paired test.

Proceedings of the BioNLP Workshop on Linking Natural Language Processing and Biology at HLT-NAACL 06, pages 93–95,
New York City, June 2006. ©2006 Association for Computational Linguistics

	Precis.	Recall	F
mouse eval			
likely-prot	0.667	0.268	0.453
possible-prot	0.304	0.566	0.396
dictionary	0.245	0.439	0.314
YAPEX test			
likely-prot	0.872	0.621	0.725
YAPEX system	0.678	0.664	0.671

Table 1: Performance of the NER systems on the mouse evaluation corpus and the YAPEX test corpus.

	Mean Average Precision (MAP)
mouse evaluation data	
likely-prot + softTFIDF	0.450
possible-prot + softTFIDF	0.626
graph-based ranking	0.513
+ extra links	0.730
+ extra links & learning	0.807

Table 2: Mean average precision of several geneId-ranking methods on the 50 abstracts from the mouse evaluation dataset.

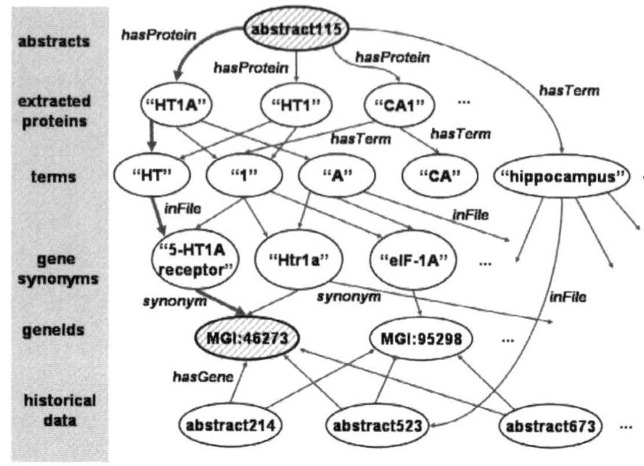

Figure 1: Part of a simplified version of the graph used for geneId ranking.

cludes the test abstracts, the extracted names, the synonym list, and the historical data. We then use *proximity in a graph* for ranking. The graph used is illustrated in Figure 1. Nodes in this graph can be either *files*, *strings*, *terms*, or *user-defined types*. Abstracts and gene synonyms are represented as *file* and *string* nodes, respectively. Files are linked to the *terms* (i.e., the words) that they contain, and terms are linked to the files that contain them.[3] File nodes are also linked to *string* nodes corresponding to the output of an NER system on that file. (*String* nodes are simply short files.) The graph also contains *geneId* nodes and *synonym* string nodes created from the dictionary, and for each historical-data abstract, we include links to its associated geneId nodes.

Given this graph, gene identifiers for an abstract are generated by traversing the graph away from the abstract node, and looking for *geneId* nodes that are "close" to the abstract according to a certain proximity measure for nodes. Similarity between two nodes is defined by a *lazy walk process*, similar to PageRank with decay. The details of this are described in the full paper and elsewhere (Minkov et al., 2006). Intuitively, however, this measures the similarity of two nodes by the weighted sum of all paths that connect the nodes, where shorter paths will be weighted exponentially higher than longer paths. One consequence of this measure is that information associated with paths like the one on the left-hand side of the graph—which represents a soft-match between a likely-protein and a synonym—can be reinforced by other types of paths, like the one on the right-hand side of the figure.

As shown in Table 2, the graph-based approach has performance intermediate between the two baseline systems. However, the baseline approaches include some information which is not available in the graph, e.g., the softTFIDF distances, and the implicit knowledge of the "importance" of paths from an abstract to a synonym via an NER-extracted string. To include this information, we inserted extra edges labeled *proteinToSynonym* between the extracted protein strings x and comparable synonyms y, and also "short-cut" edges in the graph that directly link abstracts x to *geneId* nodes reachable via one of the "important" paths described above.

As Table 2 shows, graph search with the augmented graph does indeed improve MAP performance on the mouse evaluation data: performance is better than the simple graph, and also better than

[3]In fact, all edges have inverses in the graph.

	MAP	Avg Max F
mouse test data		
likely-prot + softTFIDF	0.368	0.421
possible-prot + softTFIDF	0.611	0.672
graph-based ranking	0.640	0.695
+ extra links & learning	0.711	0.755

Table 3: Mean average precision of several geneId-ranking methods on the 250 abstracts from the mouse test dataset.

either of the baseline methods described above.

Finally we extended the lazy graph walk to produce, for each node x reached on the walk, a feature vector summarizing the walk. Intuitively, the feature vector records certain features of each edge in the graph, weighting these features according to the probability of traversing the edge. We then use a learning-to-rank method (Collins and Duffy, 2002) to rerank the top 100 nodes. Table 2 shows that learning improves performance. In combination, the techniques described have improved MAP performance to 0.807, an improvement of nearly 80% over the most natural baseline (i.e., soft-matching the dictionary to the NER method with the best F measure).

As a final prospective test, we applied these methods to the 250-abstract mouse test data. We compared their performance to the graph-based search method combined with a reranking postpass learned from the 100-abstract mouse training data. The performance of these methods is summarized in Table 3. The somewhat lower performance is probably due to variation in the two samples.[4] We also computed the maximal F-measure (over any threshold) of each ranked list produced, and then averaged these measures over all queries. This is comparable to the best F1 scores in the BioCreatIvE workshop, although the averaging for BioCreatIvE was done differently.

3 Conclusion

We evaluate several geneId-ranking systems, in which an article is associated with a ranked list of possible gene identifiers. We find that, when used in the most natural manner, the F-measure performance of an NER systems does not correlate well with MAP of the geneId-ranker based on it: rather, the NER system with higher recall, but lower overall performance, has significantly better performance when used for geneId-ranking.

We also present a graph-based scheme for combining NER systems, which allows many types of information to be combined. Combining this system with learning produces performance much better than either NER system can achieve alone. On average, 68% of the correct proteins will be found in the top two elements of the list, 84% will be found in the top five elements, and more than 90% will be found in the top ten elements. This level of performance is probably good enough to be of use in curation.

Acknowledgement

The authors with to thank the organizers of BioCreatIvE, Bob Murphy, Tom Mitchell, and Einat Minkov. The work described here is supported by NIH K25 grant DA017357-01.

References

William W. Cohen and Pradeep Ravikumar. 2003. SecondString: An open-source Java toolkit of approximate string-matching techniques. Project web page, http://secondstring.sourceforge.net.

Michael Collins and Nigel Duffy. 2002. New ranking algorithms for parsing and tagging: Kernels over discrete structures, and the voted perceptron. In *Proceedings of the ACL*.

Kristofer Franzén, Gunnar Eriksson, Fredrik Olsson, Lars Asker Per Lidén, and Joakim Coster. 2002. Protein names and how to find them. *International Journal of Medical Informatics*, 67(1-3):49–61.

Lynette Hirschman, Alexander Yeh, Christian Blaschke, and Alfonso Valencia. 2005. Overview of BioCreAtIvE: critical assessment of information extraction for biology. *BMC Bioinformatics*, 6(S1).

2004. Minorthird: Methods for identifying names and ontological relations in text using heuristics for inducing regularities from data. http://minorthird.sourceforge.net.

Einat Minkov, William Cohen, and Andrew Ng. 2006. A graph framework for contextual search and name disambiguation in email. In *SIGIR '06: Proceedings of the 29th annual international ACM SIGIR conference on research and development in information retrieval*, August. To appear.

[4] For instance, the test-set abstracts contain somewhat more proteins on average (2.2 proteins/abstract) than the evaluation-set abstracts (1.7 proteins/abstract).

Semi-supervised anaphora resolution in biomedical texts

Caroline Gasperin
Computer Laboratory,
University of Cambridge,
15 JJ Thomson Avenue,
Cambridge CB3 0FD, UK
cvg20@cl.cam.ac.uk

Abstract

Resolving anaphora is an important step in the identification of named entities such as genes and proteins in biomedical scientific articles. The goal of this work is to resolve associative and coreferential anaphoric expressions making use of the rich domain resources (such as databases and ontologies) available for the biomedical area, instead of annotated training data. The results are comparable to extant state-of-the-art supervised methods in the same domain. The system is integrated into an interactive tool designed to assist FlyBase curators by aiding the identification of the salient entities in a given paper as a first step in the aggregation of information about them.

1 Introduction

The number of articles being published in biomedical journals per year is increasing exponentially. For example, Morgan et al. (2003) report that more than 8000 articles were published in 2000 just in relation to FlyBase[1], a database of genomic research on the fruit fly *Drosophila melanogaster*.

The growth in the literature makes it difficult for researchers to keep track of information, even in very small subfields of biology. Progress in the field often relies on the work of professional curators, typically postdoctoral-level scientists, who are trained to identify important information in a scientific article. This is a very time-consuming task which first requires identification of gene, allele and protein names and their synonyms, as well as several interactions and relations between them.The information extracted from each article is then used to fill in a template per gene or allele.

To extract all information about a specific biomedical entity in the text and be able to fill in the corresponding template, a useful first step is the identification of all textual mentions that are referring to or are related with that entity. Linking all these mentions together corresponds to the task known as *anaphora resolution* in Natural Language Processing.

In this paper, we are interested in linking automatically all mentions that refer to a gene or are related to it (i.e. its 'products'). For example, in the following portion of text, we aim to link the highlighted mentions:

``` 
``... is composed of five proteins(1) encoded by the male-specific lethal genes(2) ... The MSL proteins(3) colocalize to hundreds of sites ... male animals die when they are mutant for any one of the five msl genes(4).''
```

In this work we use the output of a gene name recogniser (Vlachos et al., 2006) and information from the Sequence Ontology (Eilbeck and Lewis, 2004) to identify the entities of interest and the genomic relations among them. We also use RASP (Briscoe and Carroll, 2002), a statistical parser, to identify NPs (and their subconstituents) which may be anaphorically linked. Our system identifies coref-

[1] http://www.flybase.org

Proceedings of the BioNLP Workshop on Linking Natural Language Processing and Biology at HLT-NAACL 06, pages 96–103,
New York City, June 2006. ©2006 Association for Computational Linguistics

erential relations between biomedical entities (such as (1) and (3), and (2) and (4) above) as well as associative links (relations between different entities, e.g. the link between a gene and its protein as in (2) and (3) above). A previous version of this system was presented in (Vlachos et al., 2006); here we improve its results due to refinements on some of the steps previous to the resolution and to the anaphora resolution process itself.

The large majority of the entities in biomedical texts are referred to using non-pronominal noun phrases, like proper nouns, acronyms or definite descriptions. Hence, we focus on these NPs and do not resolve pronominal references (as pronouns represent only about 3% of the noun phrases in our domain).

In the following section, we detail the different components of the anaphora resolution system. The results are tested against hand-annotated papers, and an extensive evaluation is provided in Section 3, where the performance and errors are discussed.

2 The anaphora resolution system

Our system for anaphora resolution makes use of lexical, syntactic, semantic and positional information to link anaphoric expressions. The lexical information consists of the words themselves. The syntactic information consists of noun phrase boundaries and the distinction between head and pre-modifiers (extracted from RASP output). The distance (in words) between the anaphoric expression and its possible antecedent is taken into account as positional information. The semantic information comes from the named entity recognition (NER) process and some extra tagging based on features from the Sequence Ontology.

FlyBase is used as source of gene names, symbols and synonyms, giving rise to training data for the gene name recognition system detailed in Section 2.1. The output of this system is tagged named entities that refer to the fruit fly genes.

We then parse the text using RASP in order to extract the noun phrases and their subparts (head and modifiers). Retagging gene names as proper names before parsing improves the parser's performance, but otherwise the parser is used unmodified.

The Sequence Ontology (SO) can be used to identify words and phrases related to a gene: its subtypes (e.g. oncogene, transposable element), parts (e.g. transcript, regulatory region) and products (e.g. polypeptide, protein). Subsection 2.3 details the information extracted from SO to type the non-gene mentions.

2.1 Gene-name recognition

The NER system we use (Vlachos et al., 2006) is a replication and extension of the system developed by Morgan et al. (2004): a different training set and software were used. For training data we used a total of 16609 abstracts, which were automatically annotated by a dictionary-based gene name tagger. The dictionary consists of lists of the gene names, symbols and synonyms extracted from FlyBase. The gene names and their synonyms that were recorded by the curators from the full paper were annotated automatically in each abstract, giving rise to a large but noisy set of training data. The recognizer used is the open source toolkit LingPipe[2], implementing a 1st-order HMM model using Witten-Bell smoothing. A morphologically-based classifier was used to deal with unknown gene names (that were not present in the training data).

The performance of the trained recogniser on a revised version of the test data used in Morgan et al. (86 abstracts annotated by a biologist curator and a computational linguist) was 80.81% recall and 84.93% precision.

2.2 Parsing and NP extraction

RASP is a pipelined parser which identifies sentence boundaries, tokenises sentences, tags the tokens with their part-of-speech (PoS) and finally parses PoS tag sequences, statistically ranking the resulting derivations. We have made minor modifications to RASP's tokeniser to deal with some specific features of biomedical articles, and manually modified a small number of entries in the PoS tagger lexicon, for example to allow the use of *and* as a proper name (referring to a fruit fly gene). Otherwise, RASP uses a parse ranking module trained on a generic treebank and a grammar also developed from similar resources.

The anaphora resolution system first tags genes

[2]http://www.alias-i.com/lingpipe/

using the gene recogniser. This means that identified gene mentions can be retagged as proper names before the RASP parser is applied to the resulting PoS sequences. This improves parser performance as the accuracy of PoS tagging decreases for unknown words, especially as the RASP tagger uses an unknown word handling module which relies heavily on the similarity between unknown words and extant entries in its lexicon. This strategy works less well on gene names and other technical vocabulary from the biomedical domain, as almost no such material was included in the training data for the tagger. We have not evaluated the precise improvement in performance as yet due to the lack of extant gold standard parses for relevant text.

RASP can output grammatical relations (GRs) for each parsed sentence (Briscoe, 2006). GRs are factored into binary lexical relations between a head and a dependent of the form `(GR-type head dependent)`. We use the following GR-types to identify the head-nouns of NPs (the examples of GRs are based on the example of the first page unless specified otherwise):

- `ncsubj` encodes binary relations between non-clausal subjects and their verbal heads; e.g. (**ncsubj** colocalize proteins).
- `dobj` encodes a binary relation between verbal or prepositional head and the head of the NP to its immediate right; e.g. (**dobj** of sites).
- `obj2` encodes a binary relation between verbal heads and the head of the second NP in a double object construction; e.g. for the sentence "Xist RNA provides a mark for specific histones" we get (**dobj** provides mark) (**obj2** provides histones).
- `xcomp` encodes a binary relation between a head and an unsaturated VP complement; e.g. for the phrase "a class of regulators in Drosophila is the IAP family" we get (**xcomp** is family).
- `ta` encodes a binary relation between a head and the head of a text adjunct delimited by punctuation (quotes, brackets, dashes, commas, etc.); e.g. for "BIR-containing proteins (BIRPs)" we get (**ta** proteins BIRPs).

To extract the modifiers of the head nouns, we search the GRs typed `ncmod` which encode binary relations between non-clausal modifiers and their heads; e.g (**ncmod** genes msl).

When the head nouns take part in coordination, it is necessary to search the `conj` GRs which encode relations between a coordinator and the head of a conjunct. There will be as many such binary relations as there are conjuncts of a specific coordinator; e.g. for "CED-9 and EGL-1 belong to a large family ..." we get (**ncsubj** belong and) (**conj** and CED-9) (**conj** and EGL-1).

Last but not least, to identify definite descriptions, we search the `det` GR for a definite specifier, e.g. (**det** proteins The). By using the GR representation of the parser output we were able to improve the performance of the anaphora resolution system by about 10% over an initial version described in (Vlachos et al., 2006) that used the RASP tree output instead of GRs. GRs generalise more effectively across minor and irrelevant variations in derivations such as the X-bar level of attachment in nominal coordinations.

2.3 Semantic typing and selecting NPs

To identify the noun phrases that refer to the entities of interest, we classify the head noun as belonging to one of the five following classes: "part-of-gene", "subtype-of-gene", "supertype-of-gene", "product-of-gene" or "is-a-gene". These classes are referred to as biotypes.

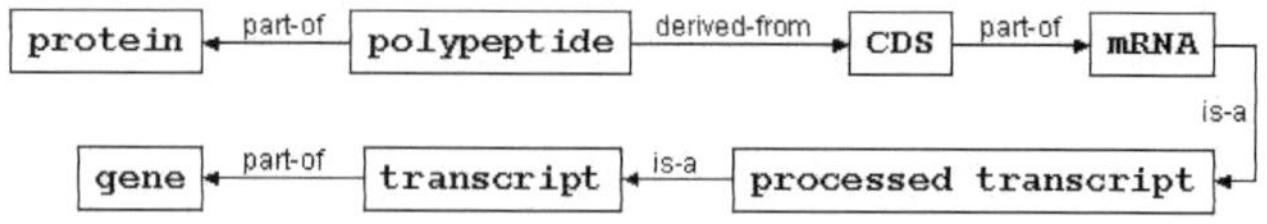

Figure 1: SO path from gene to protein.

The biotypes reflect the way the SO relates entities to the concept of the gene using the following relations: derives_from, member_of, part_of, and is_a, among others.[3] We extracted the unique path

[3]We consider the member_of relation to be the same as the part_of relation.

of concepts and relations which leads from a gene to a protein. The result is shown in Figure 1.

Besides the facts directly expressed in this path, we also assumed the following:[4]

1. Whatever is-a transcript is also part-of a gene.
2. Whatever is part-of a transcript is also part-of a gene.
3. An mRNA is part-of a gene.
4. Whatever is part-of an mRNA is also part-of a gene.
5. CDS is part-of a gene.
6. A polypeptide is a product (derived-from) of a gene.
7. Whatever is part-of a polypeptide is also a product of a gene.
8. A protein is a product of a gene.

We then used these assumptions to add new derivable facts to our original path. For example, an *exon* is a part of a transcript according to the SO, therefore, by the 2nd assumption, we add the fact that an *exon* is a part of a gene. We also extracted information about gene subtypes that is included in the ontology as an entry called "gene class". We consider NPs as supertypes of a gene when they refer to nucleotide sequences that are bigger than but include the gene.[5]

Finally, we tagged every NP whose head noun is one of the items extracted from the SO with its biotype. For instance, we would tag "the third exon" with "part-of-gene".

The NPs whose head noun is a gene name tagged in the NER phase also receive the "is-a-gene" biotype. Other NPs that still remain without biotype info are tagged as "other-bio" if any modifier of the head is a gene name.

This typing process achieves 75% accuracy when evaluated against the manually annotated corpora described in Section 3. The majority of the errors (70%) are on typing NPs that contain just a proper name, which can refer to a gene or to a protein. At the moment, all of these cases are being typed as "is-a-gene".

The biotyped NPs are then selected and considered for anaphora resolution. NPs with the same biotype can be coreferent, as well as NPs with is-a-gene and subtype-of-gene biotypes. The anaphoric relation between an is-a-gene NP and a part-of-gene or product-of-gene NP is associative rather than coreferential.

2.4 Resolving anaphora cases

We take all proper namer (PNs) and definite descriptions (DDs) among the filtered NPs as potential anaphoric expressions (anaphors) to be resolved. As possible antecedents for an anaphor we take all bio-typed NPs that occur before it in the text. For each anaphor we look for its antecedent (the closest previous mention that is related to it). For linking anaphors to their antecedents we look at:

- $head_{an}$: anaphor head noun
- $head_a$: antecedent head noun
- mod_{an}: set of anaphor pre-modifiers
- mod_a: set of antecedent pre-modifiers
- $biotype_{an}$: anaphor biotype
- $biotype_a$: antecedent biotype
- d: distance in sentences from the anaphor

The pseudo-code to find the antecedent for the DDs and PNs is given below:

- Input: a set A with all the anaphoric expressions (DDs and PNs); a set C with all the possible antecedents (all NPs with biotype information)
- For each anaphoric expression A_i:
    - Let antecedent 1 be the closest preceding NP C_j such that head(C_j)=head(A_i) and biotype(C_j)=biotype(A_i)

[4]A curator from FlyBase was consulted to confirm the validity of these assumptions.

[5]In the SO a gene holds an is-a relation to "sequence" and "region" entries.

- Let antecedent 2 be the closest preceding NP C_j such that
  biotype(C_j)$\neq$ biotype(A_i), but
  head(C_j)=head(A_i) or
  head(C_j)=mod(A_i) or
  mod(C_j)=head(A_i) or
  mod(C_j)=mod(A_i)
- Take the closest candidate as antecedent, if 1 and/or 2 are found; if none is found, the DD/PN is treated as non-anaphoric

- Output: The resolved anaphoric expressions in A linked to their antecedents.

As naming conventions usually recommend gene names to be lower-cased and protein names to be upper-cased, our matching among heads and modifiers is case-insensitive, allowing, for example, `msl gene` to be related to `MSL protein` due to their common modifiers.

Antecedent 1, if found, is considered coreferent to A_i, and antecedent 2, associative. For example, in the passage:

``Dosage compensation, which ensures that the expression of **X-linked genes**:C_j is equal in males and females ... the hypertranscription of **the X-chromosomal genes**:A_j in males ...''

the NP in bold font which is indexed as antecedent C_j is taken to be coreferential to the anaphor indexed as A_j. Additionally, in:

``... the role of **the roX genes**:C_k in this process ... which MSL proteins interact with **the roX RNAs**:A_k ...''

C_k meets the conditions to form an associative link to A_k. The same is true in the following example in which there is an associative relation between C_j and A_j:

``The expression of **reaper**:C_j has been shown to be regulated by distinct stimuli ... it was shown to bind a specific region of **the reaper promoter**:A_j ...''

If we consider the example from the first page, mention (1) is returned by the system as the coreferent antecedent for (3), as they have the same biotype and a common head noun. In the same example, (2) is returned as a coreferent antecedent to (4), and (3) as an associative antecedent to (4).

3 Evaluation

We evaluated our system against two hand-annotated full papers which have been curated in FlyBase and were taken from PubMed Central in XML format. Together they contain 302 sentences, in which 97 DDs and 217 PNs related to biomedical entities (out of 418 NPs in total) were found.

For each NP, the following information was manually annotated:

- NP form: definite NP, proper name, or NP.
- biotype: gene, part-of-gene, subtype-of-gene, supertype-of-gene, product-of-gene, other-bio, or a non-bio noun.
- coreferent antecedent: a link to the closest previous coreferent mention (if there is one).
- associative antecedent: a link to the closest previous associative anaphoric mention (if there is one, and only if there is no closer coreferent mention).

All coreferent mentions become linked together as a coreference chain, which allows us to check for previous coreferent antecedents of a mention besides the closest one.

Table 1 shows the distributions of the anaphoric expressions according to the anaphoric relations they hold to their closest antecedent.

	coreferent	associative	no ant.	Total
DDs	34	51	12	97
PNs	132	62	23	217
Total	166	113	35	314

Table 1: Anaphoric relation distribution

DDs and PNs in associative relations account for 27% of all NPs in the test data, which is almost double the number of bridging cases (associative plus coreferent cases where head nouns are not the same) reported for newspaper texts in Vieira and Poesio (2000).

Table 2 shows the distribution of the different biotypes present in the corpus.

gene	part	subtype	supertype	product
67	62	1	7	244

Table 2: Biotype distribution

	coreferent	associative	no ant.
DDs	20/+2	14/+13	7
PNs	115/+9	11/+22	16

Table 3: Resolved anaphoric relations

3.1 Results

The anaphora resolution system reaches 58.8% precision and 57.3% recall when looking for the closest antecedent for DDs and PNs, after having been provided with hand-corrected input (that is, perfect gene name recognition, NP typing and selection). If we account separately for coreference and associative relations, we get 59.47% precision and 81.3% recall for the coreferent cases, and 55.5% precision and 22.1% recall for the associative ones.

The performance of the system is improved if we consider that it is able to find an antecedent other than the closest, which is still coreferential to the anaphor. These are cases like the following:

``**five proteins** encoded by *the male-specific lethal genes* ... **The MSL proteins** ...''

where the system returns "five proteins" as the coreferent antecedent for "the MSL proteins", instead of returning "the male-specific lethal genes" as the closest (in this case, associative) antecedent. Treating these cases as positive examples we reach 77.5% precision and 75.6% recall[6]. It conforms with the goal of adding the anaphor to a coreferential chain rather than simply relating it to the closest antecedent.

Table 3 reports the number of coreferent and associative DDs and PNs that could be resolved. The numbers on the left of the slash refer to relations with the closest antecedent, and the numbers on the right refer to additional relations found when links with another antecedent are considered (all the new positive cases on the right are coreferent, since our evaluation data just contain associative links to the closest antecedent).

Most of the cases that could be resolved are coreferent, and when the restriction to find the closest antecedent is relaxed, the system manages to resolve 35 cases of DD coreference (64.7% recall). It achieves very high recall (93.9%) on coreferential PNs. All the associative relations that are hand annotated in our evaluation corpus are between an anaphor and its closest antecedent, so when the recency preference is relaxed, we get coreferent instead of associative antecedents: we got 35 coreferent antecedents for anaphors that had a closest associative antecedent that could not be recovered. This conforms to the goal of having coreference chains that link all the mentions of a single entity.

The system could resolve around 27% of the associative cases of DDs, although fewer associative antecedents could be recovered for PNs, mainly due to the frequent absence of head-noun modifiers and different forms for the same gene name (expanded vs. abbreviated).

Although associative anaphora is considered to be harder than coreference, we believe that certain refinements of our resolution algorithm (such as normalizing gene names in order to take more advantage of the string matching among NP heads and modifiers) could improve its performance on these cases too.

The anaphora resolution system is not able to find the correct antecedent when there is no head or modifier matching as in the anaphoric relation between ``Dark/HAC-1/Dapaf-1'' and ``The Drosophila homolog''.

The performance rates drop when using the output of the NER system (presented in Section 2.1), RASP parsing (Section 2.2) and SO-based NP typing (Section 2.3), resulting in 63% precision and 53.4% recall.

When the NER system fails to recognise a gene name, it can decrease the parser performance (as it would have to deal with an unknown word) and influences the semantic tagging (the NP containing such a gene name won't be selected as a possible antecedent or anaphor unless it contains another word that is part of SO). When just the NER step is corrected by hand, the system reaches 71.8% precision

[6] We are able to compute these rates since our evaluation corpus includes also a coreferent antecedent for each case where an associative antecedent was selected.

and 64.1% recall.

4 Related work

Previous approaches to solve associative anaphora have made use of knowledge resources like WordNet (Poesio et al., 1997), the Internet (Bunescu, 2003) and a corpus (Poesio et al., 2002) to check if there is an associative link between the anaphor and a possible antecedent.

In the medical domain, Castaño et al. (2002) used UMLS (Unified Medical Language System)[7] as their knowledge source. They treat coreferential pronominal anaphora and anaphoric DDs and aim to improve the extraction of biomolecular relations from MEDLINE abstracts. The resolution process relies on syntactic features, semantic information from UMLS, and the string itself. They try to resolve just the DDs that refer to relevant biotypes (corresponding to UMLS types) such as amino acids, proteins or cells. For selecting the antecedents, they calculate salience values based on string similarity, person/number agreement, semantic type matching and other features. They report precision of 74% and recall of 75% on a very small test set.

Yang et al. (2004) test a supervised learning-based approach for anaphora resolution, evaluating it on MEDLINE abstracts from the GENIA corpus. They focus only on coreferent cases and do not attempt to resolve associative links. 18 features describe the relationship between an anaphoric expression and its possible antecedent - their source of semantic knowledge is the biotype information provided by the NER component of GENIA. They achieved recall of 80.2% and precision of 77.4%. They also experiment with exploring the relationships between NPs and coreferential clusters (i.e. chains), selecting an antecedent based not just on a single candidate but also on the cluster that the candidate is part of. For this they add 6 cluster-related features to the machine-learning process, and reach 84.4% recall and 78.2% precision.

Our system makes use of extant biomedical resources focused on the relevant microdomain (fruit fly genomics), and attempts to tackle the harder problem of associative anaphora, as this constitutes a significant proportion of cases and is relevant to the curation task. Our performance rates are lower than the ones above, but did not rely on expensive training data.

5 Concluding remarks

Our system for anaphora resolution is semi-supervised and relies on rich domain resources: the FlyBase database for NER, and the Sequence Ontology for semantic tagging. It does not need training data, which is a considerable advantage, as annotating anaphora by hand is a complicated and time-demanding task, requiring very precise and detailed guidelines.

The resulting links between the anaphoric entities are integrated into an interactive tool which aims to facilitate the curation process by highlighting and connecting related bio-entities: the curators are able to navigate among different mentions of the same entity and related ones in order to find easily the information they need to curate.

We are currently working on increasing our evaluation corpus; we aim to make it available to the research community together with our annotation guidelines.

We intend to enhance our system with additional syntactic features to deal with anaphoric relations between textual entities that do not have any string overlap. We also intend to add different weights to the features. The performance of the fully-automated version of the system can be improved if we manage to disambiguate between gene and protein names and infer the correct biotype for them. The performance on associative cases could be improved by normalizing the gene names in order to find more matches among heads and modifiers.

Acknowledgements

This work is part of the BBSRC-funded FlySlip[8] project. Caroline Gasperin is funded by a CAPES award from the Brazilian government. Thanks to Nikiforos Karamanis and Ted Briscoe for their comments and help with this manuscript.

[7] http://www.nlm.nih.gov/research/umls/

[8] http://www.cl.cam.ac.uk/users/av308/Project_Index/Project_Index.html

References

Ted Briscoe and John Carroll. 2002. Robust accurate statistical annotation of general text. In *Proceedings of LREC 2002*, pages 1499–1504, Las Palmas de Gran Canaria.

Ted Briscoe. 2006. Tag sequence grammars. Technical report, Computer Laboratory, Cambridge University.

Razvan Bunescu. 2003. Associative anaphora resolution: A web-based approach. In *Proceedings of EACL 2003 - Workshop on The Computational Treatment of Anaphora*, Budapest.

José Castaño, Jason Zhang, and James Pustejovsky. 2002. Anaphora resolution in biomedical literature. In *Proceedings of International Symposium on Reference Resolution for NLP 2002*, Alicante, Spain.

Karen Eilbeck and Suzanna E. Lewis. 2004. Sequence ontology annotation guide. *Comparative and Functional Genomics*, 5:642–647.

Alex Morgan, Lynette Hirschman, Alexander Yeh, and Marc Colosimo. 2003. Gene name extraction using FlyBase resources. In *Proceedings of ACL 2003 Workshop on Natural Language Processing in Biomedicine*, Sapporo, Japan.

Alex Morgan, Lynette Hirschman, Mark Colosimo, Alexander Yeh, and Jeff Colombe. 2004. Gene name identification and normalization using a model organism database. *J. of Biomedical Informatics*, 37(6):396–410.

Massimo Poesio, Renata Vieira, and Simone Teufel. 1997. Resolving bridging descriptions in unrestricted texts. In *Proceedings of the Workshop on Operational Factors in the Practical, Robust, Anaphora Resolution for Unrestricted Texts*, Madrid.

Massimo Poesio, Tomonori Ishikawa, Sabine Schulte im Walde, and Renata Vieira. 2002. Acquiring lexical knowledge for anaphora resolution. In *Proceedings of LREC 2002*, Las Palmas De Gran Canaria.

Renata Vieira and Massimo Poesio. 2000. An empirically-based system for processing definite descriptions. *Computational Linguistics*, 26(4):525–579.

Andreas Vlachos, Caroline Gasperin, Ian Lewin, and Ted Briscoe. 2006. Bootstrapping the recognition and anaphoric linking of named entities in Drosophila articles. In *Proceedings of the PSB 2006*, Hawaii.

Xiaofeng Yang, Jian Su, Gouodong Zhou, and Chew Lim Tan. 2004. An NP-cluster based approach to coreference resolution. In *Proceedings of COLING 2004*, Geneva, Switzerland, August.

Using Dependency Parsing and Probabilistic Inference to Extract Relationships between Genes, Proteins and Malignancies Implicit Among Multiple Biomedical Research Abstracts

Ben Goertzel
Applied Research Lab for National and Homeland Security
Virginia Tech
Arlington VA 22216
ben@goertzel.org

Hugo Pinto
Novamente LLC
1405 Bernerd Place
Rockville MD 20851
hugo@vettalabs.com

Ari Heljakka
Novamente LLC
1405 Bernerd Place
Rockville MD 20851
heljakka@iki.fi

Izabela Freire Goertzel
Novamente LLC
1405 Bernerd Place
Rockville MD 20851
izabela@goertzel.org

Mike Ross
SAIC
5971 Kingstowne Village Parkway
Kingstowne, VA 22315
miross@objectsciences.com

Cassio Pennachin
Novamente LLC
1405 Bernerd Place
Rockville MD 20851
cassio@vettalabs.com

Abstract

We describe BioLiterate, a prototype software system which infers relationships involving relationships between genes, proteins and malignancies from research abstracts, and has initially been tested in the domain of the molecular genetics of oncology. The architecture uses a natural language processing module to extract entities, dependencies and simple semantic relationships from texts, and then feeds these features into a probabilistic reasoning module which combines the semantic relationships extracted by the NLP module to form new semantic relationships. One application of this system is the discovery of relationships that are not contained in any individual abstract but are implicit in the combined knowledge contained in two or more abstracts.

1 Introduction

Biomedical literature is growing at a breakneck pace, making the task of remaining current with all discoveries relevant to a given research area nearly impossible without the use of advanced NLP-based tools (Jensen et al, 2006). Two classes of tools that provide great value in this regard are those that help researchers find relevant documents and sentences in large bodies of biomedical texts (Müller, 2004; Schuler, 1996; Tanabe, 1999), and those that automatically extract knowledge from a set of documents (Smalheiser and Swanson, 1998; Rzhetsky et al, 2004). Our work falls into the latter category. We have created a prototype software system called BioLiterate, which applies dependency parsing and advanced probabilistic inference to the problem of combining semantic relationships extracted from biomedical texts, have tested this system via experimentation on research abstracts in the domain of the molecular genetics of oncology.

In order to concentrate our efforts on the inference aspect of biomedical text mining, we have built our BioLiterate system on top of a number of general NLP and specialized bioNLP components created by others. For example, we have handled entity extraction -- perhaps the most mature existing bioNLP technology (Kim, 2004) -- via incorporating a combination of existing open-source tools. And we have handled syntax parsing via integrat-

Proceedings of the BioNLP Workshop on Linking Natural Language Processing and Biology at HLT-NAACL 06, pages 104–111,
New York City, June 2006.

ing a modified version of the link parser (Sleator and Temperley, 1992).

The BioLiterate system is quite general in applicability, but in our work so far we have focused on the specific task of extracting relationships regarding interactions between genes, proteins and malignancies contained in, or implicit among multiple, biomedical research abstracts. This application is critical because the extraction of protein/gene/disease relationships from text is necessary for the discovery of metabolic pathways and non-trivial disease causal chains, among other applications (Nédellec, 2005; Davulcu, 2005, Ahmed, 2005).

Systems extracting these sorts of relationships from text have been developed using a variety of technologies, including support vector machines (Donaldson et al, 2003), maximum entropy models and graph algorithms (McDonald, 2005), Markov models and first order logic (Riedel, 2005) and finite state automata (Hakenberg, 2005). However, these systems are limited in the relationships that they can extract. Most of them focus on relationships described in single sentences. The results we report here support the hypothesis that the methods embodied in BioLiterate, when developed beyond the prototype level and implemented in a scalable way, may be significantly more powerful, particularly in the extraction of relationships whose textual description exists in multiple sentences or multiple documents.

Overall, the extraction of both entities and single-sentence-embodied inter-entity relationships has proved far more difficult in the biomedical domain than in other domains such as newspaper text (Nédellec, 2005; Jing et al, 2003; Pyysalo, 2004). One reason for this is the lack of resources, such as large tagged corpora, to allow statistical NLP systems to perform as well as in the news domain. Another is that biomedical text has many features that are quite uncommon or even nonexistent in newspaper text (Pyysalo, 2004), such as numerical post-modifiers of nouns (*Serine 38*), non-capitalized entity names (*...ftsY is solely expressed during...*), hyphenated verbs (*X cross-links Y*), nominalizations, and uncommon usage of parentheses (*sigma(H)-dependent expression of spo0A*). While recognizing the critical importance of overcoming these issues more fully, we have not addressed them in any novel way in the context of our work on BioLiterate, but have rather chosen to focus attention on the other end of the pipeline: using inference to piece together relationships extracted from separate sentences, to construct new relationships implicit among multiple sentences or documents.

The BioLiterate system incorporates three main components: an NLP system that outputs entities, dependencies and basic semantic relations; a probabilistic reasoning system (PLN = Probabilistic Logic Networks); and a collection of hand-built semantic mapping rules used to mediate between the two prior components.

One of the hypotheses underlying our work is that the use of probabilistic inference in a bioNLP context may allow the capturing of relationships not covered by existing systems, particularly those that are implicit or spread among several abstracts. This application of BioLiterate is reminiscent of the Arrowsmith system (Smalheiser and Swanson, 1998), which is focused on creating novel biomedical discoveries via combining pieces of information from different research texts; however, Arrowsmith is oriented more toward guiding humans to make discoveries via well-directed literature search, rather than more fully automating the discovery process via unified NLP and inference.

Our work with the BioLiterate prototype has tentatively validated this hypothesis via the production of interesting examples, e.g. of conceptually straightforward deductions combining premises contained in different research papers.[1] Our future research will focus on providing more systematic statistical validation of this hypothesis.

2 System Overview

For the purpose of running initial experiments with the BioLiterate system, we restricted our attention to texts from the domain of molecular genetics of oncology, mostly selected from the PubMEd subset selected for the PennBioNE project (Mandel, 2006). Of course, the BioLiterate architecture in general is not restricted to any particular type or subdomain of texts.

The system is composed of a series of components arranged in a pipeline: Tokenizer →Gene,

[1] It is worth noting that inference which appear conceptually to be "straightforward deductions" often manifest themselves within BioLiterate as PLN inference chains with 1-2 dozen inferences. This is mostly because of the relatively complex way in which logical relationships emerge from semantic mapping, and also because of the need for inferences that explicitly incorporate "obvious" background knowledge.

Protein and Malignancy Tagger → Nominalization Tagger → Sentence Extractor → Dependency Extractor → Relationship Extractor → Semantic Mapper → Probabilistic Reasoning System.

Each component, excluding the semantic mapper and probabilistic reasoner, is realized as a UIMA (Götz and Suhre, 2004) annotator, with information being accumulated in each document as each phase occurs.[2]

The gene/protein and malignancy taggers collectively constitute our "entity extraction" subsystem. Our entity extraction subsystem and the tokenizer were adapted from PennBioTagger (McDonald et al, 2005; Jin et al, 2005; Lerman et al, 2006). The tokenizer uses a maximum entropy model trained upon biomedical texts, mostly in the oncology domain. Both the protein and malignancy taggers were built using conditional random fields.

The nominalization tagger detects nominalizations that represent possible relationships that would otherwise go unnoticed. For instance, in the sentence excerpt "… intracellular signal transduction leading to transcriptional activation…" both "transduction" and "activation" are tagged. The nominalization tagger uses a set of rules based on word morphology and immediate context.

Before a sentence passes from these early processing stages into the dependency extractor, which carries out syntax parsing, a substitution process is carried out in which its tagged entities are replaced with simple unique identifiers. This way, many text features that often impact parser performance are left out, such as entity names that have numbers or parenthesis as post-modifiers.

The dependency extractor component carries out dependency grammar parsing via a customized version of the open-source Sleator and Temperley link parser (1993). The link parser outputs several parses, and the dependencies of the best one are taken.[3]

The relationship extractor component is composed of a number of template matching algorithms that act upon the link parser's output to produce a semantic interpretation of the parse. This component detects implied quantities, normalizes passive and active forms into the same representation and assigns tense and number to the sentence parts. Another way of conceptualizing this component is as a system that translates link parser dependencies into a graph of semantic primitives (Wierzbicka, 1996), using a natural semantic metalanguage (Goddard, 2002).

Table 1 below shows some of the primitive semantic relationships used, and their associated link parser links:

subj	Subject	S, R, RS
Obj	Direct object	O, Pv, B
Obj-2	Indirect object	O, B
that	Clausal Complement	TH, C
to-do	Subject Raising Complement (do)	I, TO, Pg

Table 1. Semantic Primitives and Link Parser Links

For a concrete example, suppose we have the sentences:

a) Kim kissed Pat.
b) Pat was kissed by Kim.

Both would lead to the extracted relationships:

```
subj(kiss, Kim), obj(kiss, Pat)
```

For a more interesting case consider:

c) Kim likes to laugh.
d) Kim likes laughing.

Both will have a `to-do (like, laugh)` semantic relation.

Next, this semantic representation, together with entity information, is feed into the Semantic Mapper component, which applies a series of hand-created rules whose purpose is to transform the output of the Relationship Extractor into logical relationships that are fully abstracted from their syntactic origin and suitable for abstract inference. The need for this additional layer may not be apparent a priori, but arises from the fact that the output of the Relationship Extractor is still in a sense "too close to the syntax." The rules used within the Relationship Extractor are crisp rules with little context-dependency, and could fairly easily be built into a dependency parser (though the link parser is not architected in such a way as to make this pragmatically feasible); on the other

[2] The semantic mapper will be incorporated into the UIMA framework in a later revision of the software.

[3] We have experimented with using other techniques for selecting dependencies, such as getting the most frequent ones, but variations in this aspect did not impact our results significantly.

hand, the rules used in the Semantic Mapper are often dependent upon semantic information about the words being interrelated, and would be more challenging to integrate into the parsing process.

As an example, the semantic mapping rule

```
by($X,$Y) & Inh($X, transitive_event) →
subj ($X,$Y)
```

maps the relationship `by(prevention, inhibition)`, which is output by the Relationship Extractor, into the relationship subj(prevention, inhibition), which is an abstract conceptual relationship suitable for semantic inference by PLN. It performs this mapping because it has knowledge that "prevention" inherits (`Inh`) from the semantic category `transitive_event`, which lets it guess what the appropriate sense of "by" might be.

Finally, the last stage in the BioLiterate pipeline is probabilistic inference, which is carried out by the Probabilistic Logic Networks[4] (PLN) system (Goertzel et al, in preparation) implemented within the Novamente AI Engine integrated AI architecture (Goertzel and Pennachin, 2005; Looks et al, 2004). PLN is a comprehensive uncertain inference framework that combines probabilistic and heuristic truth value estimation formulas within a knowledge representation framework capable of expressing general logical information, and possesses flexible inference control heuristics including forward-chaining, backward-chaining and reinforcement-learning-guided approaches.

Among the notable aspects of PLN is its use of two-valued truth values: each PLN statement is tagged with a truth value containing at least two components, one a probability estimate and the other a "weight of evidence" indicating the amount of evidence that the probability estimate is based on. PLN contains a number of different inference rules, each of which maps a premise-set of a certain logical form into a conclusion of a certain logical form, using an associated truth-value formula to map the truth values of the premises into the truth value of the conclusion.

The PLN component receives the logical relationships output by the semantic mapper, and performs reasoning operations on them, with the aim at arriving at new conclusions implicit in the set of relationships fed to it. Some of these conclusions may be implicit in a single text fed into the system; others may emerge from the combination of multiple texts.

In some cases the derivation of useful conclusions from the semantic relationships fed to PLN requires "background knowledge" relationships not contained in the input texts. Some of these background knowledge relationships represent specific biological or medical knowledge, and others represent generic "commonsense knowledge." The more background knowledge is fed into PLN, the broader the scope of inferences it can draw.

One of the major unknowns regarding the current approach is how much background knowledge will need to be supplied to the system in order to enable truly impressive performance across the full range of biomedical research abstracts. There are multiple approaches to getting this knowledge into the system, including hand-coding (the approach we have taken in our BioLiterate work so far) and automated extraction of relationships from relevant texts beyond research abstracts, such as databases, ontologies and textbooks. While this is an extremely challenging problem, we feel that due to the relatively delimited nature of the domain, the knowledge engineering issues faced here are far less severe than those confronting projects such as Cyc (Lenat, 1986; Guha, 1990; Guha, 1994) and SUMO (Niles, 2001) which seek to encode commonsense knowledge in a broader, non-domain-specific way.

3 A Practical Example

We have not yet conducted a rigorous statistical evaluation of the performance of the BioLiterate system. This is part of our research plan, but will involve considerable effort, due to the lack of any existing evaluation corpus for the tasks that BioLiterate performs. For the time being, we have explored BioLiterate's performance anecdotally via observing its behavior on various example "inference problems" implicit in groups of biomedical abstracts. This section presents one such example in moderate detail (full detail being infeasible due to space limitations).

Table 2 shows two sentences drawn from different PubMed abstracts, and then shows the conclusions that BioLiterate draws from the combination of these two sentences. The table shows the conclusions in natural language format, but the system

[4] Previously named Probabilistic Term Logic

actually outputs conclusions in logical relationship form as detailed below.

Premise 1	Importantly, bone loss was almost completely prevented by p38 MAPK inhibition. (PID 16447221)
Premise 2	Thus, our results identify DLC as a novel inhibitor of the p38 pathway and provide a molecular mechanism by which cAMP suppresses p38 activation and promotes apoptosis. (PID 16449637)
(Uncertain) Conclusions	DLC prevents bone loss. cAMP prevents bone loss.

Table 2. An example conclusion drawn by BioLiterate via combining relationships extracted from sentences contained in different PubMed abstracts. The PID shown by each premise sentence is the PubMed ID of the abstract from which it was drawn.

Tables 3-4 explore this example in more detail. Table 3 shows the relationship extractor output, and then the semantic mapper output, for the two premise sentences.

Premise 1 Rel Ex. Output	_subj-n(bone, loss) _obj(prevention, loss) _subj-r(almost, completely) _subj-r(completely, prevention) by(prevention, inhibition) _subj-n(p38 MAPK, inhibition)
Premise 2 Sem Map Output	subj (prevention, inhibition) obj (prevention, loss) obj (inhibition, p38_MAPK) obj (loss, bone)
Premise 1 Rel Ex Output	_subj(identify, results) as(identify, inhibitor) _obj(identify, DLC) _subj-a(novel, inhibitor) of(inhibitor, pathway) _subj-n(p38, pathway)
Premise 2 Sem Map Output	subj (inhibition, DLC) obj (inhibition, pathway) inh(pathway, p38)

Table 3. Intermediary processing stages for the two premise sentences in the example in Table 2.

Table 4 shows a detailed "inference trail" constituting part of the reasoning done by PLN to draw the inference "DLC prevents bone loss" from these extracted semantic relationships, invoking background knowledge from its knowledge base as appropriate.

The notation used in Table 4 is so that, for instance, `Inh` $inhib_1$ $inhib_2$ is synonymous with `inh(`$inhib_1$`,` $inhib_2$`)` and denotes an Inheritance relationship between the terms $inhibition_1$ and $inhibition_2$ (the textual shorthands used in the table are described in the caption). The logical relationships used are Inheritance, Implication, AND (conjunction) and Evaluation. Evaluation is the relation between a predicate and its arguments; e.g. *`Eval subj(`*$inhib_2$*`, DLC)`* means that the `subj` predicate holds when applied to the list `(`$inhib_2$`, DLC)`. These particular logical relationships are reviewed in more depth in (Goertzel and Pennachin, 2005; Looks et al, 2004). Finally, indent notation is used to denote argument structure, so that e.g.

```
R
    A
    B
```

is synonymous with `R(A,B)`.

PLN is an uncertain inference system, which means that each of the terms and relationships used as premises, conclusions or intermediaries in PLN inference come along with uncertain truth values. In this case the truth value of the conclusion at the end of Table 4 comes out to <.8,.07>, which indicates that the system guesses the conclusion is true with probability .8, and that its confidence that this probability assessment is roughly correct is .07. Confidence values are scaled between 0 and 1: .07 is a relatively low confidence, which is appropriate given the speculative nature of the inference. Note that this is far higher than the confidence that would be attached to a randomly generated relationship, however.

The only deep piece of background knowledge utilized by PLN in the course of this inference is the knowledge that:

```
Implication
    AND
        Inh X1 causal_event
        Inh X2 causal_event
        subj(X1, X3)
        subj(X2, X1)
    subj(X2,X3)
```

which encodes the transitivity of causation in terms of the `subj` relationship. The other knowledge used consisted of simple facts such as the inheritance of inhibition and prevention from the category `causal_event`.

Rule	Premises	Conclusion
Abduction	Inh inhib$_1$, inhib Inh inhib$_2$, inhib	Inh inhib$_1$, inhib$_2$ <.19, .99>
Similarity Substitution	Eval subj (prev$_1$, inhib$_1$) Inh inhib$_1$, inhib$_2$	Eval subj (prev$_1$ inhib$_2$) <1, .07>
Deduction	Inh inhib$_2$, inhib Inh inhib, causal_event	Inh inhib$_2$, causal_event <1,1>
AND	Inh inhib$_2$, causal_event Inh prev$_1$, causal_event Eval subj (prev$_1$, inhib$_2$) Eval subj (inhib$_2$, DLC)	AND <1, .07> Inh inhib$_2$, causal_event Inh prev$_1$, causal_event Eval subj (prev$_1$, inhib$_2$) Eval subj (inhib$_2$, DLC)
Unification	ForAll (X_0, X_1, X_2) Imp AND Inh X_0, causal_event Inh X_1, causal_event Eval subj (X_1, X_0) Eval subj (X_0, X_2) Eval subj (X_1, X_2) AND Inh inhib$_2$, causal_event Inh prev$_1$, causal_event Eval subj (prev$_1$, inhib$_2$) Eval subj (inhib$_2$, DLC)	Eval subj (prev$_1$, inhib$_2$) <1,.07>
Implication Breakdown (Modus Ponens)	Imp AND Inh inhib$_2$, causal_event Inh prev$_1$, causal_event Eval subj (prev$_1$, inhib$_2$) Eval subj (inhib$_2$, DLC) Eval subj (prev$_1$, DLC)	Eval subj (prev$_1$, DLC) <.8, .07>

Table 4. Part of the PLN inference trail underlying Example 1. This shows the series of inferences leading up to the conclusion that the prevention act prev1 is carried out by the subject DLC. A shorthand notation is used here: Eval = Evaluation, Imp = Implication, Inh = Inheritance, inhib = inhibition, prev = prevention. For instance, prev$_1$ and prev$_2$ denote terms that are particular instances of the general concept of prevention. Relationships used in premises along the trail, but not produced as conclusions along the trail, were introduced into the trail via the system looking in its knowledge base to obtain the previously computed truth value of a relationship, which was found via prior knowledge or a prior inference trail.

4 Discussion

We have described a prototype bioNLP system, BioLiterate, aimed at demonstrating the viability of using probabilistic inference to draw conclusions based on logical relationships extracted from multiple biomedical research abstracts using NLP technology. The preliminary results we have obtained via applying BioLiterate in the domain of the genetics of oncology suggest that the approach is potentially viable for the extraction of hypothetical interactions between genes, proteins and malignancies from sets of sentences spanning multiple abstracts. One of our foci in future research will be the rigorous validation of the performance of the BioLiterate system in this domain, via construction of an appropriate evaluation corpus.

In our work with BioLiterate so far, we have identified a number of examples where PLN is able to draw biological conclusions by combining simple semantic relationships extracted from different biological research abstracts. Above we reviewed one of these examples. This sort of application is particularly interesting because it involves software potentially creating relationships that may not have been explicitly known by any human, because they existed only implicitly in the connections between many different human-written documents. In this sense, the BioLiterate approach blurs the boundary between NLP information extraction and automated scientific discovery.

Finally, by experimenting with the BioLiterate prototype we have come to some empirical conclusions regarding the difficulty of several parts of the pipeline. First, entity extraction remains a challenge, but not a prohibitively difficult one. Our system definitely missed some important relationships because of imperfect entity extraction but this was not the most problematic component.

Sentence parsing was a more serious issue for BioLiterate performance. The link parser in its pure form had very severe shortcomings, but we were able to introduce enough small modifications to obtain adequate performance. Substituting uncommon and multi-word entity names with simple noun identifiers (a suggestion we drew from Pyysalo, 2004) reduced the error rate significantly, via bypassing problems related to wrong guessing of unknown words, improper handling of parentheses, and excessive possible-parse production. Other improvements we may incorporate in future include augmenting the parser's dictionary to include biomedical terms (Slozovits, 2003), pre-processing so as to split long and complex sentences into shorter, simpler ones (Ding et al, 2003), modifying the grammar to handle with unknown constructs, and changing the link parser's ranking system (Pyysalo, 2004).

The inferences involved in our BioLiterate work so far have been relatively straightforward for PLN once the premises have been created. More complex inferences may certainly be drawn in the biomedical domain, but the weak link inference-wise seems to be the provision of inference with the appropriate premises, rather than the inference process itself.

The most challenging aspects of the work involved semantic mapping and the supplying of relevant background knowledge. The creation of appropriate semantic mapping rules can be subtle because these rules sometimes rely on the semantic categories of the words involved in the relationships they transform. The execution of even commonsensically simple biomedical inferences often requires the combination of abstract and concrete background knowledge. These are areas we will focus on in our future work, as achieving a scalable approach will be critical in transforming the current BioLiterate prototype into a production-quality system capable of assisting biomedical researchers to find appropriate information, and of drawing original and interesting conclusions by combining pieces of information scattered across the research literature.

Acknowledgements

This research was partially supported by a contract with the NIH Clinical Center in September-November 2005, arranged by Jim DeLeo.

References

Chan-Goo Kang and Jong C. Park. 2005. *Generation of Coherent Gene Summary with Concept-Linking Sentences*. Proceedings of the International Symposium on Languages in Biology and Medicine (LBM), pages 41-45, Daejeon, Korea, November, 2005.

Claire Nédellec. 2005. *Learning Language in Logic - Genic Interaction Extraction Challenge*. Proceedings of The 22nd International Conference on Machine Learning, Bonn, Germany.

Cliff Goddard. 2002. *The On-going Development of the NSM Research Program*. Ch 5 (pp. 301-321) of *Meaning and Universal Grammar - Theory and Empirical Findings. Volume II*. Amsterdam: John Benjamins.

Davulcu, H et Al. 2005. *IntEx?: A Syntactic Role Driven Protein-Protein Interaction Extractor for Bio-Medical Text*. Proceedings of the ACL-ISMB Workshop on Linking Biological Literature, Ontologies and Databases: Mining Biological Semantics. Detroit.

Donaldson, Ian, Joel Martin, Berry de Bruijn, Cheryl Wolting et al. 2003. *PreBIND and Textomy - mining the biomedical literature for protein-protein interactions using a support vector machine*. BMC Bioinformatics, 4:11,

Friedman C, Kra P, Yu H, Krauthammer M, Rzhetsky. 2001. *A. GENIES: a natural-language processing system for the extraction of molecular pathways from journal articles*. Bioinformatics Jun;17 Suppl 1:S74-82.

Goertzel, Ben and Cassio Pennachin. 2005. *Artificial General Intelligence*. Springer-Verlag.

Goertzel, Ben, Matt Ikle', Izabela Goertzel and Ari Heljakka. 2006. *Probabilistic Logic Networks*. In preparation.

Götz, T and Suhre, O. 2004. *Design and implementation of the UIMA Common Analysis System*. IBM Systems Journal. V 43, number 3. pages 476-489 .

Guha, R. V., & Lenat, D. B. 1994. *Enabling agents to work together*. Communications of the ACM, 37(7), 127-142.

Guha, R.V. and Lenat,D.B. 1990. *Cyc: A Midterm Report*. AI Magazine 11(3):32-59.

Hakenberg, . et al. 2205. *LLL'05 Challenge: Genic Interaction Extraction -- Identification of Language Patterns Based on Alignment and Finite State Automata*. Proceedings of The 22nd International Conference on Machine Learning, Bonn, Germany. 2005.

Hoffmann, R., Valencia, A. 2005. *Implementing the iHOP concept for navigation of biomedical literature*. Bioinformatics 21(suppl. 2), ii252-ii258 (2005).

Ian Niles and Adam Pease. 2001. *Towards a Standard Upper Ontology*. In Proceedings of the 2nd International Conference on Formal Ontology in Information Systems (FOIS-2001), Ogunquit, Maine, October 2001

Jensen, L.J., Saric, J and Bork, P. 2006. *Literature Mining for the biologist: from information retrieval to biological discovery*. Nature Reviews. Vol 7. pages 119-129. Natura Publishing Group. 2006.

Jing Ding. 2003. *Extracting biomedical interactions with from medline using a link grammar parser*. Proceedings of 15th IEEE international Conference on Tools With Artificial Intelligence.

Kim, Jim-Dong et al. 2004. *Introduction to the Bio-NLP Entity Task at JNLPBA 2004*. In Proceedings of JNLPBA 2004.

Lenat, D., Prakash, M., & Shepard, M. 1986. *CYC: Using common sense knowledge to overcome brittleness and knowledge acquisition bottlenecks*. AI Magazine, 6(4), 65-85

Lerman, K , McDonal, R., Jin, Y. and Pancoast, E. University of Pennsylvania *BioTagger*. 2006. http://www.seas.upenn.edu/~ryantm/software/BioTagger/

Looks, Moshe, Ben Goertzel and Cassio Pennachin. 2004. Novamente: An Integrative Approach to Artificial General Intelligence. *AAAI Symposium on Achieving Human-Level Intelligence Through Integrated Systems and Research*, Washington DC, October 2004

Mandel, Mark. 2006. *Mining the Bibliome*. February, 2006 http://bioie.ldc.upenn.edu

Mark A. Greenwood, Mark Stevenson, Yikun Guo, Henk Harkema, and Angus Roberts. 2005. *Automatically Acquiring a Linguistically Motivated Genic Interaction Extraction System*. In Proceedings of the 4th Learning Language in Logic Workshop (LLL05), Bonn, Germany.

McDonald, F. Pereira, S. Kulick, S. Winters, Y. Jin and P. White. 2005. Simple Algorithms for Complex Relation Extraction with Applications to Biomedical IE. R. 43rd Annual Meeting of the Association for Computational Linguistics, 2005.

Müller, H. M., Kenny, E. E. and Sternberg, P. W. 2004. *Textpresso: An Ontology-Based Information Retrieval and Extraction System for Biological Literature*. PLoS Biol 2(11): e309

Pyysalo, S. et al. 2004. *Analisys of link Grammar on Biomedical Dependency Corpus Targeted at Protein-Protein Interactions*. In Proceedings of JNLPBA 2004.

Riedel, et al. 2005. *Genic Interaction Extraction with Semantic and Syntactic Chains*. Proceedings of The 22nd International Conference on Machine Learning, Bonn, Germany.

Ryan McDonald and Fernando Pereira. 2005. *Identifying gene and protein mentions in text using conditional random fields*. BMC Bioinformatics 2005, 6(Suppl 1):S6

Rzhetsky A, Iossifov I, Koike T, Krauthammer M, Kra P, Morris M, Yu H, Duboue PA, Weng W, Wilbur WJ, Hatzivassiloglou V, Friedman C. 2004. *GeneWays: a system for extracting, analyzing, visualizing, and integrating molecular pathway data*. Journal of Biomedical Informatics 37(1):43-53.

Sleator, Daniel and Dave Temperley. 1993. *Parsing English with a Link Grammar*. Third International Workshop on Parsing Technologies, Tilburg, The Netherlands.

Smalheiser, N. L and Swanson D. R. 1996. *Linking estrogen to Alzheimer's disease: an informatics approach*. Neurology 47(3):809-10.

Smalheiser, N. L and Swanson, D. R. 1998. *Using ARROWSMITH: a computer-assisted approach to formulating and assessing scientific hypotheses*. Comput Methods Programs Biomed. 57(3):149-53.

Syed Ahmed et al. 2005. *IntEx: A Syntactic Role Driven Protein-Protein Interaction Extractor for Bio-Medical Text*. Proc. of BioLink '2005, Detroit, Michigan, June 24, 2005

Szolovits, Peter. 2003. *Adding a medical lexicon to an English parser*. Proceedings of 2003 AMIA Annual Symposium. Bethesda. MD.

Tanabe, L. U. Scherf, L. H. Smith, J. K. Lee, L. Hunter and J. N. Weinstein. 1999. *MedMiner: an Internet Text-Mining Tool for Biomedical Information, with Application to Gene Expression Profiling*. BioTechniques 27:1210-1217.

Wierzbicka, Anna. 1996. *Semantics, Primes and Universals*. Oxford University Press.

Recognizing Nested Named Entities in GENIA corpus

Baohua Gu

School of Computing Science

Simon Fraser University, Burnaby, BC, Canada

bgu@cs.sfu.ca

Abstract

Nested Named Entities (nested NEs), one containing another, are commonly seen in biomedical text, e.g., accounting for 16.7% of all named entities in GENIA corpus. While many works have been done in recognizing non-nested NEs, nested NEs have been largely neglected. In this work, we treat the task as a binary classification problem and solve it using Support Vector Machines. For each token in nested NEs, we use two schemes to set its class label: labeling as the outmost entity or the inner entity. Our preliminary results show that while the *outmost labeling* tends to work better in recognizing the outmost entities, the *inner labeling* recognizes the inner NEs better. This result should be useful for recognition of nested NEs.

1 Introduction

Named Entity Recognition (NER) is a key task in biomedical text mining, as biomedical named entities usually represent biomedical concepts of research interest (e.g., protein/gene/virus, etc).

Nested NEs (also called embedded NEs, or cascade NEs) exhibit an interesting phenomenon in biomedical literature. For example, "human immuneodeficiency virus type 2 enhancer" is a DNA domain, while "human immunodeficiency virus type 2" represents a virus. For simplicity, we call the former the *outmost* entity (if it is not inside another entity), while the later the *inner* entity (it may have another one inside).

Nested NEs account for 16.7% of all entities in GENIA corpus (Kim, 2003). Moreover, they often represent important relations between entities (Nedadic, 2004), as in the above example. However, there are few results on recognizing them. Many studies only consider the outmost entities, as in BioNLP/NLPBA 2004 Shared Task (Kim, 2004).

In this work, we use a machine learning method to recognize nested NEs in GENIA corpus. We view the task as a classification problem for each token in a given sentence, and train a SVM model. We note that nested NEs make it hard to be considered as a multi-class problem, because a token in nested entities has more than one class label. We therefore treat it as a binary-class problem, using one-vs-rest scheme.

1.1 Related Work

Overall, our work is an application of machine learning methods to biomedical NER. While most of earlier approaches rely on handcrafted rules or dictionaries, many recent works adopt machine learning approaches, e.g, SVM (Lee, 2003), HMM (Zhou, 2004), Maximum Entropy (Lin, 2004) and CRF (Settles,2004), especially with the availability of annotated corpora such as GENIA, achieving state-of-the-art performance. We know only one work (Zhou,2004) that deals with nested NEs to improve the overall NER performance. However, their approach is basically rule-based and they did not report how well the nested NEs are recognized.

2 Methodology

We use SVM-light (http://svmlight.joachims.org/) to train a binary classifier on the GENIA corpus.

2.1 Data Set

The GENIA corpus (version 3.02) contains 97876 named entities (35947 distinct) of 36 types, and 490941 tokens (19883 distinct). There are 16672

Proceedings of the BioNLP Workshop on Linking Natural Language Processing and Biology at HLT-NAACL 06, pages 112–113,
New York City, June 2006.

nested entities, containing others or nested in others (the maximum embedded levels is four). Among all the outmost entities, 2342 are protein and 1849 are DNA, while there are 9298 proteins and 1452 DNAs embedded in other entities.

2.2 Features and Class Label

For each token, we generate four types of features, reflecting its characteristics on orthography, part-of-speech, morphology, and special nouns. We also use a window of (-2, +2) as its context.

For each token, we use two schemes to set the class label: *outmost labeling* and *inner labeling*. In the outmost labeling, a token is labeled +1 if the *outmost* entity containing it is the target entity, while in the inner labeling, a token is labeled +1 if *any* entity containing it is the target entity. Otherwise, the token is labeled -1.

3 Experiment And Discussion

We report our preliminary experimental results on recognizing *protein* and *DNA* nested entities. For each target entity type (e.g., protein) and each labeling scheme, we obtain a data set containing 490941 instances. We run 5-fold cross-validation, and measure performance (P/R/F) of exact match, left/right boundary match w.r.t. outmost and inner entities respectively. The results are shown in Table 1 and Table 2.

		Outmost labeling (P/R/F)	**Inner labeling (P/R/F)**
Outmost Entities Recognized	Exact	0.772 /0.014 /0.028	0.705 /0.017 /0.033
	Left	0.363 /0.373 /0.368	0.173 /0.484 /0.254
	Right	0.677 /0.199 /0.308	0.674 /0.208 /0.318
	Overall	**0.60/0.20/0.23**	**0.52/0.24/0.20**
Inner Entities Recognized	Exact	0.692 /0.229 /0.344	0.789 /0.679 /0.730
	Left	0.682 /0.289 /0.406	0.732 /0.702 /0.717
	Right	0.671 /0.255 /0.370	0.769 /0.719 /0.743
	Overall	**0.68/0.26/0.37**	**0.76/0.70/0.73**

Table 1 Performance of nested protein entities

From the tables, we can see that while the outmost labeling works (slightly) better for the outmost entities, the inner labeling works better for the inner entities. This result seems reasonable in that each labeling scheme tends to introduces more entities of its type in the training set.

It is interesting to see that the inner labeling works much better in identifying inner proteins than in inner DNAs. The reason could be due to the fact that there are about three times more inner proteins than the outmost ones, while the numbers of inner DNAs and outmost DNAs are roughly the same (see Section 2.1).

Another observation is that the inner labeling gains significantly (over the outmost labeling) in the inner entities, comparing to its loss in the outmost entities. We are not sure whether this is the general trend for other types of entities, and if so, what causes it. We will address this issue in our following work.

		Outmost labeling (P/R/F)	**Inner labeling (P/R/F)**
Outmost Entities Recognized	Exact	0.853 /0.005 /0.009	0.853 /0.005 /0.009
	Left	0.682 /0.542 /0.604	0.543 /0.555 /0.549
	Right	0.324 /0.070 /0.114	0.321 /0.070 /0.115
	Overall	**0.62/0.21/0.24**	**0.57/0.21/0.22**
Inner Entities Recognized	Exact	0.269 /0.333 /0.298	0.386 /0.618 /0.475
	Left	0.272 /0.405 /0.325	0.336 /0.618 /0.435
	Right	0.237 /0.376 /0.290	0.350 /0.694 /0.465
	Overall	**0.26/0.37/0.30**	**0.36/0.64/0.46**

Table 2 Performance of nested DNA entities

We hope these results can help in recognizing nested NEs, and also attract more attention to the nested NE problem. We are going to further our study by looking into more related issues.

References

J. Kim, et al. 2003. GENIA corpus – a semantically annotated corpus for bio-textmining. Bioinformatics, Vol 19.

J. Kim, et al. 2004. Introduction to the Bio-Entity Recognition Task at JNLPBA. Proceedings of JNLPBA.

K. Lee, et al. 2003. Two-Phase Biomedical NE Recognition based on SVMS. Proceedings of ACL Workshop on NLP in Biomedical.

Y. Lin, et al. 2004. A Maximum Entropy Approach to Biomedical Named Entity Recognition. Proceedings of KDD Workshop on Data Mining and Bioinformatics.

G. Nenadic, et al. 2004. Mining Biomedical Abstracts: What's in a Term? Proceedings of IJCNLP 2004.

B. Settles. 2004. Biomedical Named Entity Recognition Using Conditional Random Fields and Rich Feature Sets. Proceedings of Joint Workshop on NLPBA.

G. Zhou, et al. 2004. Recognizing Names in Biomedical Texts: a Machine Learning Approach. *Bioinformatics*, Vol. 20, no. 7.

Biomedical Term Recognition With the Perceptron HMM Algorithm

Sittichai Jiampojamarn and **Grzegorz Kondrak** and **Colin Cherry**
Department of Computing Science,
University of Alberta,
Edmonton, AB, T6G 2E8, Canada
{sj,kondrak,colinc}@cs.ualberta.ca

Abstract

We propose a novel approach to the identification of biomedical terms in research publications using the Perceptron HMM algorithm. Each important term is identified and classified into a biomedical concept class. Our proposed system achieves a 68.6% F-measure based on 2,000 training Medline abstracts and 404 unseen testing Medline abstracts. The system achieves performance that is close to the state-of-the-art using only a small feature set. The Perceptron HMM algorithm provides an easy way to incorporate many potentially interdependent features.

1 Introduction

Every day, new scientific articles in the biomedical field are published and made available on-line. The articles contain many new terms and names involving proteins, DNA, RNA, and a wide variety of other substances. Given the large volume of the new research articles, it is important to develop systems capable of extracting meaningful relationships between substances from these articles. Such systems need to recognize and identify biomedical terms in unstructured texts. Biomedical term recognition is thus a step towards information extraction from biomedical texts.

The term recognition task aims at locating biomedical terminology in unstructured texts. The texts are unannotated biomedical research publications written in English. Meaningful terms, which may comprise several words, are identified in order to facilitate further text mining tasks. The recognition task we consider here also involves term classification, that is, classifying the identified terms into biomedical concepts: proteins, DNA, RNA, cell types, and cell lines.

Our biomedical term recognition task is defined as follows: given a set of documents, in each document, find and mark each occurrence of a biomedical term. A term is considered to be annotated correctly only if all its composite words are annotated correctly. Precision, recall and F-measure are determined by comparing the identified terms against the terms annotated in the gold standard.

We believe that the biomedical term recognition task can only be adequately addressed with machine-learning methods. A straightforward dictionary look-up method is bound to fail because of the term variations in the text, especially when the task focuses on locating exact term boundaries. Rule-based systems can achieve good performance on small data sets, but the rules must be defined manually by domain experts, and are difficult to adapt to other data sets. Systems based on machine-learning employ statistical techniques, and can be easily re-trained on different data. The machine-learning techniques used for this task can be divided into two main approaches: the word-based methods, which annotate each word without taking previous assigned tags into account, and the sequence based methods, which take other annotation decisions into account in order to decide on the tag for the current word.

We propose a biomedical term identification

Proceedings of the BioNLP Workshop on Linking Natural Language Processing and Biology at HLT-NAACL 06, pages 114–115,
New York City, June 2006.

system based on the Perceptron HMM algorithm (Collins, 2004), a novel algorithm for HMM training. It uses the Viterbi and perceptron algorithms to replace a traditional HMM's conditional probabilities with discriminatively trained parameters. The method has been successfully applied to various tasks, including noun phrase chunking and part-of-speech tagging. The perceptron makes it possible to incorporate discriminative training into the traditional HMM approach, and to augment it with additional features, which are helpful in recognizing biomedical terms, as was demonstrated in the ABTA system (Jiampojamarn et al., 2005). A discriminative method allows us to incorporate these features without concern for feature interdependencies. The Perceptron HMM provides an easy and effective learning algorithm for this purpose.

The features used in our system include the part-of-speech tag information, orthographic patterns, word prefix and suffix character strings. The additional features are the word, IOB and class features. The orthographic features encode the spelling characteristics of a word, such as uppercase letters, lowercase letters, digits, and symbols. The IOB and class features encode the IOB tags associated with biomedical class concept markers.

2 Results and discussion

We evaluated our system on the JNLPBA Bio-Entity recognition task. The training data set contains 2,000 Medline abstracts labeled with biomedical classes in the IOB style. The IOB annotation method utilizes three types of tags: `<B>` for the beginning word of a term, `<I>` for the remaining words of a term, and `<O>` for non-term words. For the purpose of term classification, the IOB tags are augmented with the names of the biomedical classes; for example, `<B-protein>` indicates the first word of a protein term. The held-out set was constructed by randomly selecting 10% of the sentences from the available training set. The number of iterations for training was determined by observing the point where the performance on the held-out set starts to level off. The test set is composed of new 404 Medline abstracts.

Table 1 shows the results of our system on all five classes. In terms of F-measure, our system achieves the average of 68.6%, which a substantial improvement over the baseline system (based on longest string matching against a lists of terms from training data) with the average of 47.7%, and over the basic HMM system, with the average of 53.9%. In comparison with the results of eight participants at the JNLPBA shared tasks (Kim et al., 2004), our system ranks fourth. The performance gap between our system and the best systems at JNLPBA, which achieved the average up to 72.6%, can be attributed to the use of richer and more complete features such as dictionaries and Gene ontology.

Class	Recall	Precision	F-measure
protein	76.73 %	65.56 %	70.71 %
DNA	63.07 %	64.47 %	63.76 %
RNA	64.41 %	59.84 %	62.04 %
cell_type	64.71 %	76.35 %	70.05 %
cell_line	54.20 %	52.02 %	53.09 %
ALL	70.93 %	66.50 %	68.64 %

Table 1: The performance of our system on the test set with respect to each biomedical concept class.

3 Conclusion

We have proposed a new approach to the biomedical term recognition task using the Perceptron HMM algorithm. Our proposed system achieves a 68.6% F-measure with a relatively small number of features as compared to the systems of the JNLPBA participants. The Perceptron HMM algorithm is much easier to implement than the SVM-HMMs, CRF, and the Maximum Entropy Markov Models, while the performance is comparable to those approaches. In the future, we plan to experiment with incorporating external resources, such as dictionaries and gene ontologies, into our feature set.

References

M. Collins. 2004. Discriminative training methods for hidden markov models: Theory and experiments with perceptron algorithms. In *Proceedings of EMNLP*.

S. Jiampojamarn, N. Cercone, and V. Keselj. 2005. Biological named entity recognition using n-grams and classification methods. In *Proceedings of PACLING*.

J. Kim, T. Ohta, Y. Tsuruoka, Y. Tateisi, and N. Collier. 2004. Introduction to the bio-entity recognition task at JNLPBA. In *Proceedings of JNLPBA*.

Refactoring Corpora

Helen L. Johnson
Center for Computational Pharmacology
U. of Colorado School of Medicine
helen.johnson@uchsc.edu

William A. Baumgartner, Jr.
Center for Computational Pharmacology
U. of Colorado School of Medicine
william.baumgartner@uchsc.edu

Martin Krallinger
Protein Design Group
Universidad Autónoma de Madrid
martink@cnb.uam.es

K. Bretonnel Cohen
Center for Computational Pharmacology
U. of Colorado School of Medicine
kevin.cohen@gmail.com

Lawrence Hunter
Center for Computational Pharmacology
U. of Colorado School of Medicine
larry.hunter@uchsc.edu

Abstract

We describe a pilot project in semi-automatically refactoring a biomedical corpus. The total time expended was just over three person-weeks, suggesting that this is a cost-efficient process. The refactored corpus is available for download at http://bionlp.sourceforge.net.

1 Introduction

Cohen et al. (2005) surveyed the usage rates of a number of biomedical corpora, and found that most biomedical corpora have not been used outside of the lab that created them. Empirical data on corpus design and usage suggests that one major factor affecting usage is the format in which it is distributed.

These findings suggest that there would be a large benefit to the community in refactoring these corpora. *Refactoring* is defined in the software engineering community as altering the internal structure of code without altering its external behavior (Fowler et al., 1999). We suggest that in the context of corpus linguistics, refactoring means changing the *format* of a corpus without altering its *contents,* i.e. its annotations and the text that they describe. The significance of being able to refactor a large number of corpora should be self-evident: a likely increase in the use of the already extant publicly available data for evaluating biomedical language processing systems, without the attendant cost of repeating their annotation.

We examined the question of whether corpus refactoring is practical by attempting a proof-of-concept application: modifying the format of the Protein Design Group (PDG) corpus described in Blaschke et al. (1999) from its current idiosyncratic format to a stand-off annotation format (WordFreak[1]) and a GPML-like (Kim et al., 2001) embedded XML format.

2 Methods

The target WordFreak and XML-embedded formats were chosen for two reasons. First, there is some evidence suggesting that standoff annotation and embedded XML are the two most highly preferred corpus annotation formats, and second, these formats are employed by the two largest extant curated biomedical corpora, GENIA (Kim et al., 2001) and BioIE (Kulick et al., 2004).

The PDG corpus we refactored was originally constructed by automatically detecting protein-protein interactions using the system described in Blaschke et al. (1999), and then manually reviewing the output. We selected it for our pilot project because it was the smallest publicly available corpus of which we were aware. Each block of text has a deprecated MEDLINE ID, a list of actions, a list of proteins and a string of text in which the actions and proteins are mentioned. The structure and contents of the original corpus dictate the logical steps of the refactoring process:

1. Determine the current PubMed identifier, given the deprecated MEDLINE ID. Use the PubMed identifier to retrieve the original abstract.

[1] http://venom.ldc.upenn.edu/_resources/info/wordfreak_ann.html

Proceedings of the BioNLP Workshop on Linking Natural Language Processing and Biology at HLT-NAACL 06, pages 116–117,
New York City, June 2006.

2. Locate the original source sentence in the title or abstract.
3. Locate the "action" keywords and the entities (i.e., proteins) in the text.
4. Produce output in the new formats.

Between each file creation step above, human curators verify the data. The creation and curation process is structured this way so that from one step to the next we are assured that all data is valid, thereby giving the automation the best chance of performing well on the subsequent step.

3 Results

The refactored PDG corpus is publicly available at http://bionlp.sourceforge.net. Total time expended to refactor the PDG corpus was 122 hours and 25 minutes, or approximately three person-weeks. Just over 80% of the time was spent on the programming portion. Much of that programming can be directly applied to the next refactoring project. The remaining 20% of the time was spent curating the programmatic outputs.

Mapping IDs and obtaining the correct abstract returned near-perfect results and required very little curation. For the sentence extraction step, 33% of the corpus blocks needed manual correction, which required 4 hours of curation. (Here and below, "curation" time includes both visual inspection of outputs, and correction of any errors detected.) The source of error was largely due to the fact that the sentence extractor returned the best sentence from the abstract, but the original corpus text was sometimes more or less than one sentence.

For the protein and action mapping step, about 40% of the corpus segments required manual correction. In total, this required about 16 hours of curation time. Distinct sources of error included partial entity extraction, incorrect entity extraction, and incorrect entity annotation in the original corpus material. Each of these types of errors were corrected.

4 Conclusion

The underlying motivation for this paper is the hypothesis that corpus refactoring is practical, economical, and useful. Erjavec (2003) converted the GENIA corpus from its native format to a TEI P4 format. They noted that the translation process brought to light some previously covert problems with the GENIA format. Similarly, in the process of the refactoring we discovered and repaired a number of erroneous entity boundaries and spurious entities.

A number of enhancements to the corpus are now possible that in its previous form would have been difficult at best. These include but are not limited to performing syntactic and semantic annotation and adding negative examples, which would expand the usefulness of the corpus. Using revisioning software, the distribution of iterative feature additions becomes simple.

We found that this corpus could be refactored with about 3 person-weeks' worth of time. Users can take advantage of the corrections that we made to the entity component of the data to evaluate novel named entity recognition techniques or information extraction approaches.

5 Acknowledgments

The authors thank the Protein Design Group at the Universidad Autónoma de Madrid for providing the original PDG protein-protein interaction corpus, Christian Blaschke and Alfonso Valencia for assistance and support, and Andrew Roberts for modifying his jTokeniser package for us.

References

Christian Blaschke, Miguel A. Andrade, and Christos Ouzounis. 1999. Automatic extraction of biological information from scientifi c text: Protein-protein interactions.

K. Bretonnel Cohen, Lynne Fox, Philip Ogren, and Lawrence Hunter. 2005. Empirical data on corpus design and usage in biomedical natural language processing. *AMIA 2005 Symposium Proceedings*, pages 156–160.

Tomaz Erjavec, Yuka Tateisi, Jin-Dong Kim, and Tomoko Ohta. 2003. Encoding biomedical resources in TEI: the case of the GENIA corpus.

Martin Fowler, Kent Beck, John Brant, William Opdyke, and Don Roberts. 1999. *Refactoring: improving the design of existing code*. Addison-Wesley.

Jin-Dong Kim, Tomoko Ohta, Yuka Tateisi, Hideki Mima, and Jun'ichi Tsujii. 2001. Xml-based linguistic annotation of corpus. In *Proceedings of The First NLP and XML Workshop*, pages 47–53.

S. Kulick, A. Bies, M. Liberman, M. Mandel, R. McDonald, M. Palmer, A. Schein, and L. Ungar. 2004. Integrated annotation for biomedical information extraction. *Proceedings of the HLT/NAACL*.

Rapid Adaptation of POS Tagging for Domain Specific Uses

John E. Miller[1] **Michael Bloodgood**[1] **Manabu Torii**[2] **K. Vijay-Shanker**[1]

[1]Computer & Information Sciences
University of Delaware
Newark, DE 19716
{jmiller,bloodgoo,vijay}@cis.udel.edu

[2]Biostatistics, Bioinformatics and Biomathematics
Georgetown University Medical Center
Washington, DC 20057
mt352@georgetown.edu

1 Introduction

Part-of-speech (POS) tagging is a fundamental component for performing natural language tasks such as parsing, information extraction, and question answering. When POS taggers are trained in one domain and applied in significantly different domains, their performance can degrade dramatically. We present a methodology for rapid adaptation of POS taggers to new domains. Our technique is unsupervised in that a manually annotated corpus for the new domain is not necessary. We use suffix information gathered from large amounts of raw text as well as orthographic information to increase the lexical coverage. We present an experiment in the Biological domain where our POS tagger achieves results comparable to POS taggers specifically trained to this domain.

Many machine-learning and statistical techniques employed for POS tagging train a model on an annotated corpus, such as the Penn Treebank (Marcus et al, 1993). Most state-of-the-art POS taggers use two main sources of information: 1) Information about neighboring tags, and 2) Information about the word itself. Methods using both sources of information for tagging are: Hidden Markov Modeling, Maximum Entropy modeling, and Transformation Based Learning (Brill, 1995).

In moving to a new domain, performance can degrade dramatically because of the increase in the unknown word rate as well as domain-specific word use. We improve tagging performance by attacking these problems. Since our goal is to employ minimal manual effort or domain-specific knowledge, we consider only orthographic, inflectional and derivational information in deriving POS. We bypass the time, cost, resource, and content expert intensive approach of annotating a corpus for a new domain.

2 Methodology and Experiment

The initial components in our POS tagging process are a lexicon and part of speech (POS) tagger trained on a generic domain corpus. The lexicon is updated to include domain specific information based on suffix rules applied to an un-annotated corpus. Documents in the new domain are POS tagged using the updated lexicon and orthographic information. So, the POS tagger uses the domain specific updated lexicon, along with what it knows from generic training, to process domain specific text and output POS tags.

In demonstrating feasibility of the approach, we used the fnTBL-1.0 POS tagger (Ngai and Florian, 2001) based on Brill's Transformation Based Learning (Brill, 1995) along with its lexicon and contextual rules trained on the Wall Street Journal corpus.

To update the lexicon, we processed 104,322 abstracts from five of the 500 compressed data files in the 2005 PubMed/Medline database (Smith *et al*, 2004). As a result of this update, coverage of words with POS tags from the lexicon increased from 73.0% to 89.6% in our test corpus.

Suffix rules were composed based on information from Michigan State University's Suffixes and Parts of Speech web page for Graduate Record Exams (DeForest, 2000). The suffix endings indicate the POS used for new words. However, as seen in the table of suffix examples below, there can be significant lack of precision in assigning POS based just on suffixes.

Suffix	POS	#uses/ %acc
ize; izes	VB VBP; VBZ	23/100%
ous	JJ	195/100%
er, or; ers, ors	NN; NNS	1471/99.5%
ate; ates	VB VBP	576/55.7%

Proceedings of the BioNLP Workshop on Linking Natural Language Processing and Biology at HLT-NAACL 06, pages 118–119,
New York City, June 2006.

Most suffixes did well in determining the actual POS assigned to the word. Some such as "-er" and "-or" had very broad use as well. "-ate" typically forms a verb from a noun or adjective in a generic domain. However in scientific domains it often indicates a noun or adjective word form. (In work just begun, we add POS assignment confirmation tests to suffix rules so as to confirm POS tags while maintaining our domain independent and unsupervised analysis of un-annotated corpora.)

Since the fnTBL POS tagger gives preliminary assignment of POS tags based on the first POS listed for that word in the lexicon, it is vital that the first POS tag for a common word be correct. Words ending in '-ing' can be used in a verbal (VBG), adjectival (JJ) or noun (NN) sense. Our intuition is that the '-ed' form should also appear often when the verbal sense dominates. In contrast, if the ratio heavily favors the '-ing' form then we expect the noun sense to dominate.

We incorporated this reasoning into a computationally defined process which assigned the NN tag first to the following words: *binding, imaging, learning, nursing, processing, screening, signaling, smoking, training, and underlying*. Only *underlying* seems out of place in this list.

In addition to inflectional and derivational suffixes, we used rules based on orthographic characteristics. These rules defined proper noun and number or code categories.

3 Results and Conclusion

For testing purposes, we used approximately half the abstracts of the GENIA corpus (version 3.02) described in (Tateisi *et al,* 2003). As the GENIA corpus does not distinguish between common and proper nouns we dropped that distinction in evaluating tagger performance.

POS tagging accuracy on our GENIA test set (second half of abstracts) consisting of 243,577 words is shown in the table below.

Source	Accuracy
Original fnTBL lexicon	92.58%
Adapted lexicon (Rapid)	94.13%
MedPost	94.04%
PennBioIE[1]	93.98%

[1] Note that output from the tagger is not fully compatible with GENIA annotation.

The original fnTBL tagger has an accuracy of 92.58% on the GENIA test corpus showing that it deals well with unknown words from this domain. Our rapid adaptation tagger achieves a modest 1.55% absolute improvement in accuracy, which equates to a 21% error reduction.

There is little difference in performance between our rapid adaptation tagger and the MedPost (Smith *et al*, 2004) and PennBioIE (Kulick *et al*, 2004) taggers. The PennBioIE tagger employs maximum entropy modeling and was developed using 315 manually annotated Medline abstracts. The MedPost tagger also used domain-specific annotated corpora and a 10,000 word lexicon, manually updated with POS tags.

We have improved the accuracy of the fnTBL-1.0 tagger for a new domain by adding words and POS tags to its lexicon via unsupervised methods of processing raw text from the new domain. The accuracy of the resulting tagger compares well to those that have been trained to this domain using annotation effort and domain-specific knowledge.

References

Brill, E. 1995. Transformation-based error-driven learning and natural language processing: A case study in part of speech tagging. Computational Linguistics, 21(4):543-565.

DeForest, Jessica. 2000. Graduate Record Exam Suffix web page. Michigan State University. http://www.msu.edu/~defores1/gre/sufx/gre_suffx.htm.

Kulick, S., Bies, A., Liberman, M., Mandel, M., McDonald, R., Palmer, M., Schein, A., Ungar, L. 2004. Integrated annotation for biomedical information extraction. *HLT/NAACL-2004:* 61-68.

Marcus, M., Santorini, B., Marcinkiewicz, M.A. 1993. Building a large annotated corpus of English: The Penn Treebank. Computational Linguistics, 19:313-330.

Ngai, G. and Florian, R. 2001. Transformation-based learning in the fast lane. In Proceedings of North America ACL 2001(June): 40-47.

Smith, L., Rindflesch, T., Wilbur, W.J. 2004. MedPost: a part-of-speech tagger for bioMedical text. Bioinformatics 20 (14):2320-2321.

Tateisi, Y., Ohta, T., dong Kim, J., Hong, H., Jian, S., Tsujii, J. 2003. The GENIA corpus: Medline abstracts annotated with linguistic information. In: Third meeting of SIG on Text Mining, Intelligent Systems for Molecular Biology (ISMB).

Extracting Protein-Protein interactions using simple contextual features

Leif Arda Nielsen
School of Informatics
University of Edinburgh
leif.nielsen@gmail.com

1 Introduction

There has been much interest in recent years on the topic of extracting Protein-Protein Interaction (PPI) information automatically from scientific publications. This is due to the need that has emerged to organise the large body of literature that is generated through research, and collected at sites such as PubMed. Easy access to the information contained in published work is vital for facilitating new research, but the rate of publication makes manual collection of all such data unfeasible. Information Extraction approaches based on Natural Language Processing can be, and are already being used, to facilitate this process.

The dominant approach so far has been the use of hand-built, knowledge-based systems, working at levels ranging from surface syntax to full parses (Blaschke and Valencia, 2002; Huang et al., 2004; Plake et al., 2005; Rebholz-Schuhmann et al., 2005; Yakushiji et al., 2005). A similar work to the one presented here is by (Sugiyama et al., 2003), but it is not possible to compare results due to differing datasets and the limited information available about their methods.

2 Data

A gene-interaction corpus derived from the BioCreAtIvE task-1A data will be used for the experiments. This data was kindly made available by Jörg Hakenberg[1] and is described in (Plake et al., 2005). The data consists of 1000 sentences marked up for POS tags, genes (both genes and proteins are marked as 'gene'; the terms will be used interchangeably in this paper) and iWords. The corpus contains 255 relations, all of which are intra-sentential, and the "interaction word" (iWord)[2] for each relation is also marked up.

I utilise the annotated entities, and focus only on relation extraction. The data contains directionality information for each relation, denoting which entity is the 'agent' and which the 'target', or denoting that this distinction cannot be made. This information will not be used for the current experiments, as my main aim is simply to identify relations between entities, and the derivation of this information will be left for future work.

I will be using the Naive Bayes, KStar, and JRip classifiers from the Weka toolkit, Zhang Le's Maximum Entropy classifier (Maxent), TiMBL, and LibSVM to test performance. All experiments are done using 10-fold cross-validation. Performance will be measured using Recall, Precision and F1.

3 Experiments

Each possible combination of proteins and iWords in a sentence was generated as a possible relation 'triple', which combines the relation extraction task with the additional task of finding the iWord to describe each relation. 3400 such triples occur in the data. After each instance is given a probability by the classifiers, the highest scoring instance for each protein pairing is compared to a threshold to decide

[1] See http://www.informatik.hu-berlin.de/ hakenber/publ/suppl/sac05/

[2] A limited set of words that have been determined to be informative of when a PPI occurs, such as *interact, bind, inhibit, phosphorylation*. See footnote 1 for complete list.

Proceedings of the BioNLP Workshop on Linking Natural Language Processing and Biology at HLT-NAACL 06, pages 120–121,
New York City, June 2006.

the outcome. Correct triples are those that match the iWord assigned to a PPI by the annotators.

For each instance, a list of features were used to construct a 'generic' model :

interindices The combination of the indices of the proteins of the interaction; "P1-position:P2-position"

interwords The combination of the lexical forms of the proteins of the interaction; "P1:P2"

p1prevword, p1currword, p1nextword The lexical form of P1, and the two words surrounding it

p2prevword, p2currword, p2nextword The lexical form of P2, and the two words surrounding it

p2pdistance The distance, in tokens, between the two proteins

inbetween The number of other identified proteins between the two proteins

iWord The lexical form of the iWord

iWordPosTag The POS tag of the iWord

iWordPlacement Whether the iWord is between, before or after the proteins

iWord2ProteinDistance The distance, in words, between the iWord and the protein nearest to it

A second model incorporates greater domain-specific features, in addition to those of the 'generic' model :

patterns The 22 syntactic patterns used in (Plake et al., 2005) are each used as boolean features[3].

lemmas and stems Lemma and stem information was used instead of surface forms, using a system developed for the biomedical domain.

4 Results

Tables 1 and 2 show the results for the two models described above. The system achieves a peak performance of 59.2% F1, which represents a noticeable improvement over previous results on the same dataset (52% F1 (Plake et al., 2005)), and demonstrates the feasibility of the approach adopted.

It is seen that simple contextual features are quite informative for the task, but that a significant gains can be made using more elaborate methods.

Algorithm	Recall	Precision	F1
Naive Bayes	61.3	35.6	45.1
KStar	65.2	41.6	50.8
Jrip	**66.0**	**45.4**	**53.8**
Maxent	58.5	48.2	52.9
TiMBL	49.0	41.1	44.7
LibSVM	49.4	56.8	52.9

Table 1: Results using 'generic' model

Algorithm	Recall	Precision	F1
Naive Bayes	64.8	44.1	52.5
KStar	60.9	45.0	51.8
Jrip	44.3	45.7	45.0
Maxent	57.7	56.6	57.1
TiMBL	42.7	74.0	54.1
LibSVM	**54.5**	**64.8**	**59.2**

Table 2: Results using extended model

[3]These patterns are in regular expression form, i.e. "P1 word{0,n} Iverb word{0,m} P2". This particular pattern matches sentences where a protein is followed by an iWord that is a verb, with a maximum of *n* words between them, and following this by *m* words maximum is another protein. In their paper, (Plake et al., 2005) optimise the values for *n* and *m* using Genetic Algorithms, but I will simply set them all to 5, which is what they report as being the best unoptimized setting.

References

C. Blaschke and A. Valencia. 2002. The frame-based module of the suiseki information extraction system. *IEEE Intelligent Systems*, (17):14–20.

Minlie Huang, Xiaoyan Zhu, Yu Hao, Donald G. Payan, Kunbin Qu 2, and Ming Li. 2004. Discovering patterns to extract proteinprotein interactions from full texts. *Bioinformatics*, 20(18):3604–3612.

Conrad Plake, Jörg Hakenberg, and Ulf Leser. 2005. Optimizing syntax-patterns for discovering protein-protein-interactions. In *Proc ACM Symposium on Applied Computing, SAC, Bioinformatics Track*, volume 1, pages 195–201, Santa Fe, USA, March.

D. Rebholz-Schuhmann, H. Kirsch, and F. Couto. 2005. Facts from text–is text mining ready to deliver? *PLoS Biol*, 3(2).

Kazunari Sugiyama, Kenji Hatano, Masatoshi Yoshikawa, and Shunsuke Uemura. 2003. Extracting information on protein-protein interactions from biological literature based on machine learning approaches. *Genome Informatics*, 14:699–700.

Akane Yakushiji, Yusuke Miyao, Yuka Tateisi, and Jun'ichi Tsujii. 2005. Biomedical information extraction with predicate-argument structure patterns. In *Proceedings of the First International Symposium on Semantic Mining in Biomedicine*, pages 60–69.

Identifying Experimental Techniques in Biomedical Literature

Meeta Oberoi, Craig A. Struble
Dept. of Math., Stat., and Comp. Sci.
Marquette University
Milwaukee, WI 53201-1881
{meeta.oberoi,craig.struble}@marquette.edu

Sonia Sugg
Department of Surgery
Medical College of Wisconsin
Milwaukee, WI 53226
ssugg@mcw.edu

Named entity recognition of gene names, protein names, cell-lines, and other biologically relevant concepts has received significant attention by the research community. In this work, we considered named entity recognition of *experimental techniques* in biomedical articles. In our system to mine gene and disease associations, each association is categorized by the techniques used to derive the association. Categories are used to weight or remove associations, such as removing associations derived from microarray experiments.

We report on a pilot study to identify experimental techniques. Three main activities are discussed: *manual annotation*, *lexicon-based tagging*, and *document classification*. Analysis of manual annotation suggests several interesting linguistic characteristics arise. Two lexicon-based tagging approaches demonstrate little agreement, suggesting sophisticated tagging algorithms may be necessary. Document classification using abstracts and titles is compared with full-text classification. In most cases, abstracts and titles show comparable performance to full-text.

Corpus We built a corpus around our interest in gene associations with breast cancer to leverage the domain expertise of the authors. The corpus consisted of 247 sampled from 2571 papers associating breast cancer with a human gene in EntrezGene.

Manual Annotation Manual annotation was primarily performed by a graduate student in bioinformatics and a computer science Ph.D. with a research emphasis in bioinformatics. Annotators were instructed to highlight direct mentions of experimental techniques. During the study, we noted low inter-annotator agreement and stopped the manual process after annotating 102 of 247 documents.

Results were analyzed for linguistic characteristics. Experimental technique mentions appear with varying frequency in 6 typical document sections: *Title, Abstract, Introduction, Materials and Methods, Results* and *Discussion.* In some sections, such as *Introduction*, mentions are often for references and not the current document. Techniques such as *transfection* and *immunoblotting*, demonstrated diverse morphology. Other characteristics included use of synonyms and abbreviations, conjunctive phrases, and endophora.

Tagging Tagging is commonly used for named entity recognition. In our context, associations are categorized by generating a list of all tagged techniques tagged in a document.

Two taggers were tested on 247 documents to investigate the efficacy of two lexicons — MeSH and UMLS — containing experimental techniques. One approach used regular expressions for terms and permuted terms in the *Investigative Techniques* MeSH subhierarchy. The other used a natural language approach based on MetaMap Transfer (Aronson, 2001), mapping text to UMLS entries with the *Laboratory Procedure* semantic type (ID: T059).

Low inter-annotator agreement between taggers was exhibited with a maximum κ of 0.220. Both taggers exhibited limitations — failing to properly tag phrases such as "Northern and Western analyses" — and neither one is clearly superior to the other.

Proceedings of the BioNLP Workshop on Linking Natural Language Processing and Biology at HLT-NAACL 06, pages 122–123,
New York City, June 2006. ©2006 Association for Computational Linguistics

Technique	Full-Text		Abstract	
	1,000	All(59,628)	1,000	All(4,395)
Electrophoresis (144)	72.4/81.2/76.5	70.3/77.4/73.7	68.9/79.8/74.0	69.2/75.3/72.1
Western Blot Analysis (132)	71.3/83.6/77.0	71.4/77.0/74.1	67.5/79.8/73.1	68.2/76.2/72.0
Gene Transfer Technique (137)	76.3/92.1/83.4	74.6/88.6/81.0	77.0/89.6/82.8	76.2/88.3/81.8
Pedigree(10)	52.0/91.3/66.2	81.2/72.5/76.6	42.9/77.7/55.3	59.9/58.3/59.1
Sequence Alignment (24)	53.0/66.6/59.1	96.6/17.9/30.1	61.2/59.5/60.3	67.0/36.5/47.2
Statistics (107)	70.7/57.7/63.5	70.3/60.8/65.2	73.6/58.6/65.2	71.5/63.5/67.2

Table 1: Precision/Recall/F1-scores for classifiers with different vocabulary sizes.

Document Classification Document classification was also used to obtain a list of utilized experimental techniques. Each article is assigned to one or more classes corresponding to techniques used to generate results.

Two distinct questions were investigated. First, how well does classification perform if only the abstract and title of the article are available? Second, how does vocabulary size affect the classification?

Multinomial Naïve Bayes models were implemented in Rainbow (McCallum, 1996; McCallum and Nigam, 1998) for 24 MeSH experimental techniques. Document frequency in each class ranged from 10 (Pedigree) to 144 (Electrophoresis). Vocabularies consist of top information gain ranked words. Classifiers were evaluated by precision, recall, and F1-scores averaged over 100 runs. The corpus was split into 2/3 training and 1/3 testing, randomly chosen for each run.

Selected results are shown in Table 1. Full-text classifiers performed better than abstract based classifiers with a few exceptions: "Sequence Alignment" and "Gene Transfer Techniques". The performance of abstract and full-text classifiers is comparable: F1 scores often differ by less than 5 points. Smaller vocabularies tend to improve the recall and overall F1 scores, while larger ones improved precision. Classifiers for low frequency ($<$ 25) techniques generally performed poorly. One class, "Pedigree", performed surprisingly well, with a maximum F1 of 76.6.

Considering that Naïve Bayes models are often baseline models and the small size of the corpus, classification performance is good.

Related and Future Work For comprehensive reviews of current work in biomedical literature mining, refer to (Cohen and Hersh, 2005) and (Krallinger et al., 2005). As future work, we will continue manual annotation, validate the informative capacity of sections with experiments similar to Sinclair and Webber (Sinclair and Webber, 2004), and investigate improvements in tagging and classification.

References

A. Aronson. 2001. Effective mapping of biomedical text to the UMLS metathesaurus: The MetaMap program. In *Proc AMIA 2001*, pages 17–21.

Aaron M. Cohen and William R. Hersh. 2005. A survey of current work in biomedical text mining. *Briefings in Bioinformatics*, 6:57–71.

Martin Krallinger, Ramon Alonso-Allende Erhardt, and Alfonso Valencia. 2005. Text-mining approaches in molecular biology and biomedicine. *Drug Discovery Today*, 10:439–445.

Andrew McCallum and Kamal Nigam. 1998. A comparison of event models for Naive Bayes text classification. In *AAAI-98 Workshop on Learning for Text Categorization*.

Andrew Kachites McCallum. 1996. Bow: A toolkit for statistical language modeling, text retrieval, classification and clustering. http://www.cs.cmu.edu/~mccallum/bow.

Gail Sinclair and Bonnie Webber. 2004. Classification from Full Text: A Comparison of Canonical Sections of Scientific Papers. In Nigel Collier, Patrick Ruch, and Adeline Nazarenko, editors, *COLING (NLPBA/BioNLP)*, pages 69–72, Geneva, Switzerland.

A Pragmatic Approach to Summary Extraction in Clinical Trials

Graciela Rosemblat
National Library of Medicine
NIH, Bethesda, Maryland
rosem@nlm.nih.gov

Laurel Graham
National Library of Medicine
NIH, Bethesda, Maryland
lagraham@mail.nih.gov

Background and Introduction

ClinicalTrials.gov, the National Library of Medicine clinical trials registry, is a monolingual clinical research website with over 29,000 records at present. The information is presented in static and free-text fields. Static fields contain high-level informational text, descriptors, and controlled vocabularies that remain constant across all clinical studies (headings, general information). Free-text data are detailed and trial-specific, such as the Purpose section, which presents each trial's goal, with large inter-trial variability in length as well as in technical difficulty. The crux of the trial purpose is generally found in 1-3 sentences, often introduced by clearly identified natural language markers.

In the Spanish cross-language information retrieval (CLIR) ClinicalTrials.gov prototype, individual studies are displayed as abridged Spanish-language records, with Spanish static field descriptors, and a manual Spanish translation for the free-text study title. The Purpose section of these abbreviated documents only contains a link (in Spanish) to the full-text English record. The premise was that the gist could be obtained from the Spanish title, the link to the English document, and the Spanish descriptors. However, in a recently conducted user study on the Spanish CLIR prototype, Spanish-speaking consumers did not use the Purpose section link, as doing so entailed leaving a Spanish webpage to go to an English one. Further, feedback from an earlier study indicated a need for some Spanish text in the Purpose section to provide the gist of the trial while avoiding the information overload in the full-text English record. Thus, in an alternative display format, extractive summarization plus translation was used to enhance the abbreviated Spanish document and supplement the link to the English record. The trial purpose--up to three sentences--was algorithmically extracted from the English document Purpose section, and translated into Spanish via post-edited machine translation for display in the Spanish record Purpose section (Rosemblat et al., 2005).

Our extraction technique, which combines sentence boundary detection, regular expressions, and decision-based rules, was validated by the user study for facilitating user relevance judgment. All participants endorsed this alternative display format over the initial schematic design, especially when the Purpose extract makes up the entire Purpose section in the English document, as is the case in 48% of all trials. For Purpose sections that span many paragraphs and exceed 1,000 words, human translation is not viable. Machine translation is used to reduce the burden, and using excerpts of the original text as opposed to entire documents further reduces the resource cost. Human post-editing ensures the accuracy of translations. Automated extraction of key goal-describing text may provide relevant excerpts of the original text via topic recognition techniques (Hovy, 2003).

1 RegExp Detection and Pattern Matching

Linguistic analysis of the natural language expressions in the clinical trial records' Purpose section was performed manually on a large sample of documents. Common language patterns across studies introducing the purpose/goal of each trial served as cue phrases. These cue phrases contained both quality features and the rhetorical role of GOAL (Teufel and Moens, 1999). The crux of the purpose was generally condensed in 1-3 sentences within the Purpose section, showing definite patterns and a limited set of productive, straightforward linguistic markers. From these common patterns, the ClinicalTrials.gov Purpose Extractor Algorithm (PEA) was devised, and developed in Java (1.5) using the native regexp package.

Proceedings of the BioNLP Workshop on Linking Natural Language Processing and Biology at HLT-NAACL 06, pages 124–125,
New York City, June 2006.

Natural language expressions in the purpose sentences include three basic elements, making them well suited to regular expressions:

a) A small, closed set of verbs (*determine, test*)
b) Specific purpose triggers or cues (*goal, aim*)
c) Particular types of sentence constructs, as in: *This study will evaluate two medications...*

PEA incorporates sentence boundary detection (A), purpose statement matching (B), and a series of decision steps (C) to ensure the extracted text is semantically and syntactically correct:

A) To improve regexp performance and ensure that extraction occurred in complete sentences, sentence boundary detection was implemented. Grok (OpenNLP), open source Java NLP software, was used for this task, corpus-trained and validated, and supplemented with rules-based post-processing.

B) Regular expressions were rank ordered from most specific to the more general with a default expression should all others fail to match. The regexp patterns allowed for possible tense and optional modal variations, and included a range of all possible patterns that resulted from combining verbs and triggers, controlled for case-sensitivity. The default for cases that differed from the standard patterns relied solely on the verb set provided.

C) Checks were made for (a) length normalization (a maximum of 450 characters), with purpose-specific text in enumerated or bulleted lists overriding this restriction; and (b) discourse markers pointing to extra-sentential information for the semantic processing of the text. In this case, PEA determines the anchor sentence (main crux of the purpose), and then whether to include a leading and trailing sentence, or two leading sentences or two trailing ones, to reach the 3-sentence limit.

RegExp Patterns	Description	Case
PURPOSE	Sentence label (purpose)	Yes
To VERB_SET	Study action starts section	No
In THIS STUDY	General actions in study	No

Table 1. Some purpose patterns used by PEA

2 Evaluation

Manual PEA validation was done on a random sample of 300 trials. For a stricter test, the 13,110 studies with Purpose sections short enough to include in full without any type of processing or decision were not part of the random sample. Judgments were provided by the authors, one of whom was not involved in the development of PEA code. The 300 English extracts (before translation) were compared against the full-text Purpose sections in the clinical trials, with compression rate averaging 30%. Evaluation was done on a 3-point scale: perfect extraction, appropriate, wrong text. Inter-annotator agreement using Cohen's kappa was considered to be good (Kappa = 0.756987). Table 2 shows evaluation results after inter-rater differences were reconciled:

CRITERIA	TRIALS	RATIO
Perfect extraction	275	92%
Appropriate extraction	18	6%
Extraction of wrong text	7	2%

Table 2: Results: 300 Clinical trials random sample

3 Conclusion

This pragmatic approach to task-specific (purposive) summary extraction in a limited domain (ClinicalTrials.gov) using regular expressions has shown a 92% precision. Further research will determine if this method is appropriate for CLIR and query language display via machine translation and subsequent post-editing in clinical trials information systems for other registries and sponsors.

Acknowledgements

The authors thank Tony Tse and the anonymous reviewers for valuable feedback. Work supported by the NIH, NLM Intramural Research Program.

References

Eduard Hovy. 2003. Text Summarization. In Ruslan Mitkov (Ed.), The Oxford Handbook of Computational Linguistics (pp. 583-598). Oxford University Press.

Graciela Rosemblat, Tony Tse, Darren Gemoets, John E. Gillen, and Nicholas C. Ide. 2005. *Supporting Access to Consumer Health Information Across Languages.* Proceedings of the 8th International ISKO Conference. London, England. pp. 315-321

Grok part of the OpenNLP project. [Accessed at http://grok.sourceforge.net]

Simone Teufel and Marc Moens. 1999. Argumentative classification of extracted sentences as a step towards flexible abstracting. In *Advances in Automatic Text Summarization*, I. Mani and M.T. Maybury (eds.), pp. 155-171. MIT Press.

The Difficulties of Taxonomic Name Extraction and a Solution

Guido Sautter **Klemens Böhm**

Dept. of Computer Science
Universität Karlsruhe (TH)
Germany

sautter@ipd.uka.de boehm@ipd.uka.de

Abstract

In modern biology, digitization of biosystematics publications is an important task. Extraction of taxonomic names from such documents is one of its major issues. This is because these names identify the various genera and species. This article reports on our experiences with learning techniques for this particular task. We say why established Named-Entity Recognition techniques are somewhat difficult to use in our context. One reason is that we have only very little training data available. Our experiments show that a combining approach that relies on regular expressions, heuristics, and word-level language recognition achieves very high precision and recall and allows to cope with those difficulties.

1 Introduction

Digitization of biosystematics publications currently is a major issue. They contain the names and descriptions of taxonomic genera and species. The names are important because they identify the various genera and species. They also position the species in the tree of life, which in turn is useful for a broad variety of biology tasks. Hence, recognition of taxonomic names is relevant. However, manual extraction of these names is time-consuming and expensive.

The main problem for the automated recognition of these names is to distinguish them from the surrounding text, including other Named Entities (NE). Named Entity Recognition (NER) currently is a big research issue. However, conventional NER techniques are not readily applicable here for two reasons: First, the NE categories are rather high-level, e.g., names of organizations or persons (cf. common NER benchmarks such as (Carreras 2005)). Such a classification is too coarse for our context. The structure of taxonomic names varies widely and can be complex. Second, those recognizers require large bodies of training data. Since digitization of biosystematics documents has started only recently, such data is not yet available in biosystematics. On the other hand, it is important to demonstrate right away that text-learning technology is of help to biosystematics as well.

This paper reports on our experiences with learning techniques for the automated extraction of taxonomic names from documents. The various techniques are obviously useful in this context:

- Language recognition – taxonomic names are a combination of Latin or Latinized words, with surrounding text written in English,
- structure recognition – taxonomic names follow a certain structure,
- lexica support – certain words never are/may well be part of taxonomic names.

On the other hand, an individual technique in isolation is not sufficient for taxonomic name extraction. Mikheev (1999) has shown that a combining approach, i.e., one that integrates the results of several different techniques, is superior to the individual techniques for common NER. Combining approaches are also promising for taxonomic name extraction. Having said this, the article will now proceed as follows:

First, we have conducted a thorough inspection of taxonomic names. An important observation is that one cannot model taxonomic names both concisely and precisely using regular expressions. As is done in bootstrapping, we use two kinds of regular expressions: *precision rules*, whose instances are taxonomic names with very high probability, and *recall rules*, whose instances are a superset of all taxonomic names. We propose a meaningful definition of precision rules and recall rules for taxonomic names.

Proceedings of the BioNLP Workshop on Linking Natural Language Processing and Biology at HLT-NAACL 06, pages 126–133,
New York City, June 2006.

Second, the essence of a combining approach is to arrange the individual specific approaches in the right order. We propose such a composition for taxonomic name extraction, and we say why it is superior to other compositions that may appear feasible as well at first sight.

Finally, to quantify the impact of the various alternatives described so far, we report on experimental results. The evaluation is based on a corpus of biosystematics documents marked up by hand. The best solution achieves about 99.2% in precision and recall. It prompts the user for only 0.2% of the words.

The remainder of the paper is as follows: Section 2 discusses related approaches. Section 3 introduces some preliminaries. Section 4 describes one specific combining approach in some detail. Section 5 features an evaluation. Section 6 concludes.

2 Related Work

This section reviews solutions to problems related to the extraction of taxonomic names.

2.1 Named Entity Recognition

Taxonomic names are a special case of named entity. In the recent past, NER has received much attention, which yielded a variety of methods. The most common ones are list lookups, grammars, rules, and statistical methods like SVMs (Bikel 1997). All these techniques have been developed for tasks like the one presented by Carreras (2005). Thus, their focus is the recognition of somewhat common NE like locations and persons. Consequently, they are not feasible for the complex and variable structure of taxonomic names (see Section 3.3). Another problem of common NER techniques is that they usually require several hundred thousand words of pre-annotated training data.

2.2 List-based Techniques

List-based NER techniques (Palmer 1997) make use of lists to determine whether a word is a NE of the category sought. The sole use of a thesaurus as a positive list is not an option for taxonomic names. All existing thesauri are incomplete. Nevertheless, such a list allows recognizing known parts of taxonomic names.

The inverse approach would be list-based exclusion, using a common English dictionary. Koning (2005) combines such an approach with structural rules. In isolation, however, it is not an option either. First, it would not exclude proper names reliably. Second, it excludes parts of taxonomic names that are also used in common English. However, exclusion of sure negatives, i.e., words that are never part of taxonomic names, simplifies the classification.

2.3 Rule Based Techniques

Rule based techniques do not require pre-annotated training data. They extract words or word sequences based on their structure. Yoshida (1999) applies regular expressions to extract the names of proteins. He makes use of the syntax of protein names like *NG-monomethyl-L-arginine*, which is very distinctive.

There are also rules for the syntax of taxonomic names, but they are less restrictive. For instance, *Prenolepis (Nylanderia) vividula Erin subsp. guatemalensis Forel var. itinerans Forel* is a taxonomic name as well as *Dolichoderus decollatus*. Because of the wide range of optional parts, it is impossible to find a regular expression that matches all taxonomic names and at the same time provides satisfactory precision. Koning (2005) presents an approach based on regular expressions and static dictionaries. This technique performs satisfactorily compared to common NER approaches, but their conception of what is a positive is restricted. For instance, they leave aside taxonomic names that do not specify a genus. However, the idea of rule-based filters for the phrases of documents is helpful.

2.4 Bootstrapping

Instead of a large amount of labeled training data, Bootstrapping uses some labeled examples ("seeds") and an even larger amount of unlabeled data for the training. Jones (1999) has shown that this approach performs equal to techniques requiring labeled training data. However, Bootstrapping is not readily applicable to our particular problem. Niu (2003) used an unlabeled corpus of 88.000.000 words for training a named entity recognizer. For our purpose, even unlabeled training data is not available in this order of magnitude, at least right now.

2.5 Active Learning

According to Day (1997), the original idea of Active Learning was to speed up the creation of large labeled training corpora from unlabeled documents. The system uses all of its knowledge during all phases of the learning. Thus, it labels most of the data items automatically and requires user interaction only in rare cases. In order to increase data quality, we include user-interaction in our taxonomic name extractor as well.

2.6 Gene and Protein Name Extraction

In the recent past, the major focus of biomedical NER has been the recognition of gene and protein names. Tanabe (2002) gives a good overview of various approaches to this task. Frequently used techniques are structural rules, dictionary lookups and Hidden Markov Models. Most of the approaches use the output of a part-of-speech tagger as additional evidence. Both gene and protein names differ from taxonomic names in that the nomenclature rules for them are by far stricter. For instance, they never include the names of the discoverer / author of a given part. In addition, there are parts which are easily distinguished from the surrounding text based on their structure, which is not true for taxonomic names. Consequently, the techniques for gene or protein name recognition are not feasible for the extraction of taxonomic names.

3 Preliminaries

This section introduces some preliminaries regarding word-level language recognition. We also describe a measure to quantify the user effort induced by interactions.

3.1 Measure for User Effort

In NLP, the f-Measure is popular to quantify the performance of a word classifier:

```
P(P) := positives classified as positive
N(P) := positives classified as negative
P(N) := negatives classified as positive
N(N) := negatives classified as negative
```

$$\text{Precision } p := \frac{P(P)}{P(P) + P(N)} \qquad \text{Recall } r := \frac{P(P)}{P(P) + N(P)}$$

$$\text{fMeasure} := \frac{2 \times p \times r}{p + r}$$

But components that use active learning have three possible outputs. If the decision between positive or negative is narrow, they may classify a word as uncertain and prompt the user. This prevents misclassifications, but induces intellectual effort. To quantify this effort as well, there are two further measures:

```
U(P) := positives not classified (uncertain)
U(N) := negatives not classified (uncertain)
```

Given this, **Coverage C** is defined as the fraction of all classifications that are not uncertain:

$$C := \frac{P(P) + N(P) + P(N) + N(N)}{P(P) + N(P) + U(P) + P(N) + N(N) + U(N)}$$

To obtain a single measure for overall classification quality, we multiply f-Measure and coverage and define **Quality Q** as

$$Q := \text{fMeasure} \times C$$

3.2 Word-Level Language Recognition for Taxonomic Name Extraction

In earlier work (Sautter 2006), we have presented a technique to classify words as parts of taxonomic names or as common English, respectively. It is based on two statistics containing the N-Gram distribution of taxonomic names and of common English. Both statistics are built from examples from the respective languages. It uses active learning to deal with the lack of training data. Precision and recall reach a level of 98%. This is satisfactory, compared to common NER components. At the same time, the user has to classify about 3% of the words manually. In a text of 10.000 words, this would be 300 manual classifications. We deem this relatively high.

3.3 Formal Structure of Taxonomic Names

The structure of taxonomic names is defined by the rules of Linnaean nomenclature (Ereshefsky 1997). They are not very restrictive and include many optional parts. For instance, both *Prenolepis (Nylanderia) vividula Erin subsp. guatemalensis Forel var. itinerans Forel* and *Dolichoderus decollatus* are taxonomic names. There are only two mandatory parts in such a name: the genus and the species. Table 1 shows the decomposition of the two examples. The parts with their names in brackets are optional. More formally, the rules of Linnaean nomenclature define the structure of taxonomic names as follows:

- The **genus** is mandatory. It is a capitalized word, often abbreviated by its first one or two letters, followed by a dot.

- The **subgenus** is optional. It is a capitalized word, often enclosed in brackets.
- The **species** is mandatory. It is a lower case word. It is often followed by the name of the scientist who first described the species.
- The **subspecies** is optional. It is a lower case word, often preceded by ***subsp.*** or ***subspecies*** as an indicator. It is often followed by the name of the scientist who first described it.
- The **variety** is optional. It is a lower case word, preceded by ***var.*** or ***variety*** as an indicator. It is often followed by the name of the scientist who first described it.

Part		
Genus	*Prenolepis*	*Dolichoderus*
(Subgenus)	*(Nylanderia)*	
Species	*vividula*	*decollatus*
(Discoverer)	*Erin*	
(Subspecies)	*subsp. guatemalensis*	
(Discoverer)	*Forel*	
(Variety)	*var. itinerans*	
(Discoverer)	*Forel*	

Table 1: The parts of taxonomic names

4 Combining Techniques for Taxonomic Name Extraction

Due to its capability of learning at runtime, the word-level language recognizer needs little training data, but it still does. In addition, the manual effort induced by uncertain classifications is high. Making use of the typical structure of taxonomic names, we can improve both aspects. First, we can use syntax-based rules to harvest training data directly from the documents. Second, we can use these rules to reduce the number of words the classifier has to deal with. However, it is not possible to find rules that extract taxonomic names with both high precision and recall, as we will show later. But we have found rules that fulfill one of these requirements very well. In what follows, we refer to these as **precision rules** and **recall rules**, respectively.

4.1 The Classification Process

1. We apply the precision rules. Every word sequence from the document that matches such a rule is a *sure positive*.
2. We apply the recall rules to the phrases that are not sure positives. A phrase not matching one of these rules is a *sure negative*.
3. We make use of domain-specific vocabulary and filter out word sequences containing at least one known negative word.
4. We collect a set of names from the set of sure positives (see Subsection 4.5). We then use these names to both include and exclude further word sequences.
5. We train the word-level language recognizer with the surely positive and surely negative words. We then apply it to the remaining uncertain word sequences.

Figure 1 visualizes the classification process. At first sight, other orders seem to be possible as well, e.g., the language recognizer classifies each word first, and then we apply the rules. But this is not feasible: It would require external training data. In addition, the language recognizer would have to classify all the words of the document. This would incur more manual classifications.

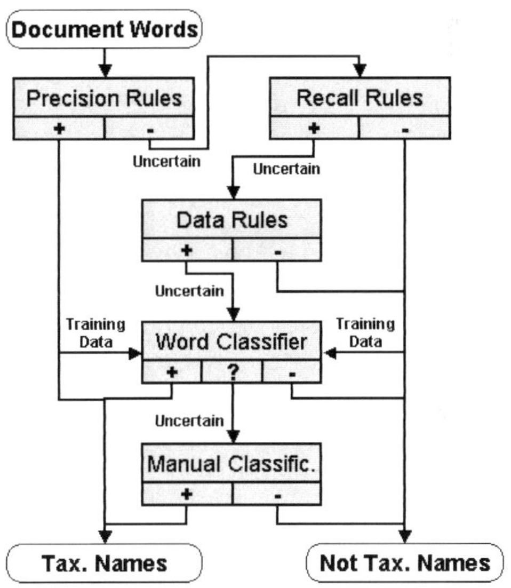

Figure 1: The Classification Process

This approach is similar to the bootstrapping algorithm proposed by Jones (1999). The difference is that this process works solely with the document it actually processes. In particular, it does not need any external data or a training phase. Average biosystematics documents contain about 15.000 words, which is less than 0.02% of the data used by Niu (2003). On the other hand, with the classification process proposed here, the accuracy of the underlying classifier has to be very high from the start.

4.2 Structural Rules

In order to make use of the structure of taxonomic names, we use rules that refer to this structure. We use regular expressions for the formal representation of the rules. In this section, we develop a regular expression matching any word sequence that conforms to the Linnaean rules of nomenclature (see 3.3). Table 2 provides some abbreviations, to increase readability. We model taxonomic names as follows:

_	one white space character
<LcW>	[a-z]$^{(3,)}$
<CapW>	[A-Z][a-z]$^{(2,)}$
<CapA>	[A-Z]{[a-z]}?.
<Name>	{<CapA>_}$^{(0,2)}$<CapW>

Table 2: Abbreviations

- The genus is a capitalized word, often abbreviated. We denote it as <genus>, which stands for {<CapW>|<CapA>}.
- The subgenus is a capitalized word, optionally surrounded by brackets. We denote it as <subGenus>, which stands for <CapW>|(<CapW>).
- The species is a lower case word, optionally followed by a name. We denote it as <species>, which stands for <LcW>{_<Name>}?.
- The subspecies is a lower case word, preceded by the indicator ***subsp.*** or ***subspecies***, and optionally followed by a name. We denote it as <subSpecies>, standing for {subsp.|subspecies}_<LcW>{_<Name>}?.
- The variety is a lower case word, preceded by the indicator ***var.*** or ***variety***, and optionally followed by a name. We denote it as <variety>, which stands for {var.|variety}_<LcW>{_<Name>}?.

A taxonomic name is now modeled as follows. We refer to the pattern as <taxName>:

```
<genus>{_<subGenus>}?
_<species>{_<subSpecies>}?
{_<variety>}?
```

4.3 Precision Rules

Because <taxName> matches any sequence of words that conforms to the Linnaean rules, it is not very precise. The simplest match is a capitalized word followed by one in lower case. Any two words at the beginning of a sentence are a match!

To obtain more precise regular expressions, we rely on the optional parts of taxonomic names. In particular, we classify a sequence of words as a sure positive if it contains at least one of the optional parts <subGenus>, <subSpecies> and <variety>. Even though these regular expressions may produce false negatives, our evaluation will show that this happens very rarely. Our set of precise regular expressions has three elements:

- <taxName> with subgenus in brackets, <subspecies> and <variety> optional:
```
<genus>_(<CapW>)
_<species>{_<subSpecies>}?
{_<variety>}?
```
- <taxName> with <subspecies> given, <subGenus> and <variety> optional:
```
<genus>{_<subGenus>}?
_<species>_<subSpecies>
{_<variety>}?
```
- <taxName> with <variety> mandatory, <subGenus> and <subSpecies> optional:
```
<genus>{_<subGenus>}?
_<species>{_<subSpecies>}?
{_<variety>}
```

To classify a word sequence as a sure positive if it matches *at least one* of these regular expressions, we combine them disjunctively and call the result <preciseTaxName>.

A notion related to that of a sure positive is the one of a *surely positive word*. A surely positive word is a part of a taxonomic name that is not part of a scientist's name. For instance, the taxonomic name *Prenolepis (Nylanderia) vividula Erin subsp. guatemalensis Forel var. itinerans Forel* contains the surely positive words *Prenolepis*, *Nylanderia*, *vividula*, *guatemalensis*, and *itinerans*. We assume that surely positive words exclusively appear as parts of taxonomic names.

4.4 Recall Rules

<taxName> matches any sequence of words that conforms to the Linnaean rules, but there is a further issue: Enumerations of several species of the same genus tend to contain the genus only once. For instance, in *Pseudomyrma arboris-sanctae Emery, latinoda Mayr and tachigalide Forel*"we want to extract *latinoda Mayr* and *tachigalide Forel* as well. To address this, we make use of the surely positive words: We use them to extract parts of taxonomic names that lack the genus.

Our technique also extracts the names of the scientists from the sure positives and collects them in a name lexicon. Based on the structure described in Section 3.3, a capitalized word in a sure positive is a name if it comes after the second position. From the sure positive *Pseudomyrma (Minimyrma) arboris-sanctae Emery*, the technique extracts *Pseudomyrma*, *Minimyrma* and *arboris-sanctae*. In addition, it would add *Emery* to the name lexicon.

We cannot be sure that the list of sure positive words suffices to find all species names in an enumeration. Hence, our technique additionally collects all lower-case words followed by a word contained in the name lexicon. In the example, we extract *latinoda Mayr* and *tachigalide Forel* if *Mayr* and *Forel* are in the name lexicon.

4.5 Data Rules

Because we want to achieve close to 100% in recall, the recall rules are very weak. In consequence, many word sequences that are not taxonomic names are considered uncertain. Before the word-level language recognizer deals with them, we see some more ways to exclude negatives.

Sure Negatives. As mentioned in Subsection 4.3, `<taxName>` matches any capitalized word followed by a word in lower case. This includes the start of any sentence. Making use of the sure negatives, we can recognize these phrases. In particular, out technique classifies any word sequence as negative that contains a word which is also in the set of sure negatives. For instance, in sentence "*Additional evidence results from ...*", *Additional evidence* matches `<taxName>`. Another sentence contains *an additional advantage*, which does not match `<taxName>`. Thus, the set of sure negatives contains *an*, *additional*, and *advantage*. Knowing that *additional* is a sure negative, we exclude the phrase *Additional evidence*.

Names of Scientists. Though the names of scientists are valid parts of taxonomic names, they also cause false matches. The reason is that they are capitalized. A misclassification occurs if they are matched with the genus or subgenus part – `<taxName>` cannot exclude this. In addition, they might appear elsewhere in the text without belonging to a taxonomic name. Similarly to sure negatives, we exclude a match of `<taxName>` if the first or second word is contained in the name lexicon. For instance, in "*..., and Forel further concludes*", *Forel further* matches `<taxName>`. If the name lexicon contains *Forel*, we know that it is not a genus, and thus exclude *Forel further*.

4.6 Classification of Remaining Words

After applying the rules, some word sequences still remain uncertain. To deal with them, we use word-level language recognition. We train the classifier with the sure positive and sure negative words. We do not classify every word separately, but compute the classification score of all words of a sequence and then classify the sequence as a whole. This has several advantages: First, if one word of a sequence is uncertain, this does not automatically incur a feedback request. Second, if a word sequence is uncertain as a whole, the user gives feedback for the entire sequence. This results in several surely classified uncertain words at the cost of only one feedback request. In addition, it is easier to determine the meaning of a word sequence than the one of a single word.

5 Evaluation

A combining approach gives rise to many questions, e.g.: How does a word-level classifier perform with training data automatically generated? How does rule-based filtering affect precision, recall, and coverage? What is the effect to dynamic lexicons? Which kinds of errors remain?

We run two series of experiments: We first process individual documents. We then process the documents incrementally, i.e., we do neither clear the sets of known positives and negatives after each document, nor the statistics of the word-level language recognizer. This is to measure the benefit of reusing data obtained from one document in the processing of subsequent ones. Finally, we take a closer look at the effects of the individual steps and heuristics from Section 4.

The platform is implemented in **`JAVA 1.4.2`**. We use the **`java.util.regex`** package to represent the rules. All tests are based on 20 issues of the *American Museum Novitates*, a natural science periodical published by the *American Museum of Natural History*. The documents contain about 260.000 words, including about 2.500 taxonomic names. The latter consist of about 8.400 words.

5.1 Tests with Individual Documents

First, we test the combined classifier with individual documents. The **Docs** column in Table 3 contains the results. The combination of rules and word-level classification provides very high precision and recall. The former is 99.7% on average, the latter 98.2%. The manual effort is very low: The average coverage is 99.7%.

5.2 Tests with Entire Corpus

In the first test the classifier did not transfer any experience from one document to later ones. We now process the documents one after another. The **Corp** column of Table 3 shows the results. As expected, the classifier performs better than with individual documents. The average recall is 99.2%, coverage is 99.8% on average. Only precision is a little less, 99.1% on average.

	Docs	Corp
<preciseTaxName>	22,6	
<taxName>	414,1	
SN excluded	78,5	
Names excluded	176,15	
Scorings	139,9	
User Feedbacks	19,6	10,35
False positives	4,25	1,5
False negatives	0,55	1,5
Precision	0,997	0,991
Recall	0,982	0,992
f-Measure	0,990	0,992
Coverage	0,997	0,998
Quality	0,987	0,990

Table 3: Test results

The effect of the incremental learning is obvious. The false positives are less than half of those in the first test. A comparison of Line `False Positives` in Table 3 shows this. The same is true for the number feedback requests (Line `User Feedbacks`). The slight decrease in precision (Line `False Negatives`) results from the propagation of misclassifications between documents. The reason for the improvement becomes clear for documents where the number of word sequences in `<preciseTaxName>` is low: experience from previous documents compensates the lack of positive examples. This reduces both false positives and manual classifications.

5.3 The Data Rules

The exclusion of word sequences containing a sure negative turns out to be effective to filter the matches of `<taxName>`. Lines `<taxName>` and `SN excluded` of Tables 3 show this. On average, this step excludes about 20% of the word sequences matching `<taxName>`. Lines `<taxName>` and `Names excluded` tell us that the rule based on the names of scientists is even more effective. On average, it excludes about 40% of the matches of `<taxName>`. Both data rules decrease the number of words the language recognizer has to deal with and eventually the manual effort. This is because they reduce the number of words classified uncertain.

5.4 Comparison to Word-Level Classifier and TaxonGrab

A word-level classifier (WLC) is the core component of the combining technique. We compare it in standalone use to the combining technique (Comb) and to the TaxonGrab (T-Grab) approach (Koning 2005). See Table 4. The combining technique is superior to both TaxonGrab and standalone word-level classification. The reason for better precision and recall is that it uses more different evidence. The better coverage results from the lower number of words that the word-level classifier has to deal with. On average, it has to classify only 2.5% of the words in a document. This reduces the classification effort, leading to less manual feedback. It also decreases the number of potential errors of the word-level classifier.

All these positive effects result in about 99% f-Measure and 99.7% coverage. This means the error is reduced by 75% compared to word-level classification, and by 80% compared to TaxonGrab. The manual effort decreases by 94% compared to the standalone word-level classifier.

	Precision	Recall	f-Measure	Coverage
T-Grab	96%	94%	95%	-
WLC	97%	95%	96%	95%
Comb	99.1%	99.2%	99%	99.7%

Table 4: Comparison to Related Approaches

5.5 Misclassified Words

Despite all improvements, there still are word sequences that are misclassified.

False Negatives. The regular expressions in `<preciseTaxName>` are intended to be 100% precise. There are, however, some (rare) exceptions. Consider the following phrase: *"... In Guadeloup (Mexico) another subspecies killed F. Smith."* Except for the word *In*, this sentence matches the regular expression from `<preciseTaxName>` where `<subSpecies>` is mandatory. Similar pathologic cases could occur for the variety part. Another class of false negatives contains two word sequences, and the first one is the name of a genus. For instance, "*Xenomyrmex varies ...*" falls into this category. The classifier (correctly) recognizes the first word as a part of a taxonomic name. The second one is not typical enough to change the overall classification of the sequence. To recognize these false negatives, one might use POS-tagging. We could exclude word sequences containing words whose meaning does not fit into a taxonomic name.

False Positives. Though `<taxName>` matches any taxonomic name, the subsequent exclusion mechanisms may misclassify a sequence of words. In particular, the word-level classifier has problems recognizing taxonomic names containing proper names of persons. The problem is that these words consist of N-Grams that are typical for common English. "*Wheeleria rogersi Smith*", for instance, is a fictitious but valid taxonomic name. A solution to this problem might be to use the scientist names for constructing and recognizing the genus and species names derived from them.

6 Conclusions

This paper has reported on our experiences with the automatic extraction of taxonomic names from English text documents. This task is essential for modern biology. A peculiarity of taxonomic name extraction is a shortage of training data. This is one reason why deployment of established NER techniques has turned out to be infeasible, at least without adaptations. A taxonomic-name extractor must circumvent that shortage. Our experience has been that designing regular expressions that generate training data directly from the documents is feasible in the context of taxonomic name extraction. A combining approach where individual techniques are carefully tuned and assigned in the right order has turned out to be superior to other potential solutions with regard to precision, recall, and number of user interactions. – Finally, is seems promising to use document and term frequencies as additional evidence. The ides is that both are low for taxonomic names.

7 References

(Bikel 1997) Daniel M. Bikel, Scott Miller, Richard Schwartz, Ralph Weischedel: *Nymble: a high-performance learning name-finder*, In Proceedings of ANLP-97, Washington, USA, 1997

(Carreras 2005) Xavier Carreras, Lluis Marquez: *Introduction to the CoNLL-2005 Shared Task: Semantic Role Labeling*, 2005

(Chieu 2002) Hai Leong Chieu, Hwee Tou Ng: *Named Entity Recognition: A Maximum Entropy Approach Using Global Information*, In Proceedings of COLING-02, Taipei, Taiwan, 2002

(Cucerzan 1999) Cucerzan, S., D. Yarowsky: *Language independent named entity recognition combining morphological and contextual evidence*, In Proceedings of SIGDAT-99, College Park, USA, 1999

(Day) David Day, John Aberdeen, Lynette Hirschman, Robyn Kozierok, Patricia Robinson, Marc Vilain: *Mixed-Initiative Development of Language Processing Systems*, In Proceedings of ANLP-97, Washington, USA, 1997

(Ereshefsky 1997) Marc Ereshefsky: *The Evolution of the Linnaean Hierarchy*, Springer Science & Business Media B.V., 1997

(Jones 1999) Rosie Jones, Andrew McCallum, Kamal Nigam, Ellen Riloff: *Bootstrapping for Text Learning Tasks*, In Proceedings of IJCAI-99 Workshop on Text Mining, 1999

(Koning 2005) Drew Koning, Neil Sarkar, Thomas Moritz: *TaxonGrab: Extractin Taxonomic Names from Text*

(Niu 2003) Cheng Niu, Wei Li, Jihong Ding, Rohini K. Srihari: *A Bootstrapping Approach to Named Entity Classification Using Successive Learners*, In Proceedings of 41st Annual Meeting of the ACL, 2003

(Palmer 1997) David D. Palmer, David S. Day: *A Statistical Profile of the Named Entity Task*, In Proceedings of ANLP-97, Washington, USA, 1997.

(Sautter 2006) G. Sautter, K. Böhm, K. Csorba: *How Helpful Is Word-Level Language Recognition to Extract Taxonomic Names?*, submitted to DILS, 2006

(Tanabe 2002) Lorraine Tanabe, W. John Wilbur: *Tagging Gene and Protein Names in Biomedical Text*, Bioinformatics, Vol. 18, 2002, pp. 1124-1132

(Yoshida 1999) Mikio Yoshida, Ken-ichiro Fukada and Toshihisa Takagi: *PDAD-CSS: a workbench for constructing a protein name abbreviation dictionary*, In Proceedings of the 32nd HICSS, 1999

Summarizing Key Concepts using Citation Sentences

Ariel S. Schwartz and **Marti Hearst**
EECS and SIMS
University of California at Berkeley
Berkeley, CA 94720
sariel@cs.berkeley.edu, hearst@sims.berkeley.edu

Citations have great potential to be a valuable resource in mining the bioscience literature (Nakov et al., 2004). The text around citations (or *citances*) tends to state biological facts with reference to the original papers that discovered them. The cited facts are typically stated in a more concise way in the citing papers than in the original. We hypothesize that in many cases, as time goes by, the citation sentences can more accurately indicate the most important contributions of a paper than its original abstract.

One can use various NLP tools to identify and normalize the important entities in (a) the abstract of the original article, (b) the body of the original article, and (c) the citances to the article. We hypothesize that grouping entities by their occurrence in the citances represents a better summary of the original paper than using only the first two sources of information.

To help determine the utility of the approach, we are applying it to the problem of identifying articles that discuss critical residue functionality, for use in *PhyloFacts* a phylogenomic database (Sjolander, 2004).

Consider the article shown in Figure 1. This paper is a prominent one, published in 1992, with nearly 500 papers citing it. For about 200 of these papers, we downloaded the sentences that surround the citation within the full text. Some examples are shown in Figure 2.

We are developing a statistical model that will group these entities into potentially overlapping groups, where each group represents a central idea in the original paper. In the example shown, some of the citances emphasize what the paper reports about the structural elements of the SH2 domain, whereas other emphasize its findings on interactions and others focus on the critical residues.

Often several articles are cited in the same citance, so it is important to untangle which entities belong to which citation; by pursuing overlapping sets, our model should be able to eliminate most spurious references.

The same entity is often described in many different ways. Prior work has shown how to use redundant information across citations to help normalize entities (Wellner et al., 2004; Pasula et al., 2003); similar techniques may work with entities mentioned in citances. This can be combined with prior work on normalizing entity names in bioscience text, e.g, (Morgan et al., 2004). For a detailed review of related work see (Nakov et al., 2004).

By emphasizing entities the model potentially misses important relationships between the entities. It remains to be determined whether or not relationships must be modeled explicitly in order to create a useful summary.

Proceedings of the BioNLP Workshop on Linking Natural Language Processing and Biology at HLT-NAACL 06, pages 134–135,
New York City, June 2006.

References

A. A. Morgan, L. Hirschman, M. Colosimo, A. S. Yeh, and J. B. Colombe. 2004. Gene name identification and normalization using a model organism database. *Journal of Biomedical Informatics*, 37(6):396–410.

P. I. Nakov, A. S. Schwartz, and M. Hearst. 2004. Citances: Citation sentences for semantic analysis of bioscience text. In *Proceedings of the SIGIR'04 workshop on Search and Discovery in Bioinformatics*.

H. Pasula, B. Marthi, B. Milch, S. Russell, and I. Shiptser. 2003. Identity uncertainty and citation matching. *Advances In Neural Information Processing Systems*, 15.

K. Sjolander. 2004. Phylogenomic inference of protein molecular function: advances and challenges. *Bioinf.*, 20(2):170–179.

B. Wellner, A. McCallum, F. Peng, and M. Hay. 2004. An integrated, conditional model of information extraction and coreference with application to citation graph construction. In *20th Conference on Uncertainty in Artificial Intelligence (UAI)*.

Waksman G, Kominos D, Robertson SC, Pant N, Baltimore D, Birge RB, Cowburn D, Hanafusa H, Mayer BJ, Overduin M, et al., *Abstract Crystal structure of the phosphotyrosine recognition domain SH2 of v-src complexed with tyrosine-phosphorylated peptides.*
Nature. 1992 Aug 20;358(6388):646-53. [PMID: 1379696]

Three-dimensional structures of complexes of the SH2 domain of the v-src oncogene product with two phosphotyrosyl peptides have been determined by X-ray crystallography at resolutions of 1.5 and 2.0 A, respectively. A central antiparallel beta-sheet in the structure is flanked by two alpha-helices, with peptide binding mediated by the sheet, intervening loops and one of the helices. The specific recognition of phosphotyrosine involves amino-aromatic interactions between lysine and arginine side chains and the ring system in addition to hydrogen-bonding interactions with the phosphate.

Figure 1: Target article for summarization.

Binding of **IFNgamma R** and **gp130 phosphotyrosine peptides** to the **STAT SH2 domains** was modeled by using the coordinates of **peptides pYIIPL (pY, phosphotyrosine)** and **pYVPML** bound to the **phospholipase C-gamma 1** and **v-src kinase SH2 domains**, respectively (#OTHER_CITATION, #TARGET_CITATION).

The ligand-binding surface of the **SH2 domain** of the **Lck nonreceptor protein tyrosine kinase** contains two pockets, one for the **Tyr(P) residue** and another for the **amino acid residue** three positions C-terminal to it, the +3 amino acid (#OTHER_CITATION, #TARGET_CITATION).

Given the inherent specificity of **SH2 phosphopeptide interactions** (#TARGET_CITATION), a high degree of selectivity is possible for **STAT dimerizations** and for **STAT activation** by different ligand-receptor combinations.

In fact, the **v-src SH2 domain** was previously shown to bind a **peptide pYVPML** of the **platelet-derived growth factor receptor** in a rather unconventional manner (#TARGET_CITATION).

Figure 2: Sample citances pointing to target article, with some key terms highlighted.

Subdomain adaptation of a POS tagger with a small corpus

Yuka Tateisi
Faculty of Informatics
Kogakuin University
Nishishinjuku 1-24-2
Shinjuku-ku, Tokyo, 163-8677, Japan

Yoshimasa Tsuruoka
School of Informatics
University of Manchester
Manchester M60 1QD, U.K.

Jun-ichi Tsujii
Dept. of Computer Science
University of Tokyo
Hongo 7-3-1, Bunkyo-ku,
Tokyo 113-0033, Japan
School of Informatics
University of Manchester
Manchester M60 1QD, U.K.

1 Introduction

For the domain of biomedical research abstracts, two large corpora, namely GENIA (Kim et al 2003) and Penn BioIE (Kulik et al 2004) are available. Both are basically in *human* domain and the performance of systems trained on these corpora when they are applied to abstracts dealing with other species is unknown. In machine-learning-based systems, re-training the model with addition of corpora in the target domain has achieved promising results (e.g. Tsuruoka et al 2005, Lease et al 2005). In this paper, we compare two methods for adaptation of POS taggers trained for GENIA and Penn BioIE corpora to *Drosophila melanogaster* (fruit fly) domain.

2 Method

Maximum Entropy Markov Models (MEMMs) (Ratnaparkhi 1996) and their extensions (Tutanova et al 2003, Tsuruoka et al 2005) have been successfully applied to English POS tagging. Here we use second-order standard MEMMs for learning POS. where the model parameters are determined with maximum entropy criterion in combination a regularization method called inequality constraints (Kazama and Tsujii 2003). This regularization method has one non-negative meta-parameter called width-factor that controls the "fitness" of the model parameters to the training data.

We used two methods of adapting a POS tagging model. One is to add the domain corpus to the training set. The other is to use the reference distribution modeling, in which the training is performed only on the domain corpus and the information about the original training set is incorporated in the form of the *reference distribution* in the maximum entropy formulation (Johnson et al 2000, Hara et al 2005).

A set of 200 MEDLINE abstracts on *D. melanogaster,* was manually annotated with POS according to the scheme of the GENIA POS corpus (Tateisi et al 2004) by one annotator. The new corpus consists of 40,200 tokens in 1676 sentences. From this corpus which we call "Fly" hereafter, 1024 sentences are randomly taken and used for training. Half of the remaining is used for development and the rest is used for testing.

We measured the accuracy of the POS tagger trained in three settings:

Original: The tagger is trained with the union of Wall Street Journal (WSJ) section of Penn Treebank (Marcus et al 1993), GENIA, and Penn BioIE. In WSJ, Sections 0-18 for training, 19-21 for development, and 22-24 for test. In GENIA and Penn BioIE, 90% of the corpus is used for training and the rest is used for test.

Combined: The tagger is trained with the union of the Original set plus *N* sentences from Fly.

Refdist: Tagger is trained with *N* sentences from Fly, plus the Original set as reference.

In Combined and Refdist settings, *N* is set to 8, 16, 32, 64, 128, 256, 512, 1024 sentences to measure the learning curve.

3 Results

The accuracies of the tagger trained in the Original setting were 96.4% on Fly, 96.7% on WSJ,

This work is partially supported by SORST program, Japan Science and Technology Agency.

Proceedings of the BioNLP Workshop on Linking Natural Language Processing and Biology at HLT-NAACL 06, pages 136–137,
New York City, June 2006.

98.1% on GENIA and 97.7% on Penn BioIE corpora respectively. In the Combined setting, the accuracies were 97.9% on Fly, 96.7% on WSJ, 98.1% on GENIA and 97.7% on Penn BioIE. With Refdist setting, the accuracy on the Fly corpus was raised but those for WSJ and Penn BioIE corpora dropped from Original. When the width factor w was 10, the accuracy was 98.1% on Fly, but 95.4% on WSJ, 98.3% on GENIA and 96.6% on Penn BioIE. When the tagger was trained only on WSJ the accuracies were 88.7% on Fly, 96.9% on WSJ, 85.0% on GENIA and 86.0% on Penn BioIE. When the tagger was trained only on Fly, the accuracy on Fly was even lower (93.1%). The learning curve indicated that the accuracies on the Fly corpus were still rising in both Combined and Refdist settings, but both accuracies are almost as high as those of the original tagger on the original corpora (WSJ, GENIA and Penn BioIE), so in practical sense, 1024 sentences is a reasonable size for the additional corpus. When the width factor was smaller (2.5 and 5) the accuracies on the Fly corpus were saturated with N=1024 with lower values (97.8% with w=2.5 and 98.0% with w=5).

The amount of resources required for the Combined and the Refdist settings were drastically different. In the Combined setting, the learning time was 30632 seconds and the required memory size was 6.4GB. On the other hand, learning in the Refdist setting took only 21 seconds and the required memory size was 157 MB.

The most frequent confusions involved the confusion between FW (foreign words) with another class. Further investigation revealed that most of the error involved Linnaean names of species. Linnaean names are tagged differently in the GENIA and Penn BioIE corpora. In the GENIA corpus, tokens that constitute a Linnaean name are tagged as FW (foreign word) but in the Penn BioIE corpus they are tagged as NNP (proper noun). This seems to be one of the causes of the drop of accuracy on the Penn BioIE corpus when more sentences from the Fly corpus, whose tagging scheme follows that of GENIA, are added for training.

4 Conclusions

We compared two methods of adapting a POS tagger trained on corpora in human domain to fly domain. Training in Refdist setting required much smaller resources to fit to the target domain, but the resulting tagger is less portable to other domains. On the other hand, training in Combined setting is slower and requires huge memory, but the resulting tagger is more robust, and fits reasonably to various domains.

References

Tadayoshi Hara, Yusuke Miyao and Jun'ichi Tsujii. 2005. Adapting a probabilistic disambiguation model of an HPSG parser to a new domain. In Proceedings of IJCNLP 2005, LNAI 3651, pp. 199-210.

Mark Johnson and Stefan Riezler. 2000. Exploiting auxiliary distributions in stochastic unification-based grammars. In Proceedings of 1st NAACL.

Jun'ichi Kazama and Jun'ichi Tsujii. 2003. Evaluation and extension of maximum entropy models with inequality constraints. In Proceedings of EMNLP 2003.

Jin-Dong Kim, Tomoko Ohta, Yuka Tateisi, and Jun'ichi Tsujii. 2003. GENIA corpus – a semantically annotated corpus for bio-textmining. Bioinformatics, 19(Suppl. 1):i180–i182.

Seth Kulick, Ann Bies, Mark Liberman, Mark Mandel, Ryan McDonald, Martha Palmer, Andrew Schein, Lyle Ungar, Scott Winters, and Pete White. 2004. Integrated annotation for biomedical information extraction. In Proceedings of BioLINK 2004, pp. 61–68.

Matthew Lease and Eugene Charniak. 2005. Parsing Biomedical Literature, In Proceedings of IJCNLP 2005, LNAI 3651, pp. 58-69.

Mitchell P. Marcus, Beatrice Sanorini and Mary Ann Marcinkiewicz. 1993. Building a large annotated corpus of English: the Penn Treebank. Computational Linguistics, Vol.19, pp. 313-330.

Adwait Ratnaparkhi. 1996. A Maximum Entropy Model for Part-Of-Speech Tagging. In Proceedings of EMNLP 1996.

Yuka Tateisi and Jun'ichi Tsujii. (2004). Part-of-Speech Annotation of Biology Research Abstracts. In the Proceedings of LREC2004, vol. IV, pp. 1267-1270.

Kristina Toutanova, Dan Klein, Christopher Manning and Yoram Singer. 2003. Feature-Rich Part-of-Speech Tagging with a Cyclic Dependency Network. In Proceedings of HLT-NAACL 2003, pp. 173-180.

Yoshimasa Tsuruoka, Yuka Tateishi, Jin-Dong Kim, Tomoko Ohta, John McNaught, Sophia Ananiadou, and Jun'ichi Tsujii. 2005. Developing a Robust Part-of-Speech Tagger for Biomedical Text. In Proceedings of 10th Panhellenic Conference on Informatics, LNCS 3746, pp. 382-392.

Bootstrapping and Evaluating Named Entity Recognition in the Biomedical Domain

Andreas Vlachos
Computer Laboratory
University of Cambridge
Cambridge, CB3 0FD, UK
av308@cl.cam.ac.uk

Caroline Gasperin
Computer Laboratory
University of Cambridge
Cambridge, CB3 0FD, UK
cvg20@cl.cam.ac.uk

Abstract

We demonstrate that bootstrapping a gene name recognizer for FlyBase curation from automatically annotated noisy text is more effective than fully supervised training of the recognizer on more general manually annotated biomedical text. We present a new test set for this task based on an annotation scheme which distinguishes gene names from gene mentions, enabling a more consistent annotation. Evaluating our recognizer using this test set indicates that performance on unseen genes is its main weakness. We evaluate extensions to the technique used to generate training data designed to ameliorate this problem.

1 Introduction

The biomedical domain is of great interest to information extraction, due to the explosion in the amount of available information. In order to deal with this phenomenon, curated databases have been created in order to assist researchers to keep up with the knowledge published in their field (Hirschman et al., 2002; Liu and Friedman, 2003). The existence of such resources in combination with the need to perform information extraction efficiently in order to promote research in this domain, make it a very interesting field to develop and evaluate information extraction approaches.

Named entity recognition (NER) is one of the most important tasks in information extraction. It has been studied extensively in various domains, including the newswire (Tjong Kim Sang and De Meulder, 2003) domain and more recently the biomedical domain (Blaschke et al., 2004; Kim et al., 2004). These shared tasks aimed at evaluating fully supervised trainable systems. However, the limited availability of annotated material in most domains, including the biomedical, restricts the application of such methods. In order to circumvent this obstacle several approaches have been presented, among them active learning (Shen et al., 2004) and rule-based systems encoding domain specific knowledge (Gaizauskas et al., 2003).

In this work we build on the idea of bootstrapping, which has been applied by Collins & Singer (1999) in the newsire domain and by Morgan et al. (2004) in the biomedical domain. This approach is based on creating training material automatically using existing domain resources, which in turn is used to train a supervised named entity recognizer.

The structure of this paper is the following. Section 2 describes the construction of a new test set to evaluate named entity recognition for *Drosophila* fly genes. Section 3 compares bootstrapping to the use of manually annotated material for training a supervised method. An extension to the evaluation of NER appear in Section 4. Based on this evaluation, section 5 discusses ways of improving the performance of a gene name recognizer bootstrapped on FlyBase resources. Section 6 concludes the paper and suggests some future work.

2 Building a test set

In this section we present a new test set created to evaluate named entity recognition for *Drosophila* fly genes. To our knowledge, there is only one other test set built for this purpose, presented in Morgan et

Proceedings of the BioNLP Workshop on Linking Natural Language Processing and Biology at HLT-NAACL 06, pages 138–145,
New York City, June 2006. ©2006 Association for Computational Linguistics

al. (2004), which was annotated by two annotators. The inter-annotator agreement achieved was 87% F-score between the two annotators, which according to the authors reflects the difficulty of the task.

Vlachos et al (2006) evaluated their system on both versions of this test set and obtained significantly different results. The disagreements between the two versions were attributed to difficulties in applying the guidelines used for the annotation. Therefore, they produced a version of this dataset resolving the differences between these two versions using revised guidelines, partially based on those developed for ACE (2004). In this work, we applied these guidelines to construct a new test set, which resulted in their refinement and clarification.

The basic idea is that *gene names* (<gn>) are annotated in any position they are encountered in the text, including cases where they are not referring to the actual gene but they are used to refer to a different entity. Names of gene families, reporter genes and genes not belonging to *Drosophila* are tagged as gene names too:

- the <gn>faf</gn> gene
- the <gn>Toll</gn> protein
- the <gn>string</gn>-<gn>LacZ</gn> reporter genes

In addition, following the ACE guidelines, for each *gene name* we annotate the shortest surrounding noun phrase. These noun phrases are classified further into *gene mentions* (<gm>) and *other mentions* (<om>), depending on whether the mentions refer to an actual gene or not respectively. Most of the times, this distinction can be performed by looking at the head noun of the noun phrase:

- <gm>the <gn>faf</gn> gene</gm>
- <om>the <gn>Reaper</gn> protein</om>

However, in many cases the noun phrase itself is not sufficient to classify the mention, especially when the mention consists of just the gene name, because it is quite common in the biomedical literature to use a gene name to refer to a protein or to other gene products. In order to classify such cases, the annotators need to take into account the context in which the mention appears. In the following examples, the word of the context that enables us to make the distinction between *gene mentions* (<gm>) and *other mentions* is underlined:

- ... ectopic expression of <gm><gn>hth</gn></gm> ...
- ... transcription of <gm><gn>string</gn></gm> ...
- ... <om><gn>Rols7</gn></om> localizes ...

It is worth noticing as well that sometimes more than one *gene name* may appear within the same noun phrase. As the examples that follow demonstrate, this enables us to annotate consistently cases of coordination, which is another source of disagreement (Dingare et al., 2004):

- <gm><gn>male-specific lethal-1</gn>, <gn>-2</gn> and <gn>-3</gn> genes</gm>

	Morgan et al.	new dataset
abstracts	86	82
tokens	16779	15703
gene-names	1032	629
unique gene-names	347	326

Table 1: Statistics of the datasets

The test set produced consists of the abstracts from 82 articles curated by FlyBase[1]. We used the tokenizer of RASP[2] (Briscoe and Carroll, 2002) to process the text, resulting in 15703 tokens. The size and the characteristics of the dataset is comparable with that of Morgan et al (2004) as it can be observed from the statistics of Table 1, except for the number of non-unique gene-names. Apart from the different guidelines, another difference is that we used the original text of the abstracts, without any post-processing apart from the tokenization. The dataset from Morgan et al. (2004) had been stripped from all punctuation characters, e.g. periods and commas. Keeping the text intact renders this new dataset more realistic and most importantly it allows the use of tools that rely on this information, such as syntactic parsers.

The annotation of *gene names* was performed by a computational linguist and a FlyBase curator.

[1] www.flybase.net

[2] http://www.cogs.susx.ac.uk/lab/nlp/rasp/

We estimated the inter-annotator agreement in two ways. First, we calculated the F-score achieved between them, which was 91%. Secondly, we used the Kappa coefficient (Carletta, 1996), which has become the standard evaluation metric and the score obtained was 0.905. This high agreement score can be attributed to the clarification of what *gene name* should capture through the introduction of *gene mention* and *other mention*. It must be mentioned that in the experiments that follow in the rest of the paper, only the *gene names* were used to evaluate the performance of bootstrapping. The identification and the classification of mentions is the subject of ongoing research.

The annotation of mentions presented greater difficulty, because computational linguists do not have sufficient knowledge of biology in order to use the context of the mentions whilst biologists are not trained to identify noun phrases in text. In this effort, the boundaries of the mentions where defined by the computational linguist and the classification was performed by the curator. A more detailed description of the guidelines, as well as the corpus itself in IOB format are available for download[3].

3 Bootstrapping NER

For the bootstrapping experiments presented in this paper we employed the system developed by Vlachos et al. (2006), which was an improvement of the system of Morgan et al. (2004). In brief, the abstracts of all the articles curated by FlyBase were retrieved and tokenized by RASP (Briscoe and Carroll, 2002). For each article, the gene names and their synonyms that were recorded by the curators were annotated automatically on its abstract using longest-extent pattern matching. The pattern matching is flexible in order to accommodate capitalization and punctuation variations. This process resulted in a large but noisy training set, consisting of 2,923,199 tokens and containing 117,279 gene names, 16,944 of which are unique. The abstracts used in the test set presented in the previous section were excluded. We used them though to evaluate the performance of the training data generation process and the results were 73.5% recall, 93% precision and 82.1% F-score.

[3]www.cl.cam.ac.uk/users/av308/Project_Index/node5.html

Training	Recall	Precision	F-score
std	75%	88.2%	81.1%
std-enhanced	76.2%	87.7%	81.5%
BioCreative	35.9%	37.4%	36.7%

Table 2: Results using Vlachos et al. (2006) system

This material was used to train the HMM-based NER module of the open-source toolkit LingPipe[4]. The performance achieved on the corpus presented in the previous section appears in Table 2 in the row "std". Following the improvements suggested by Vlachos et al. (2006), we also re-annotated as gene-names the tokens that were annotated as such by the data generation process more than 80% of the time (row "std-enhanced"), which slightly increased the performance.

In order to assess the usefulness of this bootstrapping method, we evaluated the performance of the HMM-based tagger if we trained it on manually annotated data. For this purpose we used the annotated data from BioCreative-2004 (Blaschke et al., 2004) task 1A. In that task, the participants were requested to identify which terms in a biomedical research article are gene and/or protein names, which is roughly the same task as the one we are dealing with in this paper. Therefore we would expect that, even though the material used for the annotation is not drawn from the exact domain of our test data (FlyBase curated abstracts), it would still be useful to train a system to identify gene names. The results in Table 2 show that this is not the case. Apart from the domain shift, the deterioration of the performance could also be attributed to the different guidelines used. However, given that the tasks are roughly the same, it is a very important result that manually annotated training material leads to so poor performance, compared to the performance achieved using automatically created training data. This evidence suggests that manually created resources, which are expensive, might not be useful even in slightly different tasks than those they were initially designed for. Moreover, it suggests that the use of semi-supervised or unsupervised methods for creating training material are alternatives worth-exploring.

[4]http://www.alias-i.com/lingpipe/

4 Evaluating NER

The standard evaluation metric used for NER is the F-score (Van Rijsbergen, 1979), which is the harmonic average of Recall and Precision. It is very successful and popular, because it penalizes systems that underperform in any of these two aspects. Also, it takes into consideration the existence multi-token entities by rewarding systems able to identify the entity boundaries correctly and penalizing them for partial matches. In this section we suggest an extension to this evaluation, which we believe is meaningful and informative for trainable NER systems.

Two are the main expectations from trainable systems. The first one is that they will be able to identify entities that they have encountered during their training. This is not as easy as it might seem, because in many domains token(s) representing entity names of a certain type can appear as common words or representing an entity name of a different type. Using examples from the biomedical domain, "to" can be a gene name but it is also used as a preposition. Also gene names are commonly used as protein names, rendering the task of distinguishing between the two types non-trivial, even if examples of those names exist in the training data. The second expectation is that trainable systems should be able to learn from the training data patterns that will allow it to generalize to unseen named entities. Important role in this aspect of the performance play the features that are dependent on the context and on observations on the tokens. The ability to generalize to unseen named entities is very significant because it is unlikely that training material can cover all possible names and moreover, in most domains, new names appear regularly.

A common way to assess these two aspects is to measure the performance on seen and unseen data separately. It is straightforward to apply this in tasks with token-based evaluation, such as part-of-speech tagging (Curran and Clark, 2003). However, in the case of NER, this is not entirely appropriate due to the existence of multi-token entities. For example, consider the case of the gene-name "head inhibition defective", which consists of three common words that are very likely to occur independently of each other in a training set. If this gene name appears in the test set but not in the training set, with a token-based evaluation its identification (or not) would count towards the performance on seen tokens if the tokens appeared independently. Moreover, a system would be rewarded or penalized for each of the tokens. One approach to circumvent these problems and evaluate the performance of a system on unseen named entities, is to replace all the named entities of the test set with strings that do not appear in the training data, as in Morgan et al. (2004). There are two problems with this evaluation. Firstly, it alters the morphology of the unseen named entities, which is usually a source of good features to recognize them. Secondly, it affects the contexts in which the unseen named entities occur, which don't have to be the same as that of seen named entities.

In order to overcome these problems, we used the following method. We partitioned the correct answers and the recall errors according to whether the named entity at question have been encountered in the training data as a named entity at least once. The precision errors are partitioned in seen and unseen depending on whether the string that was incorrectly annotated as a named entity by the system has been encountered in the training data as a named entity at least once. Following the standard F-score definition, partially recognized named entities count as both precision and recall errors.

In examples from the biomedical domain, if "to" has been encountered at least once as a gene name in the data but an occurrence of in the test dataset is erroneously tagged as a gene name, this will count as a precision error on seen named entities. Similarly, if "to" has never been encountered in the training data as a gene name but an occurrence of it in the test dataset is erroneously tagged as a common word, this will count as a recall error on unseen named entities. In a multi-token example, if "head inhibition defective" is a gene name in the test dataset and it has been seen as such in the training data but the NER system tagged (erroneously) "head inhibition" as a gene name (which is not the training data), then this would result in a recall error on seen named entities and a precision error on unseen named entities.

5 Improving performance

Using this extended evaluation we re-evaluated the named entity recognition system of Vlachos et

	Recall	Precision	F-score	# entities
seen	95.9%	93.3%	94.5%	495
unseen	32.3%	63%	42.7%	134
overall	76.2%	87.7%	81.5%	629

Table 3: Extended evaluation

Training	Recall	Precision	F-score	cover
bsl	76.2%	87.7%	81.5%	69%
sub	73.6%	83.6%	78.3%	69.6%
bsl+sub	82.2%	83.4%	82.8%	79%

Table 4: Results using substitution

al. (2006) and Table 3 presents the results. The big gap in the performance on seen and unseen named entities can be attributed to the highly lexicalized nature of the algorithm used. Tokens that have not been seen in the training data are passed on to a module that classifies them according to their morphology, which given the variety of gene names and their overlap with common words is unlikely to be sufficient. Also, the limited window used by the tagger (previous label and two previous tokens) does not allow the capture of long-range contexts that could improve the recognition of unseen gene names.

We believe that this evaluation allows fair comparison between the data generation process that creating the training data and the HMM-based tagger. This comparison should take into account the performance of the latter only on seen named entities, since the former is applied only on those abstracts for which lists of the genes mentioned have been compiled manually by the curators. The result of this comparison is in favor of the HMM, which achieves 94.5% F-score compared to 82.1% of the data generation process, mainly due to the improved recall (95.9% versus 73.5%). This is a very encouraging result for bootstrapping techniques using noisy training material, because it demonstrates that the trained classifier can deal efficiently with the noise inserted.

From the analysis performed in this section, it becomes obvious that the system is rather weak in identifying unseen gene names. The latter contribute 31% of all the gene names in our test dataset, with respect to the training data produced automatically to train the HMM. Each of the following subsections describes different ideas employed to improve the performance of our system. As our baseline, we kept the version that uses the training data produced by re-annotating as gene names tokens that appear as part of gene names more than 80% of times. This version has resulted in the best performance obtained so far.

5.1 Substitution

A first approach to improve the overall performance is to increase the coverage of gene names in the training data. We noticed that the training set produced by the process described earlier contains 16944 unique gene names, while the dictionary of all gene names from FlyBase contains 97227 entries. This observation suggests that the dictionary is not fully exploited. This is expected, since the dictionary entries are obtained from the full papers while the training data generation process is applied only to their abstracts which are unlikely to contain all of them.

In order to include all the dictionary entries in the training material, we substituted in the training dataset produced earlier each of the existing gene names with entries from the dictionary. The process was repeated until each of the dictionary entries was included once in the training data. The assumption that we take advantage of is that gene names should appear in similar lexical contexts, even if the resulting text is nonsensical from a biomedical perspective. For example, in a sentence containing the phrase "the sws mutant", the immediate lexical context could justify the presence of any gene name in the place "sws", even though the whole sentence would become untruthful and even incomprehensible. Although through this process we are bound to repeat errors of the training data, we expect the gains from the increased coverage to alleviate their effect. The resulting corpus consisted of 4,062,439 tokens containing each of the 97227 gene names of the dictionary once. Training the HMM-based tagger with this data yielded 78.3% F-score (Table 4, row "sub"). 438 out of the 629 genes of the test set were seen in the training data.

The drop in precision exemplifies the importance of using naturally occurring training material. Also, 59 gene names that were annotated in the training data due to the flexible pattern matching are not in-

Training	Recall	Precision	F score	unseen F score
bsl	76.2%	87.7%	81.5%	42.7%
bsl-excl	80.8%	81.1%	81%	51.3%

Table 5: Results excluding sentences without entities

cluded anymore since they are not in the dictionary, which explains the drop in recall. Given these observations, we trained HMM-based tagger on both versions of the training data, which consisted of 5,527,024 tokens, 218,711 gene names, 106,235 of which are unique. The resulting classifier had seen in its training data 79% of the gene names in the test set (497 out of 629) and it achieved 82.8% F-score (row "bsl+sub" in Table 4). It is worth pointing out that this improvement is not due to ameliorating the performance on unseen named entities but due to including more of them in the training data, therefore taking advantage of the high performance on seen named entities (93.7%). Direct comparisons between these three versions of the system on seen and unseen gene names are not meaningful because the separation in seen and seen gene names changes with the the genes covered in the training set and therefore we would be evaluating on different data.

5.2 Excluding sentences not containing entities

From the evaluation of the dictionary based tagger in Section 3 we confirmed our initial expectation that it achieves high precision and relatively low recall. Therefore, we anticipate most mistakes in the training data to be unrecognized gene names (false negatives). In an attempt to reduce them, we removed from the training data sentences that did not contain any annotated gene names. This process resulted in keeping 63,872 from the original 111,810 sentences. Apparently, such processing would remove many correctly identified common words (true negatives), but given that the latter are more frequent in our data we expect it not to have significant impact. The results appear in Table 5.

In this experiment, we can compare the performances on unseen data because the gene names that were included in the training data did not change. As we expected, the F-score on unseen gene names rose substantially, mainly due to the improvement in recall (from 32.3% to 46.2%). The overall F-score deteriorated, which is due to the drop in precision. An error analysis showed that most of the precision errors introduced were on tokens that can be part of gene names as well as common words, which suggests that removing from the training data sentences without annotated entities, deprives the classifier from contexts that would help the resolution of such cases. Still though, such an approach could be of interest in cases where we expect a significant amount of novel gene names.

5.3 Filtering contexts

The results of the previous two subsections suggested that improvements can be achieved through substitution and exclusion of sentences without entities, attempting to include more gene names in the training data and exclude false negatives from them. However, the benefits from them were hampered because of the crude way these methods were applied, resulting in repetition of mistakes as well as exclusion of true negatives. Therefore, we tried to filter the contexts used for substitution and the sentences that were excluded using the confidence of the HMM based tagger.

In order to accomplish this, we used the "std-enhanced" version of the HMM based tagger to re-annotate the training data that had been generated automatically. From this process, we obtained a second version of the training data which we expected to be different from the original one by the data generation process, since the HMM based tagger should behave differently. Indeed, the agreement between the training data and its re-annotation by the HMM based tagger was 96% F-score. We estimated the entropy of the tagger for each token and for each sentence we calculated the average entropy over all its tokens. We expected that sentences less likely to contain errors would be sentences on which the two versions of the training data would agree and in addition the HMM based tagger would annotate with low entropy, an intuition similar to that of co-training (Blum and Mitchell, 1998). Following this, we removed from the dataset the sentences on which the HMM-based tagger disagree with the annotation of the data generation process, or it agreed with but the average entropy of their tokens was above a certain threshold. By setting this threshold at

Training	Recall	Precision	F-score	cover
filter	75.6%	85.8%	80.4%	65.5%
filter-sub	80.1%	81%	80.6%	69.6%
filter-sub +bsl	83.3%	82.8%	83%	79%

Table 6: Results using filtering

0.01, we kept 72,534 from the original 111,810 sentences, which contained 61798 gene names, 11,574 of which are unique. Using this dataset as training data we achieved 80.4% F-score (row "filter" in Table 6). Even though this score is lower than our baseline (81.5% F-score), this filtered dataset should be more appropriate to apply substitution because it would contain fewer errors.

Indeed, applying substitution to this dataset resulted in better results, compared to applying it to the original data. The performance of the HMM-based tagger trained on it was 80.6% F-score (row "filter-sub" in Table 6) compared to 78.3% (row "sub" in Table 4). Since both training datasets contain the same gene names (the ones contained in the FlyBase dictionary), we can also compare the performance on unseen data, which improved from 46.7% to 48.6%. This improvement can be attributed to the exclusion of some false negatives from the training data, which improved the recall on unseen data from 42.9% to 47.1%. Finally, we combined the dataset produced with filtering and substitution with the original dataset. Training the HMM-based tagger on this dataset resulted in 83% F-score, which is the best performance we obtained.

6 Conclusions - Future work

In this paper we demonstrated empirically the efficiency of using automatically created training material for the task of *Drosophila* gene name recognition by comparing it with the use of manually annotated material from the broader biomedical domain. For this purpose, a test dataset was created using novel guidelines that allow more consistent manual annotation. We also presented an informative evaluation of the bootstrapped NER system that revealed that indicated its weakness in identifying unseen gene names. Based on this result we explored ways to improve its performance. These included taking fuller advantage of the dictionary of gene names from FlyBase, as well as filtering out likely mistakes from the training data using confidence estimations from the HMM-based tagger.

Our results point out some interesting directions for research. First of all, the efficiency of bootstrapping calls for its application in other tasks for which useful domain resources exist. As a complement task to NER, the identification and classification of the mentions surrounding the gene names should be tackled, because it is of interest to the users of biomedical IE systems to know not only the gene names but also whether the text refers to the actual gene or not. This could also be useful to anaphora resolution systems. Future work for bootstrapping NER in the biomedical domain should include efforts to incorporate more sophisticated features that would be able to capture more abstract contexts. In order to evaluate such approaches though, we believe it is important to test them on full papers which present greater variety of contexts in which gene names appear.

Acknowledgments

The authors would like to thank Nikiforos Karamanis and the FlyBase curators Ruth Seal and Chihiro Yamada for annotating the dataset and their advice in the guidelines. We would like also to thank MITRE organization for making their data available to us and in particular Alex Yeh for the BioCreative data and Alex Morgan for providing us with the dataset used in Morgan et al. (2004). The authors were funded by BBSRC grant 38688 and CAPES award from the Brazilian Government.

References

ACE. 2004. Annotation guidelines for entity detection and tracking (EDT).

Christian Blaschke, Lynette Hirschman, and Alexander Yeh, editors. 2004. *Proceedings of the BioCreative Workshop*, Granada, March.

Avrim Blum and Tom Mitchell. 1998. Combining labeled and unlabeled data with co-training. In *Proceedings of COLT 1998.*

E. J. Briscoe and J. Carroll. 2002. Robust accurate statistical annotation of general text. In *Proceedings of the*

3rd International Conference on Language Resources and Evaluation, pages 1499–1504.

Jean Carletta. 1996. Assessing agreement on classification tasks: The kappa statistic. *Computational Linguistics*, 22(2):249–254.

M. Collins and Y. Singer. 1999. Unsupervised models for named entity classification. In *Proceedings of the Joint SIGDAT Conference on EMNLP and VLC.*

J. Curran and S. Clark. 2003. Investigating gis and smoothing for maximum entropy taggers. In *Proceedings of the 11th Annual Meeting of the European Chapter of the Association for Computational Linguistics.*

S. Dingare, J. Finkel, M. Nissim, C. Manning, and C. Grover. 2004. A system for identifying named entities in biomedical text: How results from two evaluations reflect on both the system and the evaluations. In *The 2004 BioLink meeting at ISMB.*

R. Gaizauskas, G. Demetriou, P. J. Artymiuk, and P. Willet. 2003. Protein structures and information extraction from biological texts: The "PASTA" system. *BioInformatics*, 19(1):135–143.

L. Hirschman, J. C. Park, J. Tsujii, L. Wong, and C. H. Wu. 2002. Accomplishments and challenges in literature data mining for biology. *Bioinformatics*, 18(12):1553–1561.

J. Kim, T. Ohta, Y. Tsuruoka, Y. Tateisi, and N. Collier, editors. 2004. *Proceedings of JNLPBA, Geneva.*

H. Liu and C. Friedman. 2003. Mining terminological knowledge in large biomedical corpora. In *Pacific Symposium on Biocomputing*, pages 415–426.

A. A. Morgan, L. Hirschman, M. Colosimo, A. S. Yeh, and J. B. Colombe. 2004. Gene name identification and normalization using a model organism database. *J. of Biomedical Informatics*, 37(6):396–410.

D. Shen, J. Zhang, J. Su, G. Zhou, and C. L. Tan. 2004. Multi-criteria-based active learning for named entity recognition. In *Proceedings of ACL 2004*, Barcelona.

Erik F. Tjong Kim Sang and Fien De Meulder. 2003. Introduction to the conll-2003 shared task: Language-independent named entity recognition. In Walter Daelemans and Miles Osborne, editors, *Proceedings of CoNLL-2003*, pages 142–147. Edmonton, Canada.

C. J. Van Rijsbergen. 1979. *Information Retrieval, 2nd edition.* Dept. of Computer Science, University of Glasgow.

A. Vlachos, C. Gasperin, I. Lewin, and T. Briscoe. 2006. Bootstrapping the recognition and anaphoric linking of named entities in drosophila articles. In *Proceedings of PSB 2006.*

Author Index

Association for Computational Linguistics
209 N. Eighth Street
Stroudsburg, Pennsylvania 18360